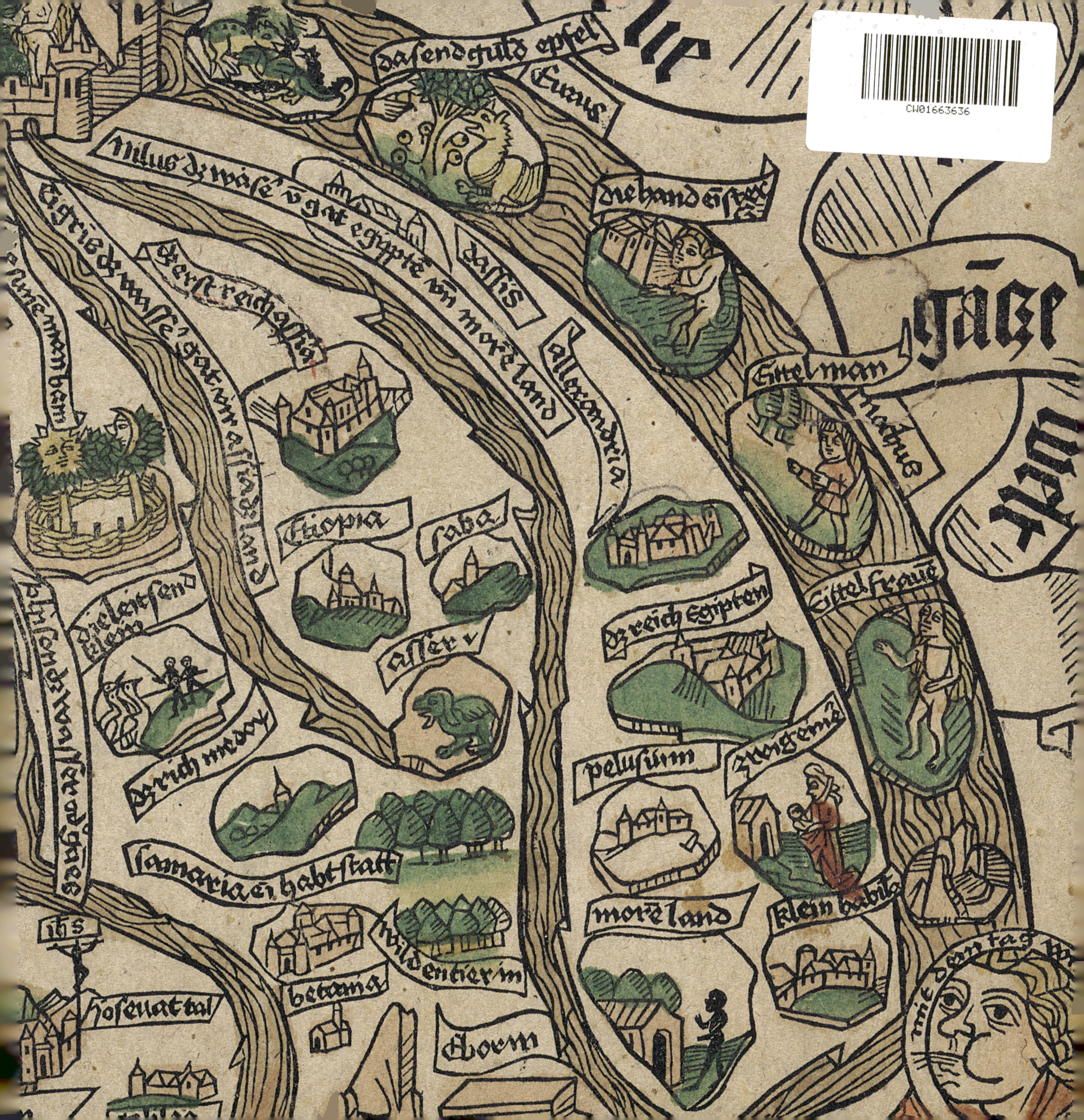

da send guld epfel
die hand essen
Etiopia
saba
alexandria
dassis
dz reich egipten
pelusium
dz rich medon
samaria ein habtstatt
more land
betania
ebron
ihs
wilden tier im

The Book of Marvels

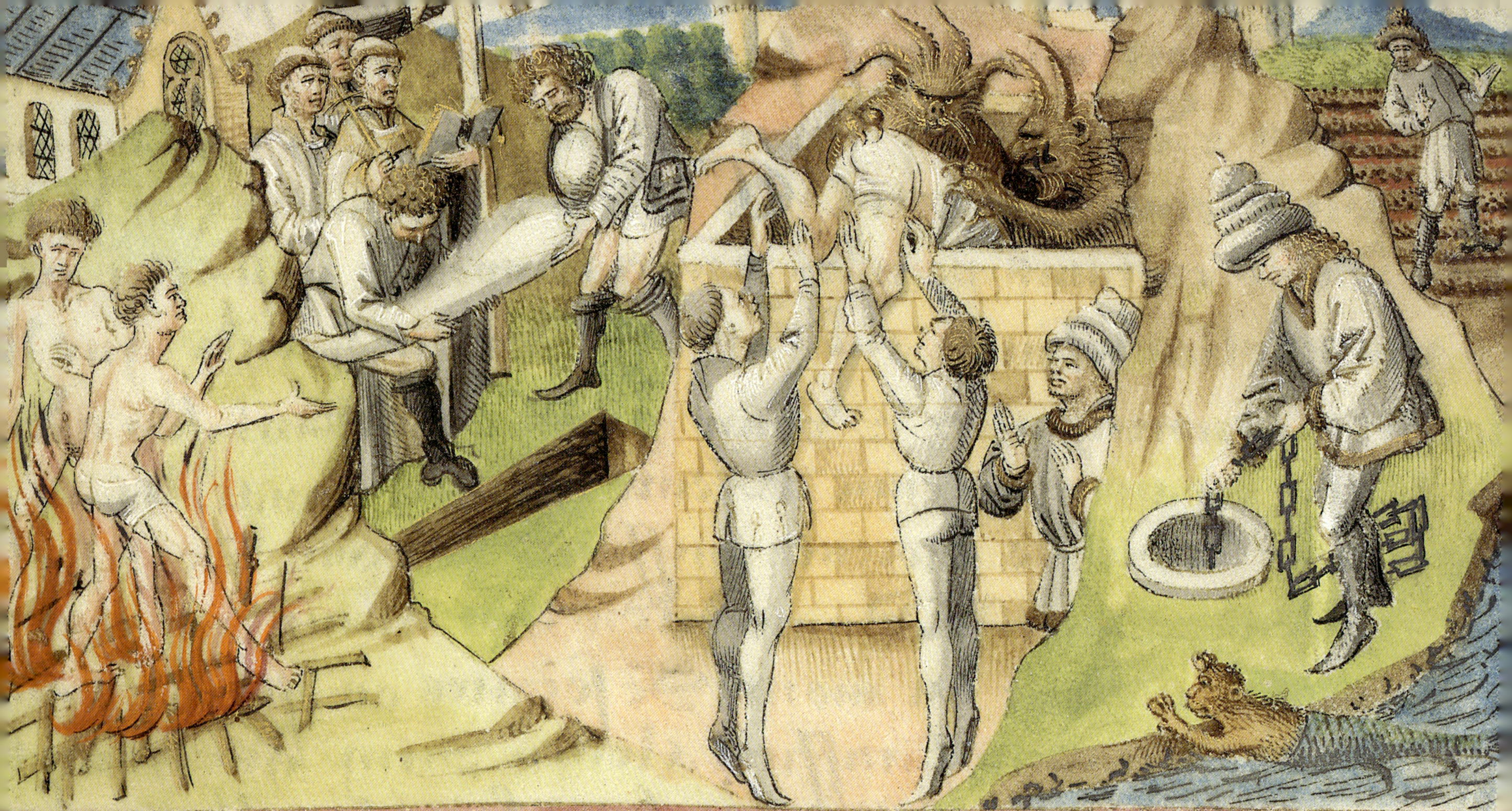

Ytalie est une tres noble & grant partie de Europe
est une province de hault & grant renom laquelle
moult bien garnie & aornee de moult grans et nob
tez qui sont moult bien peuplees et plaines de grant riches
La terre de telle province est si fertille & plantureuse
ains & en fruitz & en fleurs moult bien ordonnans. Et si
oult bien aornee & garnie de bois de forestz de fontaines
vieres de lacz & destancqs de prez de vignes & de terres lab
bles.
En ceste province sont advenues & adviennent
jour en jour moult de merveilleuses adventures & mo

The Book of Marvels

A Medieval Guide to the Globe

LARISA GROLLEMOND
KELIN MICHAEL
ELIZABETH MORRISON
JOSHUA O'DRISCOLL

With an epilogue by
NOEL B. SALAZAR

J. Paul Getty Museum, Los Angeles

This publication is issued on the occasion of the exhibitions *The Book of Marvels: Wonder and Fear in the Middle Ages*, on view at the J. Paul Getty Museum at the Getty Center, Los Angeles, from June 11 to August 25, 2024, and *The Book of Marvels: Imagining the Medieval World*, on view at the Morgan Library & Museum, New York, from January 24 to May 25, 2025.

The Morgan Library & Museum's presentation of *The Book of Marvels: Imagining the Medieval World* is made possible with support from the New York Medieval Society and an anonymous donor.

Published by the J. Paul Getty Museum, Los Angeles
Getty Publications
1200 Getty Center Drive, Suite 500
Los Angeles, California 90049-1682
getty.edu/publications

Rachel Barth, *Project Editor*
Alexandra Bonfante-Warren, *Manuscript Editor*
Jon Grizzle, *Designer*
Molly McGeehan, *Production*
Nancy Rivera, *Image and Rights Acquisition*

Distributed in the United States and Canada by the University of Chicago Press
Distributed outside the United States and Canada by Yale University Press, London

Printed in Singapore

Library of Congress Cataloging-in-Publication Data
Names: Grollemond, Larisa, author. | Michael, Kelin, author. | Morrison, Elizabeth, 1968- author. | O'Driscoll, Joshua, author. | Salazar, Noel B., 1973- writer of epilogue. | J. Paul Getty Museum, host institution, issuing body. | Pierpont Morgan Library, host institution.
Title: The book of marvels : a medieval guide to the globe / Larisa Grollemond, Kelin Michael, Elizabeth Morrison, Joshua O'Driscoll ; with an epilogue by Noel B. Salazar.
Description: Los Angeles : J. Paul Getty Museum, [2024] | Published on the occasion of the exhibition The Book of Marvels: Wonder and Fear in the Middle Ages, on view at the J. Paul Getty Museum at the Getty Center, Los Angeles, from June 11 to August 25, 2024, and The Book of Marvels: Imagining the Medieval World, on view at the Morgan Library & Museum, New York, from January 24 to May 25, 2025. | Includes bibliographical references and index. | Summary: "A study of the medieval manuscript The Book of Marvels of the World, a fifteenth-century French illustrated guide to the globe"—Provided by publisher.
Identifiers: LCCN 2023040606 (print) | LCCN 2023040607 (ebook) | ISBN 9781606069035 (hardcover) | ISBN 9781606069042 (adobe pdf)
Subjects: LCSH: J. Paul Getty Museum. Manuscript. 124—Illustrations—Exhibitions. | Pierpont Morgan Library. Manuscript. M.461—Illustrations—Exhibitions. | Livre des merveilles du monde (Compilation)—Exhibitions. | Livre des merveilles du monde (Compilation)—Illustrations—Exhibitions. | Curiosities and wonders—Early works to 1800—Exhibitions. | Curiosities and wonders in art—Exhibitions. | Illumination of books and manuscripts, Medieval—France—Exhibitions. | Illumination of books and manuscripts, French—Exhibitions.
Classification: LCC ND3399.L59 G76 2024 (print) | LCC ND3399.L59 (ebook) | DDC 741.6/470944—dc23/eng/20231212
LC record available at https://lccn.loc.gov/2023040606
LC ebook record available at https://lccn.loc.gov/2023040607

Front cover: Master of the Geneva Boccaccio, *Traponee* (*Sri Lanka*), France, probably Angers, ca. 1460–65, in the *Book of the Marvels of the World*, Los Angeles, J. Paul Getty Museum, Ms. 124, fol. 32r (detail, plate 19)
Back cover: Master of the Geneva Boccaccio, *Seres* (*China*), France, probably Angers, ca. 1460, in the *Book of the Marvels of the World*, New York, Morgan Library & Museum, Ms. M.461, fol. 75r (detail, plate 17)
Endpapers: Hanns Rüst, *Map of the World*, Germany, Augsburg, ca. 1480. New York, Morgan Library & Museum, PML 19921 (detail, fig. 23)
Page ii: Detail, plate 13 (Morgan)
Page viii: Detail, plate 10 (Getty)
Page x: Detail, plate 19 (Getty)
Page 14: Detail, plate 3
Page 36: Detail, plate 8
Page 54: Detail, figure 43
Page 78: Detail, plate 20 (Getty)
Page 80: Master of the Geneva Boccaccio, *Island (Isle)*, France, probably Angers, ca. 1460–65, in the *Book of the Marvels of the World*, Los Angeles, J. Paul Getty Museum, Ms. 124, fol. 13r (detail)
Page 84: Master of the Geneva Boccaccio, *Saba (in Arabia)*, France, probably Angers, ca. 1460–65, in the *Book of the Marvels of the World*, Los Angeles, J. Paul Getty Museum, Ms. 124, fol. 24v (detail)
Page 136: Detail, plate 18 (Getty)

The complete manuscript of this work was peer reviewed through a single-masked process in which the reviewers remained anonyous.

Illustration Credits
Every effort has been made to contact the owners and photographers of illustrations reproduced here whose names do not appear in the captions or in the illustration credits listed below. Anyone having further information concerning copyright holders is asked to contact Getty Publications so this information can be included in future printings.

Plates 1–20; figs. 1, 34, 46: The Morgan Library & Museum, New York / Photos: Janny Chiu
Figs. 3, 5, 7, 24, 37–41: Bibliothèque nationale de France
Figs. 4, 6, 8, 9, 11–14, 17–21, 23 (endpapers), 25–27, 30, 35, 43, 48: The Morgan Library & Museum, New York / Photos: Carmen González Fraile
Fig. 10: © Victoria and Albert Museum, London
Fig. 15: Leiden University Libraries, MS VGG F 3 A, fol. 41r
Fig. 22: British Library, London, UK © British Library Board. All Rights Reserved / Photo: Bridgeman Images
Fig. 42: © Ville d'Angers
Fig. 45: Bibliothèque de Genève
Fig. 47: The Morgan Library & Museum, New York
Fig. 49: Entertainment Pictures / Photo: Alamy Stock Photo
Fig. 50: Glasshouse Images / Photo: Alamy Stock Photo
Fig. 51: Shutterstock / Photo: Sandra van der Steen
Fig. 52: Moviestore Collection / Photo: Alamy Stock Photo

FSC www.fsc.org
MIX
Paper from responsible sources
FSC® C167869

Contents

Directors' Foreword

Many have seen murky photographs claiming to show the Loch Ness Monster in Scotland, or heard tales of alligators in the sewers of New York City, or wondered if it really is possible to see the Great Wall of China from space. These stories and others like them can be considered the modern counterparts of medieval marvels, describing—or, perhaps better, imagining—the unexpected, inexplicable, and astounding phenomena of a particular region. While every age has its own sense of what constitutes a marvel, what remains the same is the powerful sense of wonder and fascination that they evoke in their beholders.

Because of their inherent appeal, marvels were one of the primary ways that medieval Europeans learned about distant lands and their "exotic" cultures. The manuscript tradition at the heart of this publication centers around the *Book of the Marvels of the World*, a fifteenth-century illustrated guide to the globe that catalogues the remarkable inhabitants, customs, and natural phenomena of various regions around the world, as it was then known to Europeans. Written in France by an unidentified author, the text describes these regions from the perspective of a medieval armchair traveler. Weaving together tales from ancient sources, traditional folklore, and the supposed reports of eyewitnesses, its compelling but mostly fictitious accounts were intended both to educate and to titillate its medieval readers. The images accompanying each location in the *Book of Marvels* translate the stories into vibrant visual compositions that readily appealed to medieval audiences.

For more than a century, one of the main copies of this text was kept in a private collection, largely inaccessible to scholars, much less the public. The acquisition of this long-understudied manuscript by the J. Paul Getty Museum in 2022 presented a unique opportunity to reunite the book with its near twin, preserved since 1911 in the collection of the Morgan Library & Museum. Perhaps for the first time since their creation some five hundred years ago, these sister manuscripts will be displayed next to each other in both Los Angeles and New York, offering visitors an unprecedented opportunity to see firsthand how medieval people marveled at their world.

Building on this core pairing, the exhibitions at the Getty and the Morgan bring to life the rich varieties of geographic knowledge in the Middle Ages and the impact that the *Book of Marvels* would have had on medieval viewers. Drawing on historical, literary, scientific, and societal traditions, the exhibitions introduce visitors to medieval European conceptions and misconceptions of a global world. In their exploration of "foreignness," they extend our ability to understand deeply rooted Eurocentric notions of difference and the perception of otherness. Ultimately, the medieval manuscripts on view in these exhibitions and explored in this volume demonstrate the long origins of cultural stereotypes and xenophobia, not only in terms of geography but also of race and religion.

The present volume provides an accessible and up-to-date introduction to the *Book of Marvels*, exploring the rich traditions of the imagery of marvels in the Middle Ages; the social and cultural implications of depicting foreign peoples and practices; and the role of copying and creativity in the production of these closely related manuscripts. After a brief epilogue reflecting on the contemporary relevance of medieval marvels, the volume ends with a series of plates that links excerpts from the text to their corresponding scenes in the miniatures, thus enabling modern readers to discover the manuscripts' marvels firsthand.

For the development and execution of this project, thanks and congratulations are due to Elizabeth Morrison, senior curator of manuscripts at the J. Paul Getty Museum; Joshua O'Driscoll, associate curator of medieval and Renaissance manuscripts at the Morgan Library & Museum; Larisa Grollemond, assistant curator of manuscripts, J. Paul Getty Museum; and Kelin Michael, former graduate intern of manuscripts, J. Paul Getty Museum. Noel B. Salazar, professor of social and cultural anthropology at Katholieke Universiteit Leuven, Belgium, generously provided the volume's epilogue. In addition, our thanks go out to all our colleagues who contributed to realizing the publication and the exhibitions at both institutions.

This project continues a long history of collaboration between the J. Paul Getty Museum and the Morgan Library & Museum, which resulted most recently in the groundbreaking exhibition *Holbein: Capturing Character* (2021–22). One aspect that connects both institutions is their renowned collections of medieval and Renaissance European manuscripts, making them natural partners for collaborations that combine the diverse strengths of our respective curators. The Morgan Library & Museum is additionally grateful for support from the New York Medieval Society and from an anonymous donor, and from other gracious donors who supported the exhibition after the printing of this publication.

Timothy Potts
Maria Hummer-Tuttle and Robert Tuttle Director
J. Paul Getty Museum

Colin B. Bailey
Director
The Morgan Library & Museum

es la terre. Il comment quelles perillet ou autrement elles p
rroient paistre. Item dit Colin que en affrique e
r Isle ou semblez bestes sont. et sont appellees altides et
genoilz se vondes quelles ne les pueent plaier. et pource ne
ent couchier. et combien quelles aient les jambes rondes to
es couvent si tost quon ne les scet prendre se non que qu
s se veullent reposer elles se appuient contre ung arbre et
gneur du pais qscevent larbre la scient par le pie pres d
ite lors quant celle beste se cuide apuier contre larbre elle ch
et larbre et ne se puet relever. et ainsi est prinse.

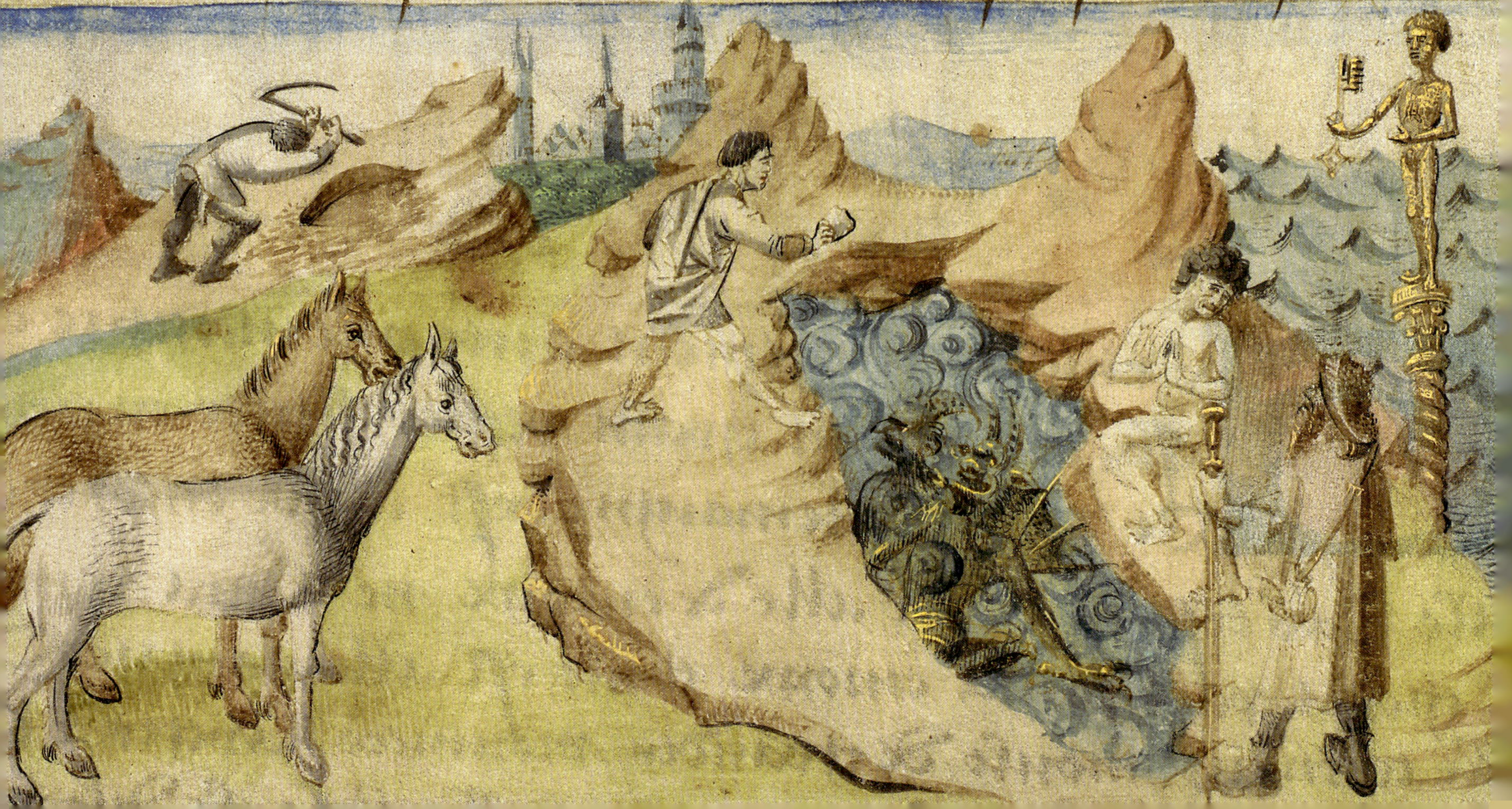

Note to the Reader

This book accompanies complementary exhibitions at the J. Paul Getty Museum, Los Angeles, and the Morgan Library & Museum, New York. The exhibitions present two illuminated French manuscripts of the *Book of the Marvels of the World* (*Livre des merveilles du monde*), one in the Getty's collection, the other in the Morgan's. Both manuscripts were probably created in Angers, in northwest France, around 1460–65. Pairing vivid descriptions with lively illuminations, the manuscripts explore dozens of locations around the globe, providing unique insight into how an elite French Christian audience imagined the world in the fifteenth century.

Some of the tales and their accompanying images may trouble modern viewers. At times, the text and miniatures demean religions, peoples, and customs, enabling the reader-viewers of their day to perceive them as not only different but also inferior. These manuscripts actively disseminated stereotypes of the kind that stoke the fires of prejudice to this day. Although the manuscripts describe mythical lands like Amazonia or Pygmy, most of the entries correspond to actual locations around the world, whose peoples had no voice in the characterization of their cultures. Thus, the text and imagery ought to be understood as historical artifacts shaped by deeply rooted cultural and social biases that privileged the perspective of white, elite, heteronormative, able-bodied, cisgendered Christian Europeans. These manuscripts describe the marvels of the globe, but in so doing they reveal much about the specific worldview of their sources, makers, and audiences. An awareness of how this narrow perspective informs the characterization of peoples and places in the *Marvels* serves as an important lesson on how the implicit biases of language and imagery play a formative role in defining and reinforcing social norms.

Introduction to the *Book of Marvels*

JOSHUA O'DRISCOLL, with LARISA GROLLEMOND, KELIN MICHAEL, and ELIZABETH MORRISON

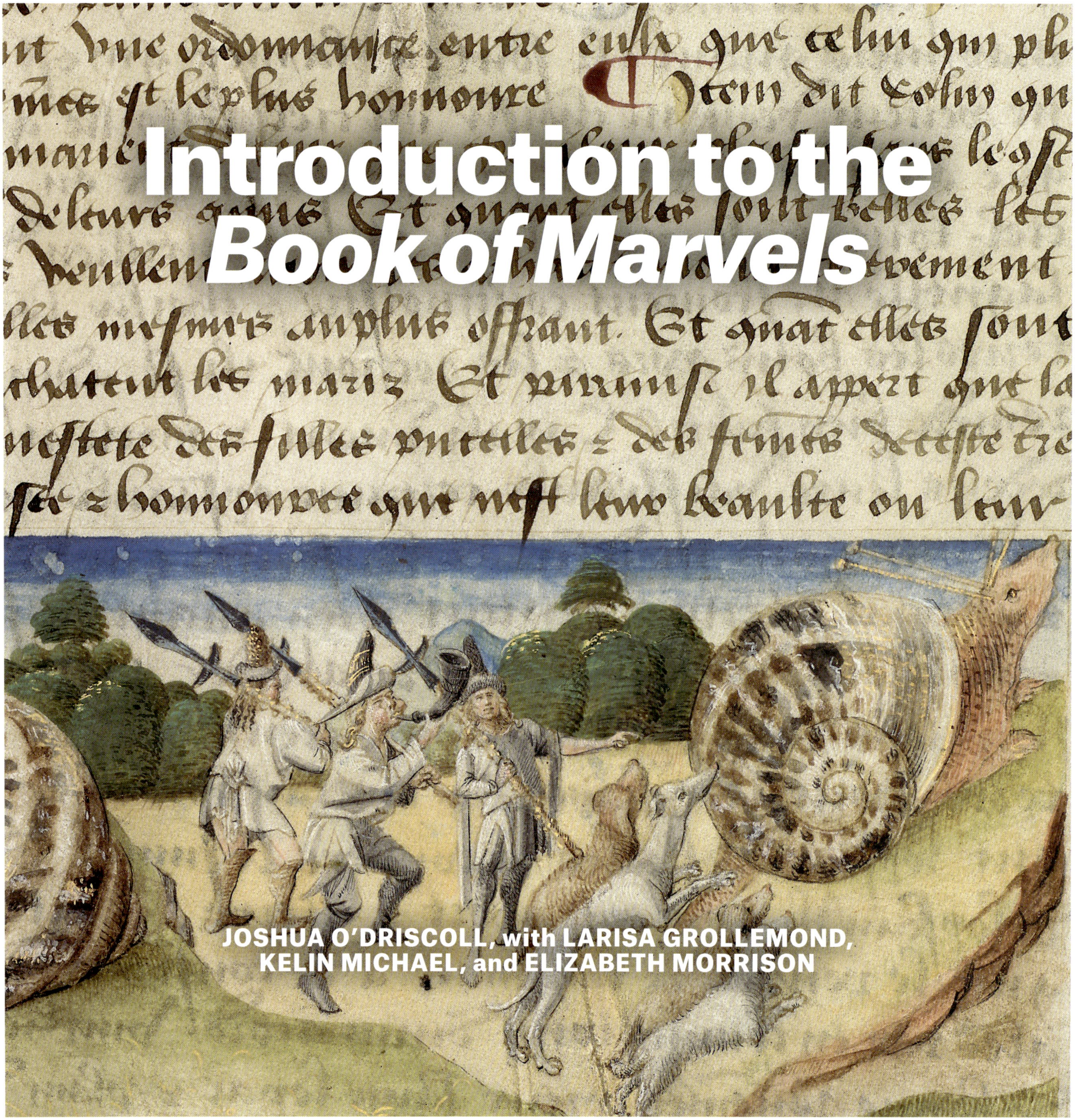

Medieval writings about the world were often based on a mixture of factual accounts, ancient traditions, and fantastic tales. One of the most fascinating examples of this genre is the *Book of the Marvels of the World* (*Livre des merveilles du monde*, hereafter *Marvels*), a fifteenth-century illustrated guide to the wonders of the globe, composed in France for a wealthy Christian audience.[1] Appealing to the tastes and expectations of its readers, it presents in great detail the remarkable inhabitants, customs, and natural phenomena of regions both near and far, from incredible accounts of cannibalism and giant snails to more mundane marvels like flames that cannot be extinguished or water that never boils (figs. 1, 2). In describing the inhabitants of various locales, the text goes beyond the usual medieval definitions of marvels, which were often regarded as natural occurrences that defy explanation. The English scholar Gervase of Tilbury (ca. 1150–1220), for example, offers one of the most concise statements on what constitutes a marvel: "[W]e call those things marvels which are beyond our comprehension, even though they are natural: in fact the inability to explain why a thing is so, constitutes a marvel."[2] Gervase goes on to differentiate between marvels and miracles: both result in wonder, but the former are natural phenomena while the latter, "being preternatural, we ascribe to divine power."[3] The fifteenth-century manuscripts that are the subject of this book take a much broader approach to the category of marvels, encompassing not only natural phenomena, but also peoples, cultural and religious practices, and man-made objects.[4] The prime characteristic uniting these marvels was the very wonder that they engendered in medieval European readers.

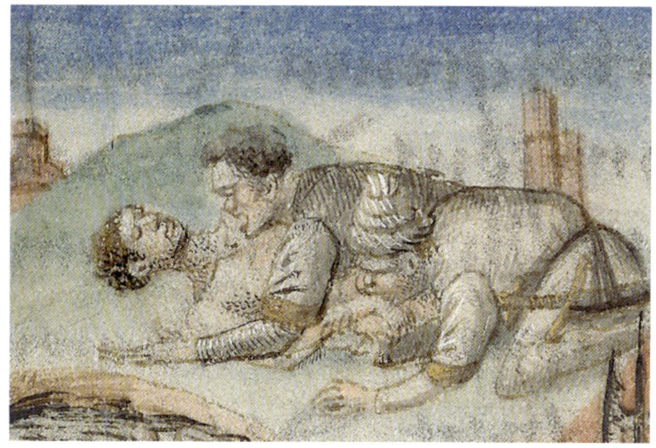

FIGURE 1 Master of the Geneva Boccaccio, *Scythia*, in the *Book of the Marvels of the World*. France, Angers, ca. 1460. New York, Morgan Library & Museum, Ms. M.461, fol. 70r (detail)

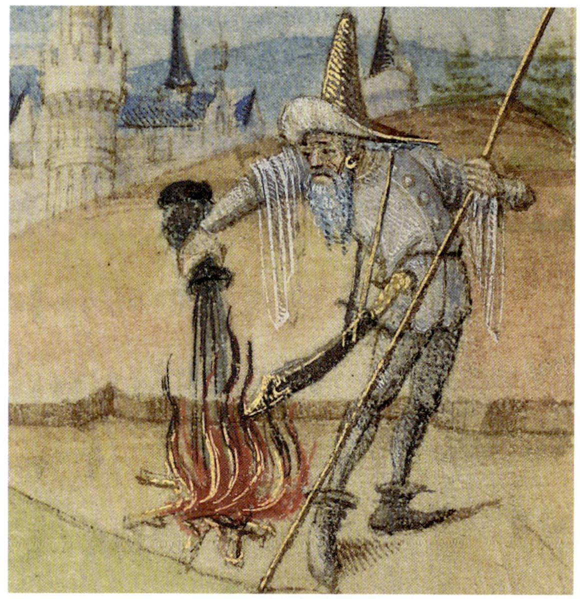

FIGURE 2 Master of the Geneva Boccaccio, *Moesia*, in the *Book of the Marvels of the World*. France, Angers, ca. 1460–65. Los Angeles, J. Paul Getty Museum, Ms. 124, fol. 18v (detail)

While many of the stories in the *Marvels* were passed down in ancient and medieval encyclopedias, some anecdotes give the impression of having being drawn instead from folklore. Examples include the story of a young man named Nicholas from Apulia who desired to live his life in the sea, as if a fish, or a woman from Brittany who lived for twenty years without eating or drinking anything except the Eucharist.[5] Bringing together a vast assortment of global wonders, compiled from various types of sources and experiences, the *Marvels* text routinely crosses the boundaries of subjects that today would be considered geography, ethnography, and the natural sciences. Unlike other European manuscripts focusing on the wonders of the world, which were only occasionally illustrated, all the surviving *Marvels* manuscripts contain an extensive sequence of images. Working together, the text and images of the *Marvels* manuscripts offered medieval readers a chance to vicariously encounter the world around them and to experience—as if firsthand—the wonders of creation. Moreover, the manuscripts provide today's readers with valuable insights into the worldview of their medieval audience and a lens through which to understand the inheritance of that viewpoint in the modern world.

Manuscripts of the *Marvels*

The *Marvels* text survives in four manuscript copies and one set of fragments, all richly illuminated. The earliest copy, preserved at the Bibliothèque nationale de France, Paris, Ms. fr. 1377–1379 (hereafter, BnF *Marvels*), is dated by an inscription to 1428. A second copy, now at the Morgan Library & Museum, New York, Ms. M.461 (hereafter, Morgan *Marvels*), is the most complete of the *Marvels* manuscripts and can be dated stylistically to a few decades later. A third manuscript, recently acquired by the J. Paul Getty Museum, Los Angeles, Ms. 124 (hereafter, Getty *Marvels*), contains about half of the expected text and illuminations, the rest having been removed at some point in its past. Based on stylistic analyses of the images in the Morgan and Getty *Marvels*, which can be considered twin manuscripts owing to their close correspondences, scholars have suggested that the two manuscripts were produced in Angers, in western France, around 1460–65 (see "Descriptions of the Morgan and Getty Manuscripts" at the end of this volume for further information). The latest surviving copy of the *Marvels*, painted by the prominent court artist Robinet Testard (active ca. 1470–1531), is also preserved at the Bibliothèque nationale de France, Ms. fr. 22971, and dates to around 1480–85. For this manuscript, Testard revised the shared pictorial cycle of the earlier copies to such an extent that it may be considered an outlier of the earlier group and will not be a focus of this volume.[6] In addition to these four manuscripts, two cuttings from a previously unknown copy emerged on the art market in 2017. Recently acquired by the Bibliothèque municipale in Angers, Rés. Ms. 2850, these fragments are closely related to the BnF copy and to the Morgan and Getty copies, further suggesting that the core group of *Marvels* manuscripts belonged to a particular time and place.

Frustratingly little is known about the patrons who commissioned the *Marvels* manuscripts, but a few clues provide some information about their early owners. An inscription at the end of the BnF *Marvels* states that the manuscript was made in Bourges for an otherwise unknown merchant named Renaud. It may be meaningful that this earliest copy was owned by someone involved in mercantile pursuits, as both the *Marvels* text and images refer to trade and goods on several occasions. The presence of the Anjou coat of arms in two of the images in the Morgan *Marvels* (Campania, fol. 15v; Ululand, fol. 79r, plate 20) indicates that it may have been made for someone in the entourage of the noted bibliophile Duke René of Anjou (1409–1480), or perhaps even for the duke himself. Furthermore, this heraldic evidence reinforces the association of the Morgan *Marvels* with Angers, the capital of the province of Anjou.[7] Because the Getty manuscript is so closely related to its counterpart at the Morgan, scholars have also linked it with Angers, although a sixteenth-century inscription places the manuscript just over one hundred kilometers away, in Rennes, where it may have been owned by a certain Jean Bregerault ("Dom[inus] Jehan Bregerault"), possibly a nobleman or a cleric. As with the Morgan *Marvels*, we can speculate that a high-ranking member in the courtly circle of René of Anjou may have been the original patron of the Getty copy.[8] The fragments of the Angers *Marvels* provide no information about the manuscript's patron or subsequent owners.

Based on these few pieces of evidence, it stands to reason that the patrons and early readers of the *Marvels* manuscripts were wealthy, well-educated members of the elite. Like Renaud, they may have engaged in the kind of commerce and travel depicted in the images, or perhaps, like René of Anjou, they may have been consumers of luxury items from distant places like China and the Middle East. For such readers, the pairing of a catalogue of wonders with an extensive program of engaging images must have been quite desirable. In this respect, the *Marvels* manuscripts can be understood in the context of a broader shift that took place in French culture during the late fourteenth and early fifteenth centuries, when scholarly texts were increasingly being translated from Latin into French and adapted to suit the interests of an urban elite.[9] The *Marvels* manuscripts responded to both a growing desire for knowledge among the French nobility and a burgeoning market for deluxe illuminated manuscripts.

Text of the *Marvels*

In terms of its structure, the first half of the text classifies marvels by the regions in which they occur. Its fifty-six short chapters are arranged alphabetically (see the "List of Locations in the *Book of Marvels*"), from Africa to Ululand (in Norway). Taking a different approach, the second half of the book consists of seventeen lengthier chapters in which marvels are grouped into conceptual categories ranging from humans and animals to buildings, monsters, and poisons. Throughout the work, the author generally refrains from adding personal opinions or remarks. Occasionally, however, it seems to have been impossible to avoid comment, as in the reference to the alleged practice of child sacrifice in pre-Christian Provence—a tradition described in the text as "very odious."[10] For most medieval Christians, such a story would have played into longstanding anti-Semitic prejudices, as it purposefully recalled the false conspiracy that Jews engaged in the ritual murder of Christian children (plate 15, no. 1).[11] Another example of authorial intervention can be found in the chapter on the marvels of England. When discussing a wonder created by the wizard Merlin, described as a "great round dance of giants in stone" (likely a reference to Stonehenge), the author warns readers about the dangers of dancing, which is "the way and the path to hell."[12]

These are exceptions, however, and for the most part the author lists one marvel after the other, with no overarching narrative and only minimal use of transitions or overt moralizations. In this respect, it reads more like a catalogue or encyclopedia than a guidebook or travel narrative. Despite this apparently neutral stance, the text was clearly intended for a specific audience of elite, white, Christian Europeans. Given this framework, the narratives within the *Marvels* consistently reinforced notions of civility, superiority, beauty, and propriety from that perspective.

In terms of its sources, the text of the *Marvels* manuscripts was closely modeled on an earlier, much larger work in Latin that was adapted, revised, and translated into French by an unknown individual (hereafter, "Translator") in the late fourteenth or early fifteenth century. This source text was a vast encyclopedia composed about a century earlier by a French monastic scholar named Pierre Bersuire (d. 1362).[13] As a young monk, Bersuire was called to the papal court at Avignon, where he served in the retinue of the powerful and well-connected Cardinal Pierre des Prés (1288–1361), vice-chancellor to the pope. It was there—no doubt profiting from the immense resources and intellectual climate of the papal library—that Bersuire began a decades-long project of composing and compiling his two great works (ca. 1320–45), which together sought to categorize and explain all the visible and invisible aspects of the world. The first is his encyclopedia known as the *Moral Reduction* (*Reductorium morale*), which he divided into sixteen sections, or "books"; the fourteenth book (the main source for the Translator) was entirely devoted to the marvels of the world. The second work, the *Moral Repertory* (*Repertorium morale*), is a catalogue of thousands of biblical words, arranged alphabetically.[14] As their titles indicate, Bersuire's twin compendia provided a moralization—that is, a Christian moral or allegorical interpretation—for each entry. Bersuire explicitly states on several occasions that he considers preachers and clerics to be his core audience, and that he intended these dense tomes (taking up about one thousand pages each) to aid in the art of preaching and composing sermons.

The success of Bersuire's project in no way matched his ambitions. A few dozen manuscripts preserve various portions of the text, but only one set of early fifteenth-century manuscripts contains a complete copy of the two tomes. Belonging to the monastic library of the Augustinian Friars (*Grands Augustins*) in Paris, the set's first volume opens with a frontispiece that shows the monastic author kneeling before his patron, Cardinal Pierre des Prés. Bersuire presents his work to the cardinal while pointing up to a representation of Adam and Eve standing between Heaven and Hell, an image that encapsulates the cosmic scale of Bersuire's scholarship (fig. 3).[15] Apart from the frontispiece to this set of manuscripts, no other copy of the *Reduction* was illustrated, and the majority belonged to the libraries of religious institutions, as one would expect given Bersuire's intended audience of preachers and clerics.

In adapting this source material, the Translator did more than just bring Bersuire's encyclopedia into the vernacular. A close comparison of the two texts reveals that the Translator systematically removed Bersuire's long moralizations and occasionally even left out certain marvels, for reasons that are never stated.[16] In other cases, the Translator substituted venerable ancient authorities such as Pliny the Elder or Solinus where Bersuire cited more contemporary sources or

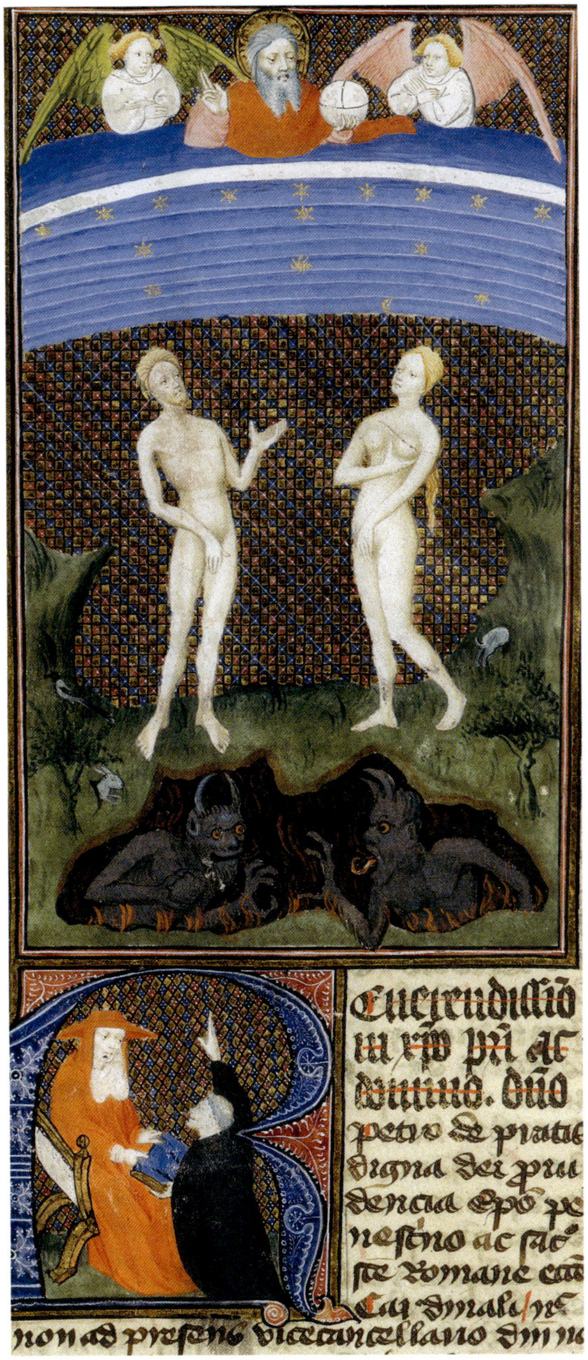

even his own firsthand experience in vouching for a marvel's authenticity.

Little is known about the Translator apart from what is stated in a prologue that survives only in the Morgan *Marvels*.[17] Preceding this short text is the portrait of a male scribe, set within an architectural space that is both ecclesiastical and scholarly (fig. 4). An ornate lectern occupies the center of the composition, behind which hangs a bookshelf on a recessed wall. These same elements appear in a much celebrated earlier drawing that served as the frontispiece for an unfinished copy of the *Moralized Bible* (*Bible moralisée*) made for Duke Philip the Bold of Burgundy (1342–1404) shortly before his death (fig. 5).[18] Attributable to a leading artist of the time—Paul van Lymborch (also known as Paul de Limbourg)—or a close follower, the drawing features Saint Jerome, who translated the Bible into Latin. He reads from a lectern while receiving divine inspiration from two sources: the dove—representing the Holy Spirit—speaking into his ear and the beams of light streaming into the space from on high. Flipping the composition, the Morgan artist removed any overt sign of divine inspiration and emphasized instead the scholarly aspects of an author at work. However generic it may seem, the image conveyed at least two distinct messages to its fifteenth-century audience. First, the text at hand is the product of careful study and learning—a point repeatedly emphasized in the prologue. Second, these are deluxe commissions,

FIGURE 3 Initial *R*: *Pierre Bersuire Presents His Work to Cardinal Pierre des Prés* and *Adam and Eve Standing between Heaven and Hell*, in Pierre Bersuire, *Moral Reduction*. France, Paris, ca. 1400–1425. Paris, Bibliothèque nationale de France, Ms. lat. 16785, fol. 1r (detail)

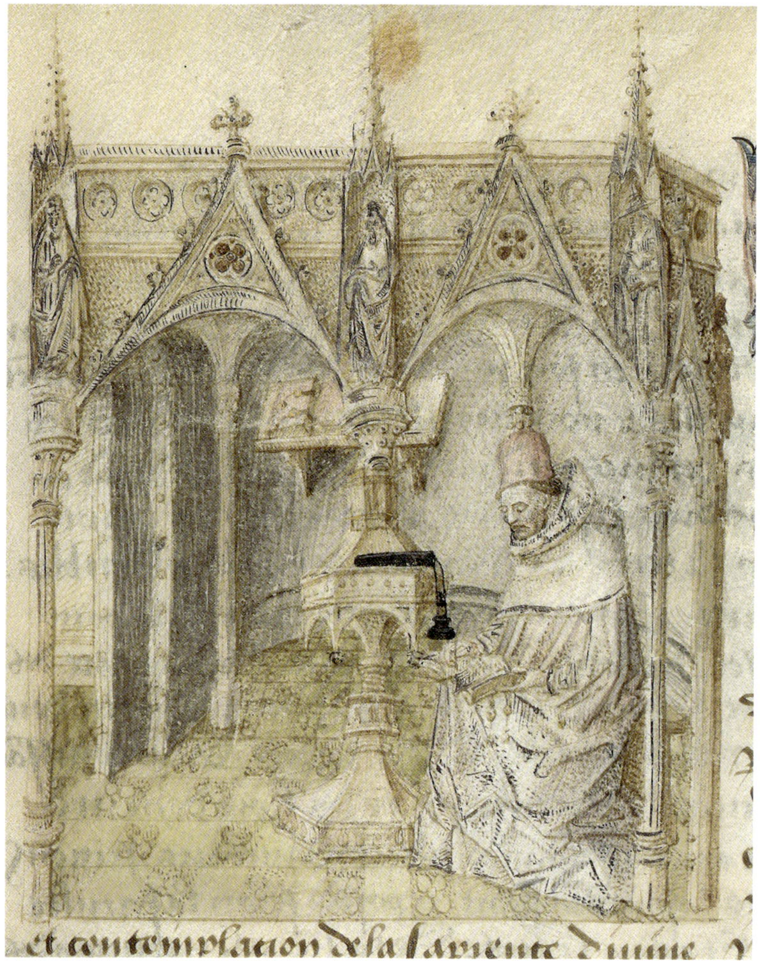

FIGURE 4 Master of the Geneva Boccaccio, Author Portrait, in the *Book of the Marvels of the World*. France, Angers, ca. 1460. New York, Morgan Library & Museum, Ms. M.461, fol. 3r (detail)

a status evident in the physical characteristics of both the Morgan and Getty manuscripts, from the quality of their parchment to their calligraphic script with numerous flourishes gracing the top of most pages and, not least, their sophisticated images, which are marvels in their own right.

Images of the *Marvels*

One of the unusual aspects of the *Marvels* manuscripts is the fact that all known copies are illuminated, even though the source text, Bersuire's encyclopedia, had no such visual tradition. The insistence on imagery in the *Marvels* manuscripts

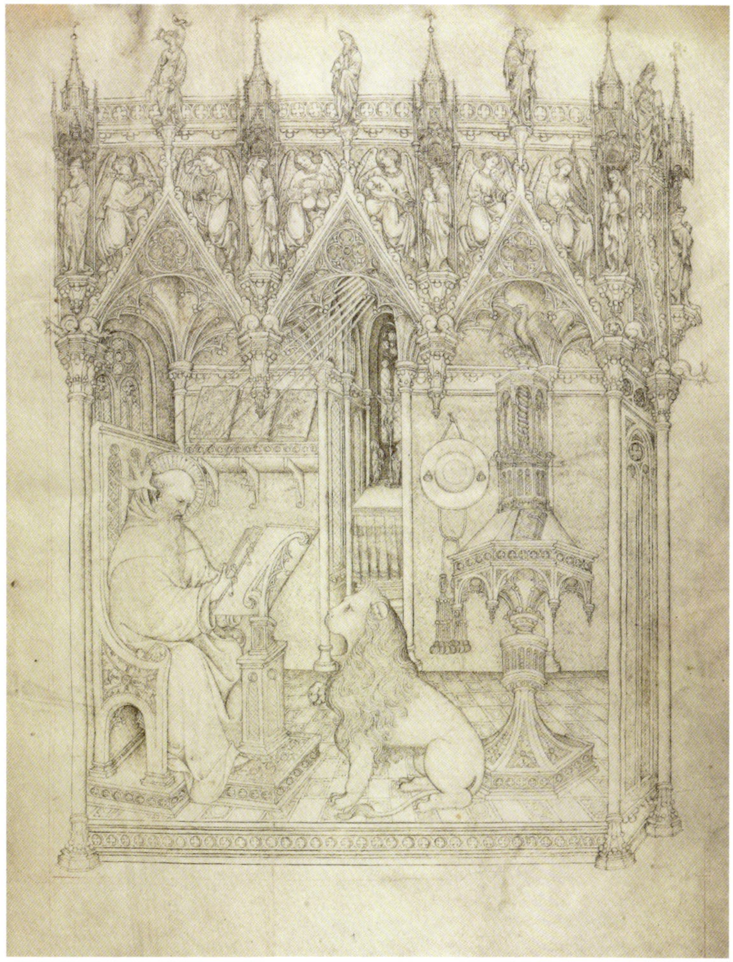

FIGURE 5 Paul van Lymborch, *Saint Jerome in His Study*, in the *Moralized Bible*. France, Paris, ca. 1402–4. Paris, Bibliothèque nationale de France, Ms. fr. 166 (unfoliated frontispiece)

indicates that the illumination was integral to the manuscripts' overall function. As the Translator explains in the prologue, marvels are a continual source of "delectation and pleasure" because people, by their very nature, "delight in hearing things that are new and unaccustomed."[19] The Translator goes on to explain that learning about marvels is a way of understanding the world, which is, in turn, a way of knowing God. Following this logic, the images not only enhance the "delectation and pleasure" of the reader, but also—and more importantly—they actively shape how readers encounter the text. Indeed, the chapter on India states, "There are many marvels and various things that seem unbelievable to men who have not previously seen and read the stories."[20] It is precisely this combined experience of seeing and reading about wonders that makes them believable. Seeing, in fact, precedes reading, just as the illuminations precede each of the geographic locations in the manuscripts. Essentially, the manuscripts themselves, with their detailed images and texts, served as testamentary witnesses to the existence of the marvels they describe.

Introducing each of the fifty-six chapters on the various regions of the known world, the images distill and reflect core elements from their accompanying entries. The systematic arrangement gives the text an air of encyclopedic detachment and scientific authority. Yet the entries themselves are filled with stand-alone anecdotes that succeed each other in a seemingly haphazard fashion. The program of images mirrors this overall approach, whereby each new place or category is introduced by a painted representation, thus reinforcing the sense of order created by the textual divisions. The viewer, however, is often hard pressed to identify and comprehend the marvels presented within each image. Akin to a collage, the disparate elements are combined into a single composition, creating what one scholar has referred to as "menu pictures," which can only be deciphered by a reader thoroughly acquainted with the text.[21] The complexity of a given image often parallels the length of its corresponding chapter. For places with very long entries, such as India and Scythia (north of the Black Sea), for example, the corresponding images contain a panoply of visualizations (plates 12 and 16). Other images, like that of Thule (possibly Orkney, the Hebrides, Shetland, or Iceland), focus on fewer anecdotes (plate 18), hewing closely to the level of detail provided by the entries. Very occasionally, as in the image of Asia, the composition is nothing more than an empty landscape, devoid of figures but nevertheless evocative, inviting the reader's imagination to fill the space (fig. 6).

For the most part, the artists produced faithful representations of the marvels as they are described in the text. In one instance, however, the representation departs from the text in a way that is as striking as it is troubling to today's viewer. Citing the ancient Greek historian Herodotus (fifth century BCE) as a source, the short text on Europe characterizes the appearance and habits of Europeans in direct juxtaposition to their counterparts in Africa.[22] Unsurprisingly for a prejudicial medieval European text, the inhabitants of Europe are described as "handsomer, stronger, bigger, and bolder" than the inhabitants of Africa, because the latter's continual exposure to the sun causes "their vital spirits to escape from their bodies."[23] The text goes on to state that Africans "are short, thin, dry, and black as coal, and they have kinky hair . . . they are lacking in courage, cowardly, and without boldness. And quite otherwise are the Europeans . . . [who are] more courageous."[24] In the BnF *Marvels*, the artist used this text as a point of departure to render the scene as a meeting between a group of Europeans and a group of Africans, who hold their hands up to each other as if in greeting (fig. 7). Later, the Morgan artist altered the scene significantly, with the two groups confronting each other across a noticeable gap between them (fig. 8). The buildings behind each group serve as symbols of the artist's imagined idea of the corresponding regions. Clad in shining armor, a group of Europeans approaches from the

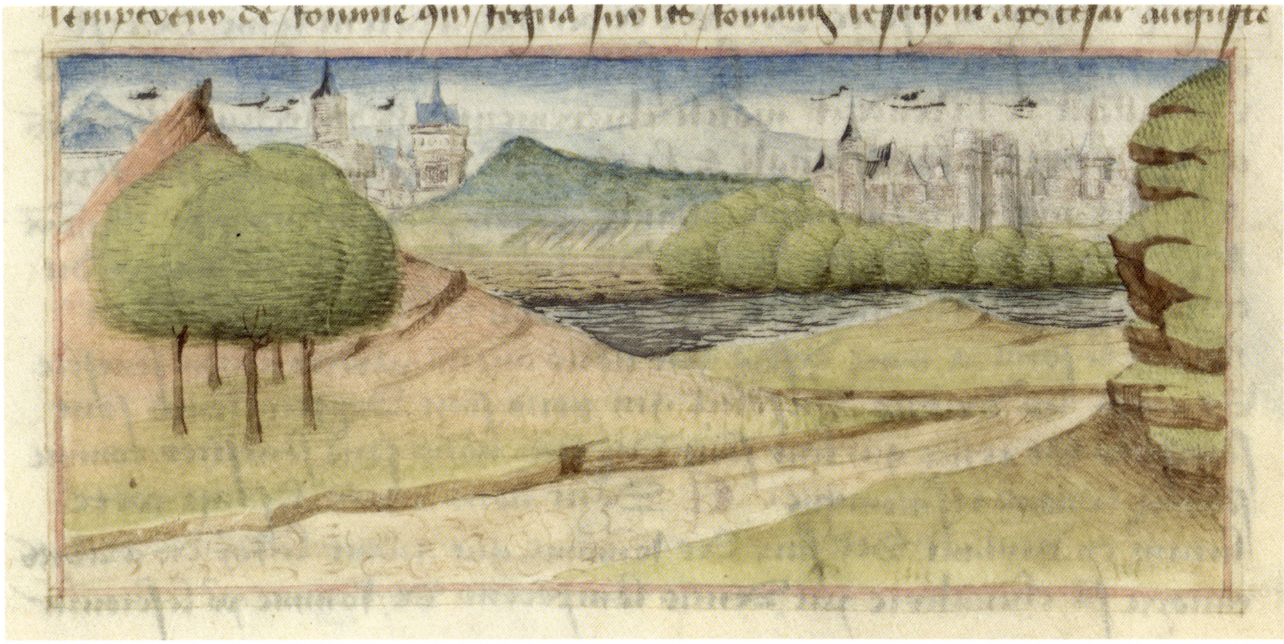

FIGURE 6 Master of the Geneva Boccaccio, *Asia*, in the *Book of the Marvels of the World*. France, Angers, ca. 1460. New York, Morgan Library & Museum, Ms. M.461, fol. 11v (detail)

left, led by two figures elegantly dressed in the latest courtly French fashions. Advancing from the right, a group of Africans are depicted with distinctive headgear and weaponry, like the prominent scimitar, suggesting they are Muslims, known pejoratively as "Moors."[25] Those in front are turbaned white men, while the soldiers in back are Black Africans, with racially stereotyped facial features that were intended to be perceived as unappealing by white Europeans of the time.[26] Revealing of the religious and racial bigotry that was widespread in Christian Europe, the image no doubt recalled the incessant battles initiated by Christians over hundreds of years to wrest the Holy Land from Muslim rule. These Crusades were unsuccessful and were still felt with a sense of bitter loss on the part of a fifteenth-century French Christian audience. Moreover, the destructive legacy of this overt Islamophobia and racism can still be seen today in the abhorrent rhetoric of white supremacy movements across Europe and North America.

The confrontation between Europe and Africa in the Morgan manuscript is merely the most blatant example of a consistent and pervasive approach to staging marvels as a juxtaposition between a presumed "us" and an othered "them." In other

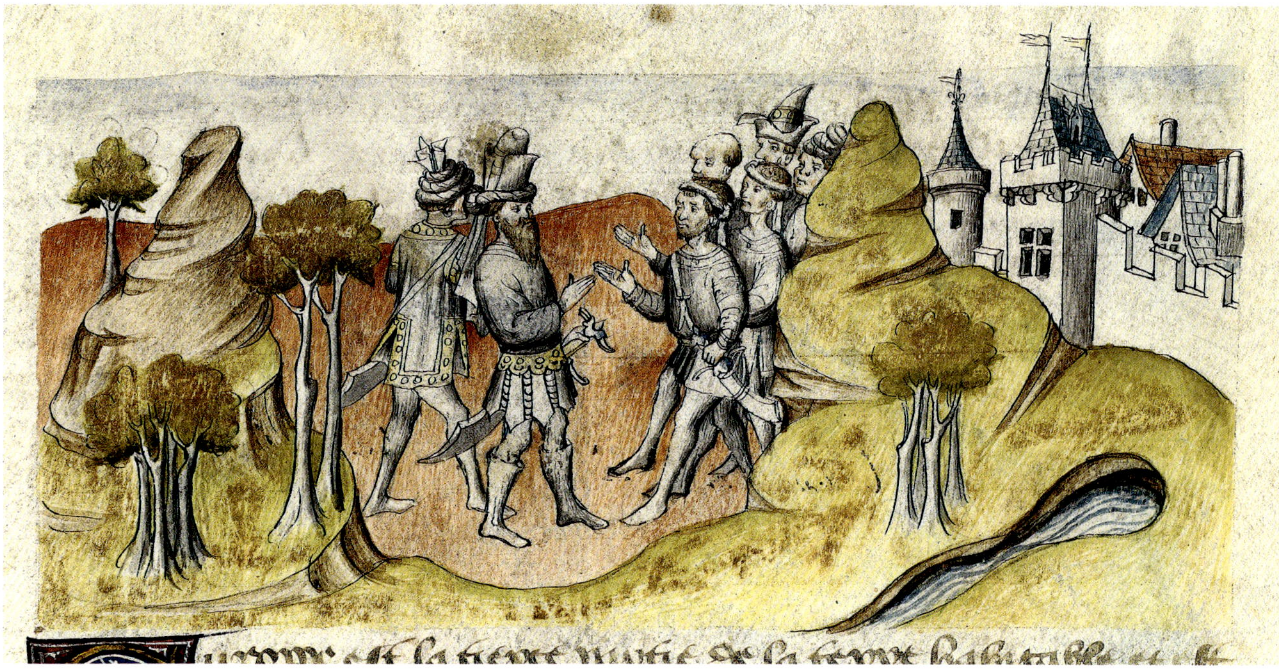

FIGURE 7 Master of Marguerite d'Orléans, *Europe*, in the *Book of the Marvels of the World*. France, Bourges, 1428. Paris, Bibliothèque nationale de France, Ms. fr. 1378, fol. 1r (detail)

words, throughout the *Marvels* manuscripts, European regions are often presented as places of normalcy, beauty, and civility, where marvels are wondrous rather than potentially threatening, such as a remarkable people in Italy who can walk through fire untouched by the flames (plate 13, no. 1) or vineyards that spring up across France without grapes ever being planted (plate 9, no. 1). This is in stark contrast to those regions distant from Europe, which are often depicted in ways that exaggerate or invent differences in appearance, customs, and religious practices.

Depictions of racial diversity are generally not a feature of the *Marvels* manuscripts, making the few exceptions, such as the one discussed above, all the more remarkable. Another example

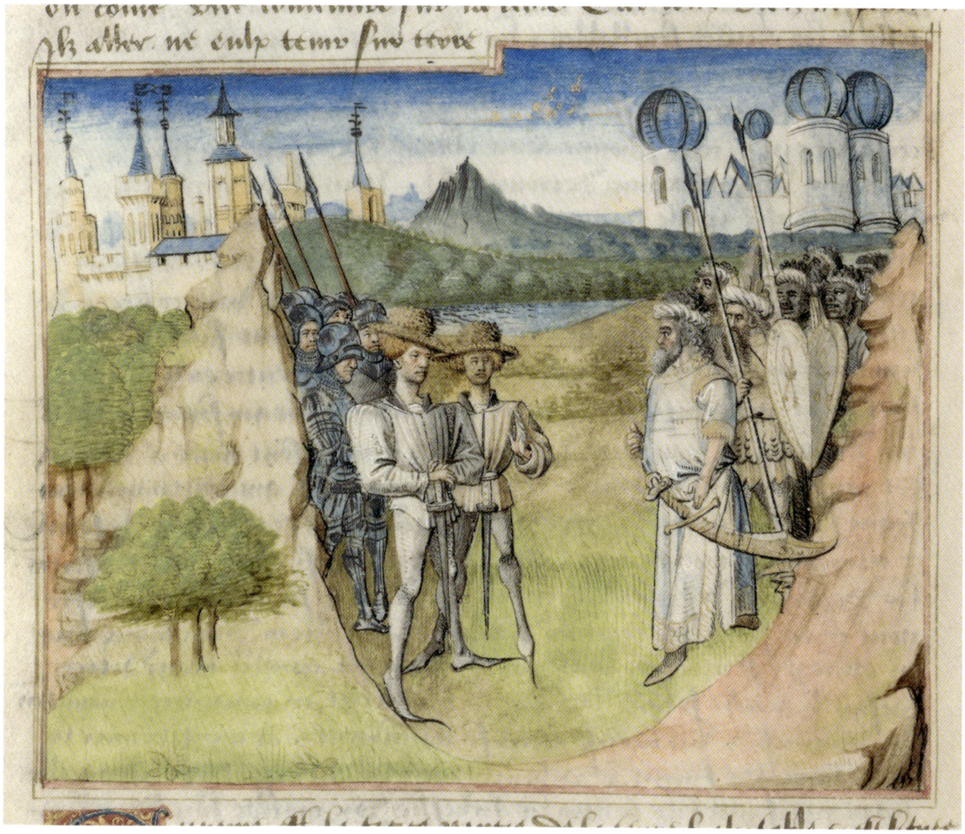

FIGURE 8 Master of the Geneva Boccaccio, *Europe*, in the *Book of the Marvels of the World*. France, Angers, ca. 1460. New York, Morgan Library & Museum, Ms. M.461, fol. 31v (detail)

occurs in the section of the manuscript discussing the wonders of the human body, where the text recounts a story relating to the importance of imagination during pregnancy: "We can take the example of a woman who conceived and gave birth to a child who was all black like a Moor from the land of the Moors, and this woman was accused of having sexual relations with an Ethiopian—even though she was a worthy woman. But later it was found and verified that at the instant the child was conceived she thought of an Ethiopian that she had seen the previous day, because she had never seen such a man before."[27] The text never states that the mother is white and Christian, but the reader is meant to presume so, as she is "accused" of sexual relations with a Black man, despite being "a worthy woman." In the accompanying image, the parents are both depicted as white, while the artist only painted the baby's head black, as if to emphasize the point that it really was the child of two white parents (plate 21, fol. 35r).[28] The illuminator's choice to depict the parents as white also carried with it the assumption that the family was Christian, as the distinct categories of race and religion that we acknowledge today were far more intertwined in the Middle Ages, with one often standing in for the other. An example is the fact that in the story, the terms "Moor" and "Ethiopian" are used as if they were interchangeable.[29] Implicit in this anecdote is the assumed superiority of white European Christians, and the resulting fear of such a woman having sexual relations with a Black Muslim man.

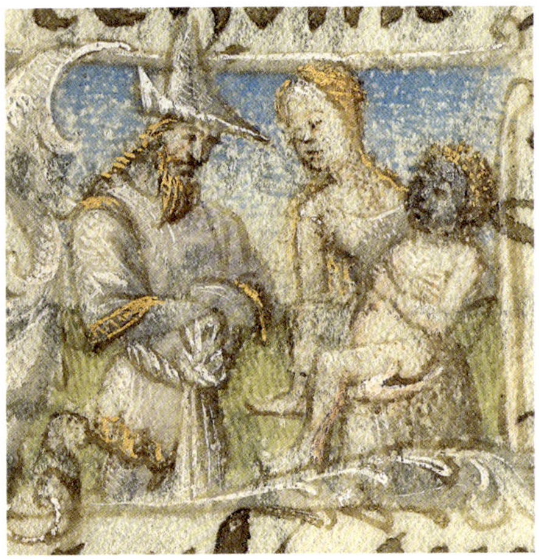
DETAIL, PLATE 21, WONDERS OF THE HUMAN BODY

Other images in the *Marvels* manuscripts were just as key in shaping the readers' understanding of the text. None of the images depict everything described in their corresponding entries, but each presents a selection or interpretation of the individual stories told in the text that depicts their essential points. The artists seem to have selected vignettes that were easy to visualize and most readily recognizable as marvels. Peoples with physical differences, fabulous animals, valuable natural resources, violent encounters, religious practices, and visually distinct customs are among the most frequently depicted imagery. Because each image precedes the written description of the place, the images help to focus the viewer's attention on particular aspects of the text that follows. Most French manuscripts of the period that feature illuminations at beginnings of chapters simply visualize the first story found in the subsequent text. The arrangement of the *Marvels* manuscripts, by contrast, encouraged readers to hunt through the text to seek out the individual stories they had already been primed to expect by the images, creating an interactive relationship between image and text. The "menu picture" format also provides something the text on its own cannot: the striking visual impact of seeing an array of marvels all at once, which is quite distinct from the experience of reading the linear text.

Complex and often densely coded, the *Marvels* manuscripts provide a glimpse into how a specific audience—in this case, wealthy Christian Europeans—imagined the larger medieval world. The images transform what would otherwise be an encyclopedic catalogue of marvels into a lively visual tour of the globe. It is important for modern viewers looking back at these wondrous tales not to think of them in terms of a strict division between empirically true and patently false, but rather to strive for a more nuanced understanding of medieval marvels as creative "non-impossibilities," as one scholar recently described them.[30] The wondrous events, peoples, and places described by the *Marvels* were intended both to instruct and to entertain, igniting the imagination of their medieval viewers in a way that is very much at odds with the need for categorization that is so prevalent in the modern world.

The remainder of this volume examines the *Marvels* manuscripts from a variety of perspectives, turning first to the rich encyclopedic traditions from which these manuscripts emerged; then exploring how the interrelationship of text and images may have evoked not only overt wonder but also covert fears in the manuscripts' wealthy and powerful audience; followed by an examination of the circumstances of the manuscripts' production in fifteenth-century France; and finally an epilogue briefly assessing how a group of medieval manuscripts can help shed light on today's world. Accompanied by a representative set of plates and corresponding excerpts from the text, these essays aim to provide a fuller understanding of the multifaceted role of marvels in the medieval world. This volume also provides a chance to reflect on what marvels say about their beholders, both then and now.

NOTES

1 The popular myth that those in the Middle Ages did not realize the earth was a globe, but rather thought it was a flat disk, originated in the early modern period as a way to denigrate medieval education and learning. In fact, the idea of the world as a globe was widespread during the medieval period.

2 Banks and Binns 2002, 559. Note that Figg and Friedman 2018 spell his name Gervaise, as can be seen throughout the plates section.

3 However, medieval authors, including Gervase himself, often conflated "miracles" and "marvels" (Bynum 1999, 815).

4 Unless otherwise identified, all manuscripts described in the essays are on parchment.

5 Figg and Friedman 2018, 214 and 229; neither of these marvels is depicted in the accompanying images.

6 For more on this manuscript, see Friedman, Giogoli, and Figg 2018.

7 König 2009.

8 König 2009.

9 See Fourcade 2021; Hedeman 2022, 1–13.

10 Figg and Friedman 2018, 271.

11 See Teter 2020. In this essay, when quotations appear in an entry illustrated in the plates section of this volume, the plate number and the number of the excerpt are given (see the "Plates with Translations" at the end of this volume). For quotations taken from entries that cannot be read in a plate, the translation is cited directly.

12 Figg and Friedman 2018, 185.

13 Samaran 1962, 304–49; Tesnière 1994.

14 A third work, the *Directorium morale*, was either never finished or has been lost. Bersuire also composed a popular French translation of Livy, and a now-lost map of the world.

15 Samaran 1962, 434–35; Tesnière 1994, 230.

16 Figg and Friedman 2018, 24–32; Friedman 2019, 11.

17 Figg and Friedman 2018, 395–98. This text may also have been in the other three copies, which have suffered losses.

18 König 2018.

19 Figg and Friedman 2018, 397.

20 Figg and Friedman 2018, 237.

21 Figg and Friedman 2018, 46.

22 On race in Herodotus, see Samuels 2015. In the BnF *Marvels*, there are no Black figures depicted in the image for Europe. This image has been lost from the Getty *Marvels*, and the image from the Testard *Marvels* is completely different.

23 The construction and meaning of race in the Middle Ages form a complex topic and the subject of substantial research by specialists. The following is just a sample of the most recent discussions of the topic: Ramey 2014, Heng 2018, Vernon 2018, Whitaker 2019, and Collins and Keene 2022.

24 Figg and Friedman 2018, 220. In the Getty and Morgan manuscripts, this is the only place in the section of the *Marvels* devoted to geographical places where Black people are depicted, despite the number of locations where one would expect to encounter such individuals. This lack of racial distinction in the imagery of the *Marvels* manuscripts is also true more generally (as in depictions of regions in Asia and the Middle East).

25 The term "Moor" derives from the name of the ancient kingdom of Mauretania in North Africa. In the Middle Ages, Moors were specifically the Muslim inhabitants of Iberia (al-Andalus; present-day Spain and Portugal) as well as North Africa (the Maghreb). The term was more generally used throughout Europe, however, to refer to anyone of Arab or African descent with the derogatory sense of being an "infidel," meaning non-Christian.

26 See Akbari 2009.

27 Figg and Friedman 2018, 297.

28 The section devoted to natural phenomena in the Morgan *Marvels* is unillustrated. However, in the Morgan *Marvels*, the image devoted to Great Britain features two women who have dyed their faces with herbs to appear as "black as the Moors of Mauritania" (plate 4, no. 3). Great Britain is one of the lost images in the Getty *Marvels*.

29 See Mittman 2015; Heng 2018 (esp. chap. 4); Whitaker 2019; and Patton 2019, 185–88.

30 Karnes 2022, 16–17 and 85–92.

Envisioning the Medieval World

Encyclopedias, Maps, and Travel Writing

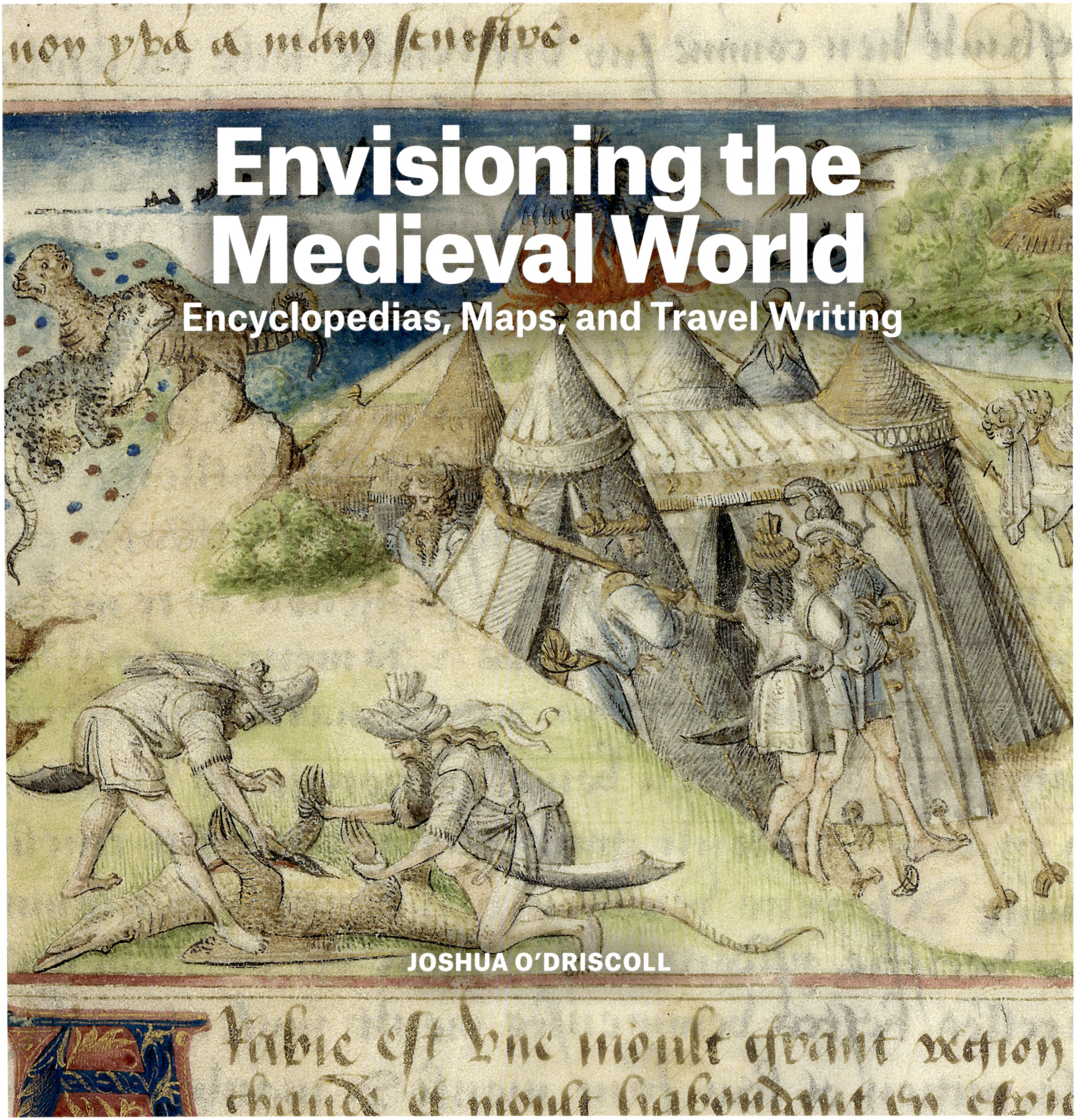

JOSHUA O'DRISCOLL

The *Book of the Marvels of the World* (*Livre des merveilles du monde*, hereafter *Marvels*) presents its readers with a collection of the most wondrous tales from around the world. From a modern perspective, it may be difficult to see how such books could serve an educational, much less spiritual purpose. Yet this is precisely the function given to the text in the prologue added by the text's Translator. Citing a key passage from Paul's epistle to the Romans (1:20), the Translator emphasizes that studying the visible things of the world leads to a better understanding of "higher and heavenly things that are invisible and spiritual."[1] The prologue explains further that "marvels and the diversity of the world" offer an ideal subject matter for this type of inquiry, since people naturally derive pleasure from hearing about new and unaccustomed things. In other words, marvels are an inherently enjoyable way of learning, and this increase in knowledge should, in turn, result in a greater love of the divine. While the prologue is emphatic about the book's important spiritual benefits, the text itself almost entirely refrains from drawing any moral lessons or religious interpretations from the marvels it so carefully details. Instead, the text follows a well-established practice of cataloguing wonders or marvels (*mirabilia*)—a practice with deep roots in the long tradition of ancient and medieval encyclopedias. Indeed, the three main authors cited as sources in the prologue—Pliny the Elder (23/24–79 CE), Solinus (ca. 300 CE), and Gervase of Tilbury (ca. 1150–1220)—all wrote encyclopedic compilations that were in many ways themselves books of marvels.[2] By exploring the illustrated traditions of encyclopedias, as well as the closely related categories of maps and travel writing, this essay examines how looking at marvels was a characteristically medieval way of encountering the world.

Studying the World

The *Marvels* text mentions the famous Roman scholar Pliny the Elder well over four hundred times, making him by far the book's most-cited source. Known modestly and somewhat misleadingly as the *Natural History* (*Historia naturalis*), Pliny's magisterial encyclopedia could more aptly be titled "Inquiry into Everything," as it aims to condense into one work the totality of human knowledge.[3] As critics have observed for centuries, however, Pliny's encyclopedia is notoriously difficult to read in its entirety, not just because of its terse style and obscure vocabulary, but more so because of the text's endless and unpredictable digressions.[4] The section on grains, for example, includes detailed histories of Roman agriculture and economics, whereas Pliny's famous discussions of ancient art appear tangentially in the entries on stones, metals, and pigments.[5] The unwieldiness of the text, combined with its immense importance as an authoritative repository of ancient knowledge, meant that Pliny's encyclopedia was a constant source for successive generations of medieval compilers and encyclopedists—like Pierre Bersuire and the *Marvels* Translator—who continually mined the *Natural History* for nuggets of ancient lore that could be reused and reworked for their own texts.[6]

Pliny's encyclopedia was influential throughout the Middle Ages not just for its contents but also for its conceptual approach to classifying knowledge according to principles of contrast and antithesis. A particularly relevant example for the *Marvels* text is Pliny's approach to ethnography—that is, the practice of describing the habits, customs, and characteristics of diverse cultures. While ethnographic anecdotes can be found throughout the *Natural History*, the greatest concentration occurs in Book 7, on human beings. Rather than offering a systematic description of the known cultures of the world, Pliny begins by contrasting the nature of humans versus animals. He then launches into a lengthy descriptive catalogue of the most distinct varieties of people from across the globe: like the mouthless Astomi, who eat by smelling (plate 12, no. 5), or the headless Blemmyes, with faces in their chests (plate 8, no. 4), or people from Scythia with one eye in the center of their head (plate 16, no. 6). By structuring his presentation of human diversity as a contrast between "generic" human beings on the one hand, and drastically different varieties of marvelous people on the other, Pliny set an important precedent for medieval approaches to ethnography, which likewise focused on the most distinctive examples of human diversity as a way of defining—by contrast—expected norms of appearance and behavior.[7]

By some estimates, well over two hundred manuscripts of Pliny's *Natural History* survive from the Middle Ages, most of which were read and copied by medieval scholars and their students. Among the very earliest surviving copies is a ninth-century manuscript from the abbey of Lorsch (in present-day Germany), home to one of the most important monastic libraries of the early Middle Ages (fig. 9).[8] Like the Lorsch Pliny, shown here at the beginning of Book 7, most manuscript copies of the *Natural History*—and indeed, of any medieval encyclopedia—were unillustrated. As scholarly reference works, medieval encyclopedias were designed for clarity and ease of use rather than visual splendor. Beginning in the fourteenth and fifteenth centuries, however, a shift occurred, in which wealthy patrons began to commission deluxe copies of encyclopedias like Pliny's. In the 1460s, for example, Gregorio Lolli Piccolomini, secretary to Pope Pius II, commissioned an illuminated copy of the *Natural History* from Giuliano di Amadeo, a monastic painter who worked on several projects for the papal court.[9] In this manuscript, each of the thirty-seven books of Pliny's encyclopedia is introduced by an image contained within the initial letter of the first word. All but four of these initials contain figural scenes that relate to the contents of their respective sections. The initial *M* at the beginning of Book 7,

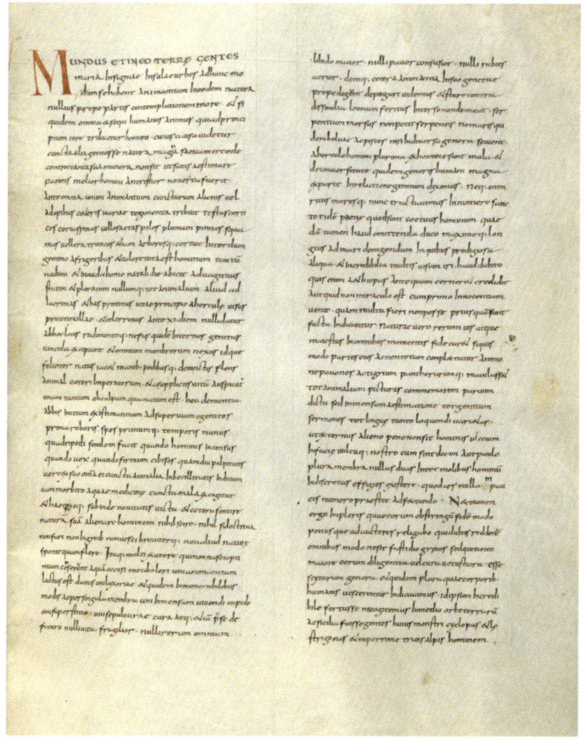

FIGURE 9 Initial *M* for Book 7 (On Humans), in Pliny the Elder, *Natural History*. Germany, Lorsch, ca. 830–40. New York, Morgan Library & Museum, Ms. M.871, fol. 74r

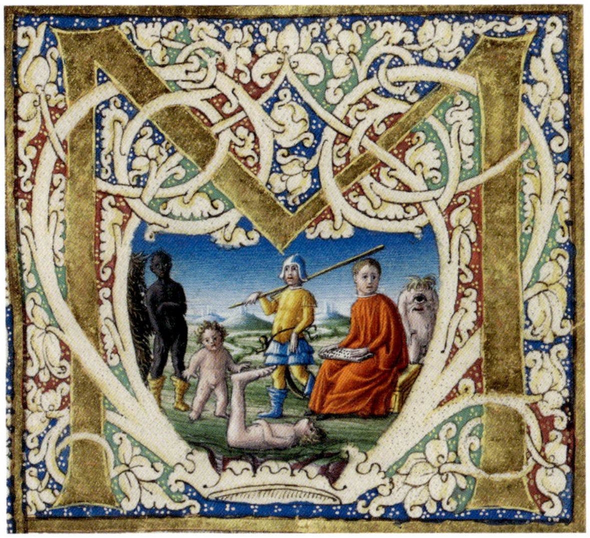

FIGURE 10 Historiated initial *M* for Book 7 (On Humans), in Pliny the Elder, *Natural History*. Italy, Rome, ca. 1460–70. London, Victoria & Albert Museum, MSL/1896/1504, fol. 94v (detail)

for example, features a display of human diversity as described in Pliny's text (fig. 10). At left, a Black man (described as Ethiopian in the text) converses with a figure completely covered in hair. Nearby, a Pygmy stands behind a Sciapod, whose single, large foot offers protection from the sun. At right, a Blemmy stares out at the viewer with its one eye. Dressed in conventional European garb, the soldier and the seated figure at center have no obvious links to the text. They may, however, represent what a fifteenth-century Italian reader would consider to be generic human beings. Understood in such a way, the miniature exemplifies Pliny's approach to ethnography by depicting human diversity as either "normal" or "different." It is important to note that medieval scholars, following Pliny, regularly grouped people of African descent—often labeled "Ethiopians"—within this latter category, thus sowing the seeds for the explicitly racist ideologies of subsequent centuries. Moreover, medieval notions of bodily diversity do not align with modern conceptions of race.[10] According to the prevalent medieval European understanding, the harsh climates of distant lands resulted in correspondingly drastic differences in human bodies. The implicit corollary of this prejudicial understanding is that the temperate climate of Europe resulted in "normal" human bodies.

With Pliny as a model, subsequent medieval encyclopedias provided additional content for the texts of Bersuire and his Translator. Yet this tradition served as an important source for the illuminators of the *Marvels* manuscripts as well. Their use of collage-like "menu pictures," already alluded to in the introduction, is deeply rooted in the practice of didactic images found in deluxe copies of encyclopedic texts. The pictorial cycles of the immensely popular encyclopedia *On the Properties of Things* (*De proprietatibus rerum*), compiled in Latin by the Franciscan friar Bartholomew of England around the middle of the thirteenth century, offer a particularly representative example.[11]

Bartholomew was, among other things, a professor at the University of Paris, and his success there no doubt contributed to his encyclopedia being listed as a required title for Parisian

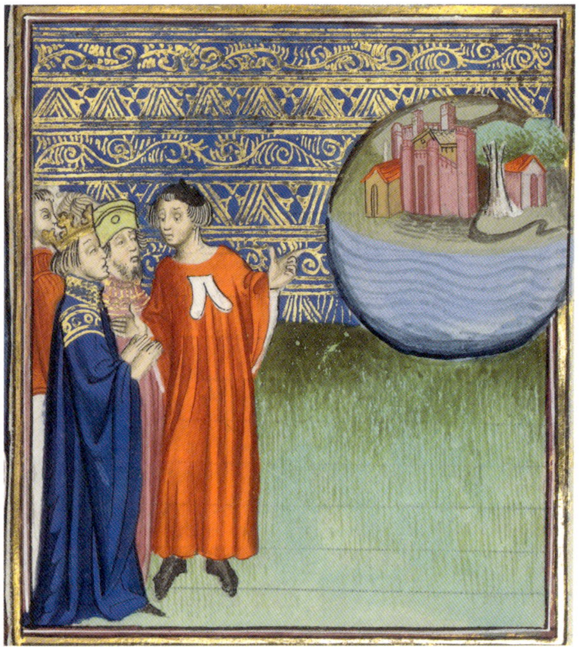

FIGURE 11 Associate of the Boethius Illuminator, Illustration for Book 8 (On the World), in Bartholomew of England, *On the Properties of Things*. France, Paris, ca. 1410. New York, Morgan Library & Museum, Ms. M.537, fol. 159r (detail)

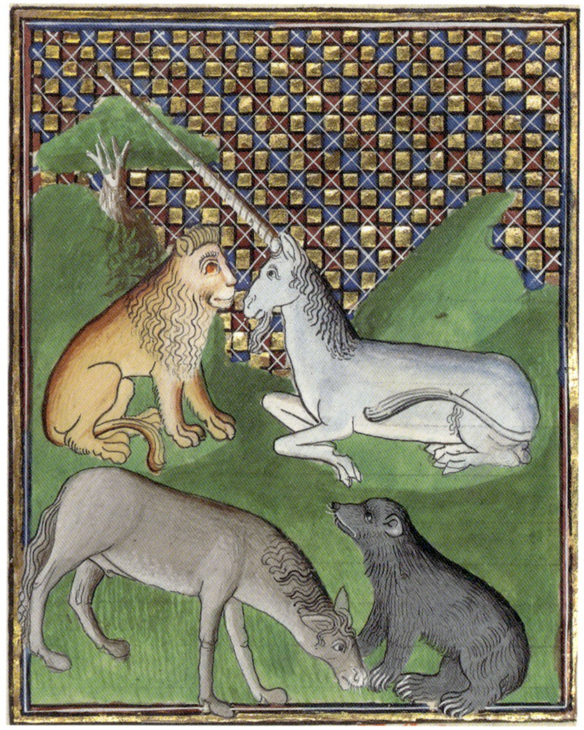

FIGURE 12 Associate of the Boethius Illuminator, Illustration for Book 18 (On Animals), in Bartholomew of England, *On the Properties of Things*. France, Paris, ca. 1410. New York, Morgan Library & Museum, Ms. M.537, fol. 353r (detail)

booksellers to stock. Coinciding with its translation into French in 1372, on order of King Charles V of France, *On the Properties of Things* began to appear in deluxe illuminated copies created for aristocratic patrons. The artists responsible for these commissions were tasked with composing a cycle of single miniatures placed at the beginning of each of the encyclopedia's nineteen books.[12] Faced with this challenge, the illuminators could design each miniature either as a single motif that represents the entire contents of a given section or as a composite image, by stitching together a number of different details mentioned in the text. In fact, these two visual strategies apply to the illustration of medieval encyclopedias in general, and both approaches can be seen in illuminated copies of Bartholomew's text. In an early fifteenth-century copy of his encyclopedia, now at the Morgan, the miniature beginning Book 8, devoted to understanding the world, depicts a scholar accompanying a king and his entourage in a landscape (fig. 11). The scholar converses with

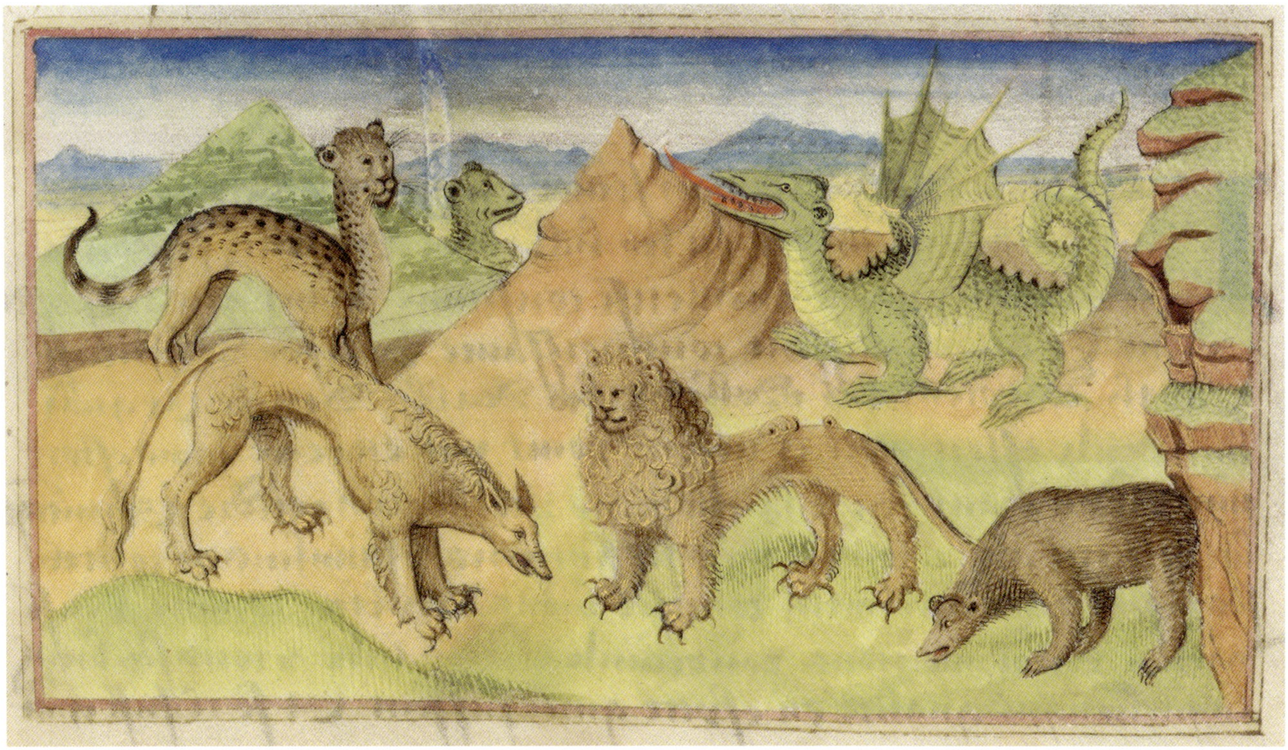

FIGURE 13 Master of the Geneva Boccaccio, *Libya*, in the *Book of the Marvels of the World*. France, Angers, ca. 1460. New York, Morgan Library & Museum, Ms. M.461, fol. 55r (detail)

the king while pointing to a schematic representation of the globe that floats within a nondescript setting. The subject matter of the scene—and of the accompanying text—is immediately clear to the reader, who may have identified with the royal figure receiving instruction. An example of the second approach can be found in the miniature opening Book 18, on animals (fig. 12). With this scene, the artist has combined into a single setting an assortment of beasts discussed in the text—in this case, a lion, unicorn, horse, and bear. In its approach to composition, the miniature resembles the scene of Libya from the *Marvels* manuscripts, which likewise features an assemblage of ferocious beasts mentioned in the text (fig. 13).

A more complex example of this visual approach can be found in a sumptuously illuminated hunting manual produced in Paris around the same time as the Morgan copy of Bartholomew's encyclopedia. Known as the *Book of the Hunt* (*Livre de la chasse*), the manuscript contains eighty-seven miniatures that cover a variety of topics, including the types of

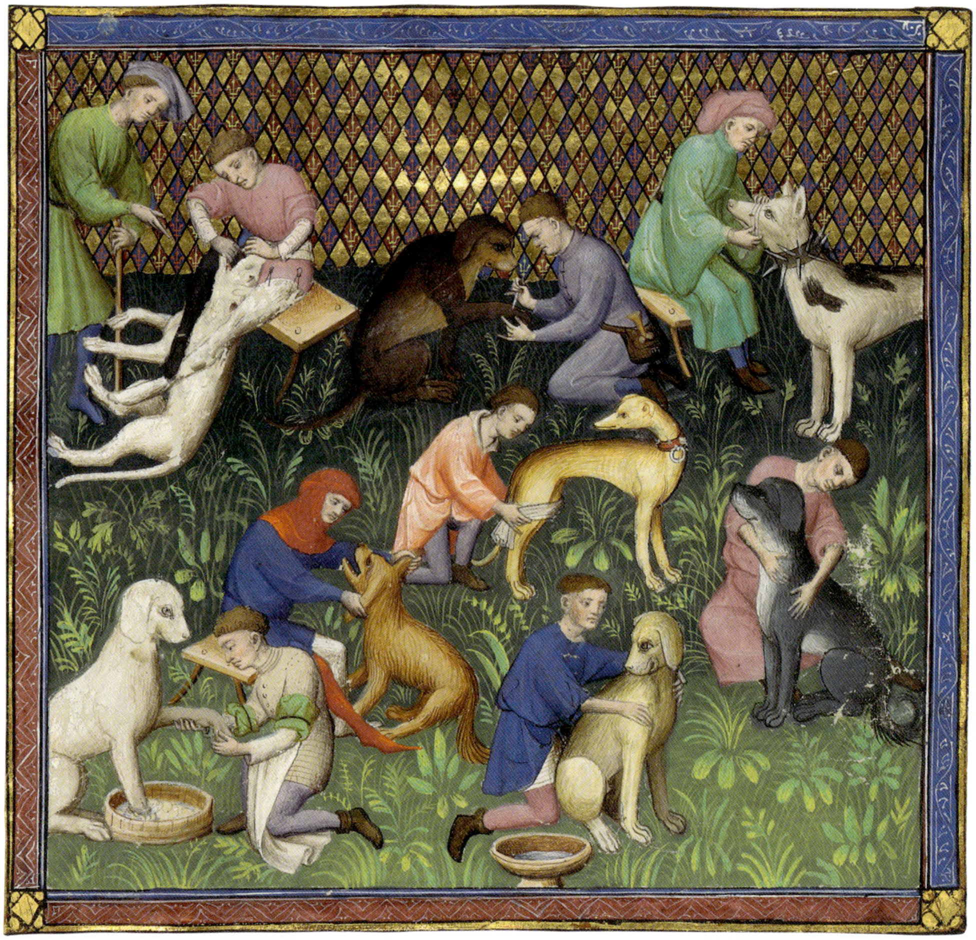

FIGURE 14 Bedford Master, *Canine Illnesses*, in Gaston Phoebus, *Book of the Hunt*. France, Paris, ca. 1406–7. New York, Morgan Library & Museum, Ms. M.1044, fol. 31v (detail)

animals that can be hunted with dogs; the various breeds of hunting dogs and their proper care; strategies for hunting; and the main types of nets and traps.[13] The miniature beginning the section on canine illnesses and their cures depicts eight different scenarios described in the text, integrated by the artist into a coherent composition (fig. 14). This is precisely the approach that one finds in the densest miniatures from the *Marvels* manuscripts, scenes like Ethiopia or India (plates 8 and 12). The structure of these composite images is itself inherently didactic—in other words, the very process of looking at the miniatures and making sense of their various components compels the viewer to develop a more profound understanding of the accompanying text.

Illustrated encyclopedias also constituted an important source for depicting the marvels of the world. A pertinent example comes from one of the most ambitious encyclopedic projects of the entire Middle Ages. Under the aegis of King Louis IX of France, a Dominican friar named Vincent of Beauvais compiled a vast encyclopedia known as the *Great Mirror* (*Speculum maius*) around the middle of the thirteenth century. Reworked and expanded upon continually until Vincent's death in 1264, his encyclopedia is in fact a set of three somewhat independent compilations, which often circulated separately: the *Mirror of History*, the *Mirror of Nature*, and the *Mirror of Doctrine*. The reason for this tripartite structure was as much practical as conceptual: at the most conservative estimate, a complete copy of the *Great Mirror* required at least ten large manuscripts, amounting to well over three million words.[14]

In its original Latin form, the *Great Mirror* was intended as a reference work for clergy and scholars. However, a dramatic shift occurred when Joan of Burgundy, queen of France and granddaughter of Louis IX, commissioned a French translation of the *Mirror of History* from Jean de Vignay. Likely intended as a gift for her son—the future King John II of France—Vignay's translation became immensely popular among the French aristocracy.[15] As a result, a number of deluxe copies were produced throughout the fourteenth and fifteenth centuries, all richly illuminated. To meet this increased demand, medieval artists had to create, essentially from scratch, extensive picture cycles often comprising several hundred miniatures. Judging from the surviving copies, however, there was no overarching logic to illustrating the *Mirror of History*: some passages of the text were more heavily illustrated than others, and the cycles of any two manuscripts are never quite the same. Among expected subjects like the story of Creation or episodes from Roman history, the miniatures also depict the tales of Alexander the Great as well as the marvels of the world.

Directly following a discussion of terrestrial paradise, Book 2 of Vignay's translation describes the various regions of the world, focusing first on the wonders of India and Asia. Perhaps unsurprisingly, given the fantastical accounts of these areas in the text, it was precisely these two regions that were most often illustrated in deluxe copies of the *Mirror of History*. In the manuscript made for King John II, for example, a miniature of the wonders of India begins a short cycle depicting marvelous regions of the world (fig. 15).[16] A griffon, a dragon, and two ornery elephants guard a mountain of gold studded with precious gems, while representative inhabitants of the region converse and observe from their vantage point in cities on either side of the central scene. The inhabitants have blue skin, which demonstrates that the artist was closely following the French text. Deviating from his Latin source, Vignay mistakenly conflated the name of the region (India, *Ynde*) with the color of the inhabitants' skin (indigo, *Ynde*).[17]

A later fifteenth-century copy of the *Mirror of History*, now at the Getty, develops the cycle of marvels in interesting ways. In addition to depictions of India and Scythia, the cycle includes a remarkable miniature of China (fig. 16).[18] Drawing on Solinus as a source, the text mentions that the region's inhabitants have the "bad habit" of bathing nude in front of each other, regardless of

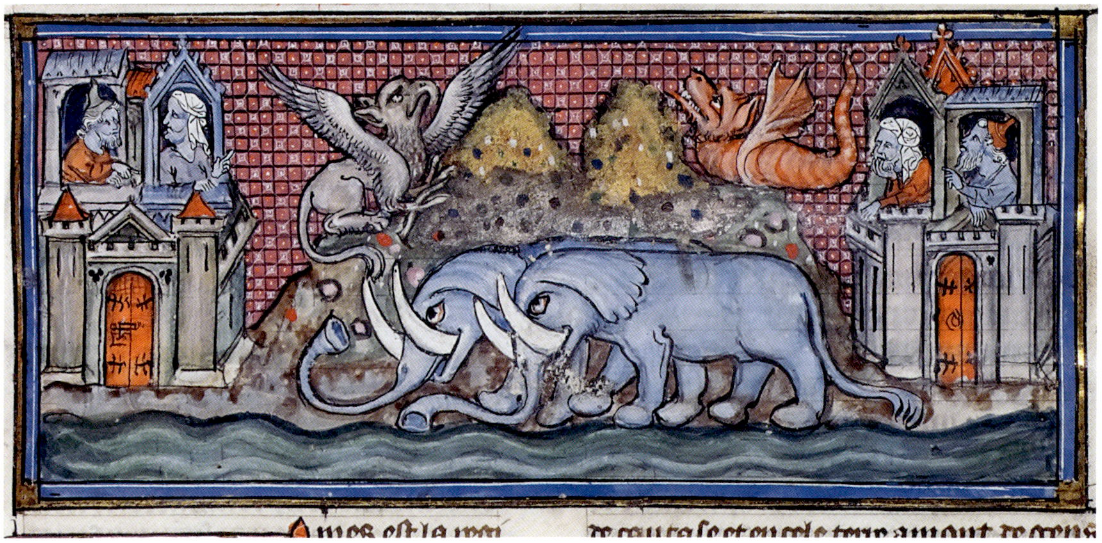

FIGURE 15 Papeleu Master and assistants, *India*, in Vincent of Beauvais, *Mirror of History*. France, Paris, ca. 1332–35. Leiden, Universiteitsbibliotheek, Ms. VGG F 3 A, fol. 41r (detail)

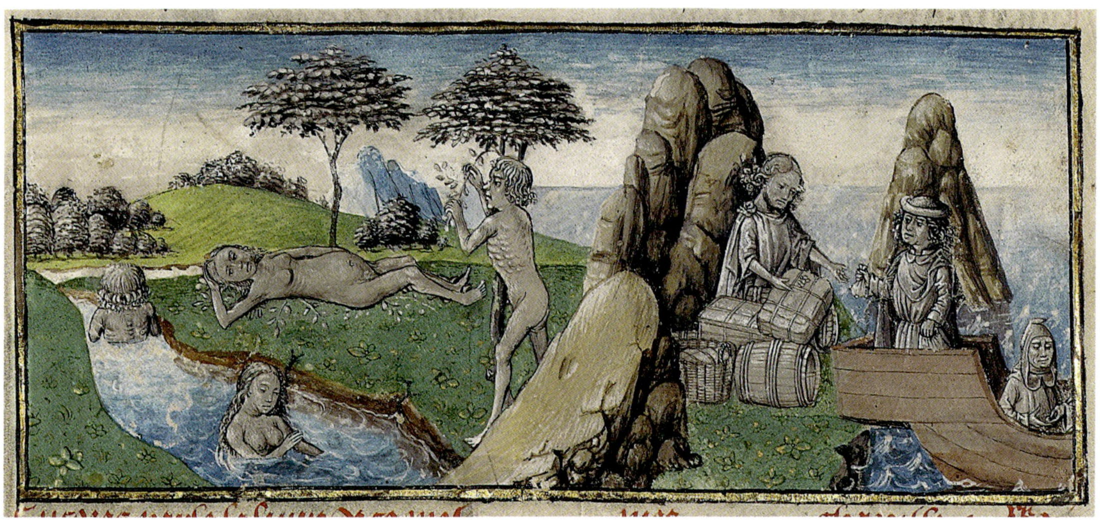

FIGURE 16 *China*, in Vincent of Beauvais, *Mirror of History*. Belgium, Ghent, ca. 1475. Los Angeles, J. Paul Getty Museum, Ms. Ludwig XIII 5, vol. 1, fol. 65r (detail)

their gender, after which they use tree branches to dry off.[19] The text goes on to explain that China is known for silk production, and that foreign merchants do not dare to set foot in the region because the local language is "unlike any other." In the left half of the miniature, a nude man grabs a tree branch while pointedly staring at a reclining nude woman. Their tense exchange offers a visual representation of how morally questionable this custom would have appeared to medieval European audiences. In the right half of the miniature, locals trade with foreign merchants, who remain on their ship, underscoring the practical difficulties of long-distance trade alluded to in the text. A variation on this anecdote forms the main scene in the miniatures of Seres (China) from the *Marvels* manuscripts (plate 17, no. 3). Here, however, the story has been altered and the difficulty in trading is ascribed to the shyness of the locals rather than to any linguistic barrier.

An interest in merchants, trade, and luxury goods was by no means restricted to stories of China. In the *Marvels* manuscripts alone, the theme also appears in the entries on Arabia, Media (in Persia), Offir (in India), Saba (in Arabia), Scythia (north of the Black Sea), Syria, and Ululand (in Norway). Most of these accounts focus on the difficulties and dangers faced by merchants attempting to acquire precious materials like gems or spices for a European market. The description of Arabia, for example, features three such anecdotes. The *Marvels* text refers to the region as "the source of precious stones," which can be seen dotting the hills guarded by dragons in the upper left corner of the accompanying miniature (plate 3). At bottom left, two men cut open the belly of a dragon in search of gems that can be sold "at a very high price." At right, two men scale lofty trees, using long hooks to pry out cinnamon twigs from the nests of the legendary Cinnamologus bird. The text specifically mentions that the high cost of this popular spice relates to the difficulty in procuring these delicate twigs. The same story appears frequently in other encyclopedic sources, such as medieval books of beasts. In a twelfth-century English manuscript known as the Worksop Bestiary, the story of cinnamon forms the subject of a splendid miniature that takes up nearly the entire page (fig. 17).[20] As in the *Marvels* example, the bestiary miniature emphasizes the great height of the cinnamon tree, implying how immensely difficult it was to harvest the spice. Similarly, a fourteenth-century Italian herbal features several scenes depicting how precious metals and other materials are sourced from the earth.[21] On the verso of its first page, for instance, two workers extract gold and quicksilver (mercury) from the side of a mountain (fig. 18). The miners' fanciful garb, combined with the idealized setting of a pristine wilderness—rather than a quarry—lends the scenes a wondrous quality. Such visual representations emphasized for medieval audiences how precious materials and luxury goods are, by their very nature, marvels of the world.

Drawing deeply on medieval encyclopedic traditions, the *Marvels* manuscripts presented their fifteenth-century readers with an immense amount of information about the world around them. Most of these stories, however, would likely have been familiar to educated audiences from a number of other sources. Thus, what is so innovative about the *Marvels* manuscripts is not so much their textual contents, but rather how the manuscripts shape and present that information through their highly developed pictorial cycles. Giving visual expression to the text, these illuminated manuscripts

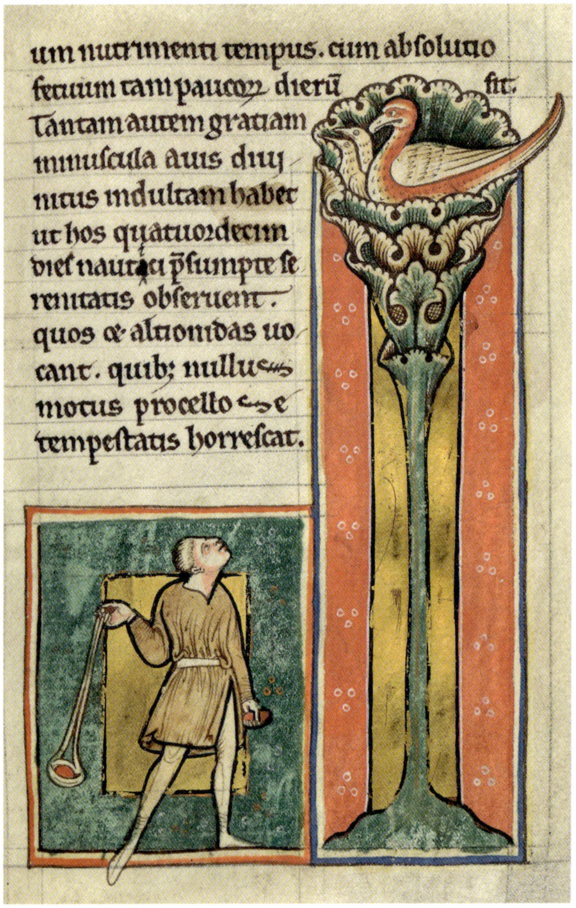

FIGURE 17 *Cinnamologus Bird*, in the Worksop Bestiary. England, Lincoln (?), ca. 1185. New York, Morgan Library & Museum, Ms. M.81, fol. 52r

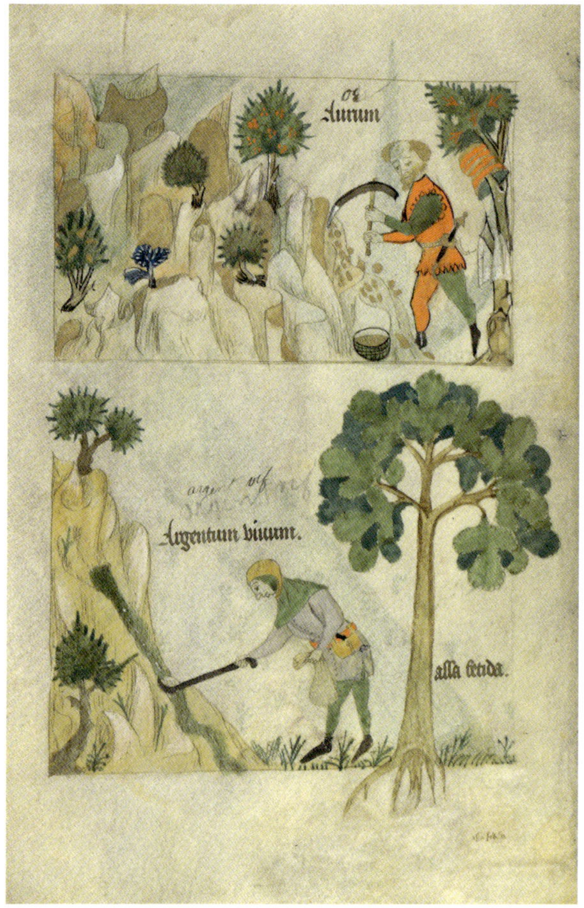

FIGURE 18 Mining Scenes, in the *Salerno Compendium.* Italy, Venice (?), ca. 1350–75. New York, Morgan Library & Museum, Ms. M.873, fol. 1v

demonstrate that the medieval interest in marvels was inseparable from a broader interest in understanding and encountering the world.

Picturing the World

Much like medieval encyclopedias, which were themselves considered to be images or representations of the world, medieval maps reflected an understanding of the world that was based more on authoritative tradition than direct observation. Throughout the Middle Ages, the most common types of maps were the so-called T-O diagrams, schematic renderings of the three continents known at the time: Asia, Africa, and Europe

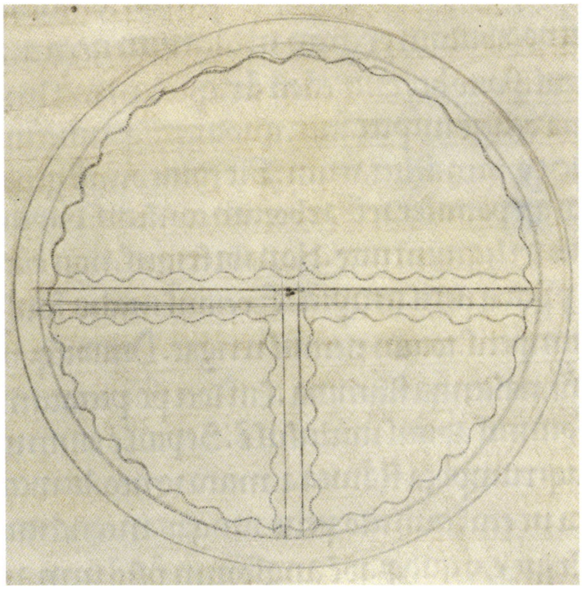

FIGURE 19 T-O Diagram, in the Worksop Bestiary. England, Lincoln (?), ca. 1185. New York, Morgan Library & Museum, Ms. M.81, fol. 113r (detail)

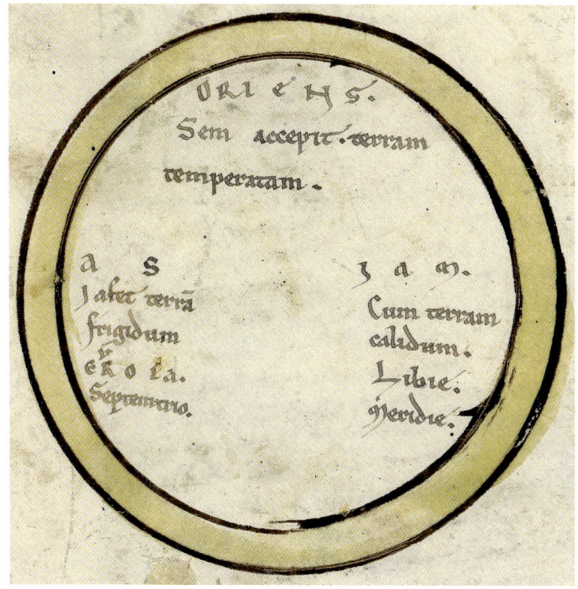

FIGURE 20 T-O Diagram, in the Las Huelgas Beatus. Spain, Burgos, 1220. New York, Morgan Library & Museum, Ms. M.429, fol. 8v (detail)

(fig. 19). These diagrams depict an east-oriented representation of Earth surrounded by water (hence, the O shape), with Asia taking up the entire eastern (upper) hemisphere. Europe and Africa constitute the northern and southern parts of the western (lower) hemisphere, respectively, and are divided from each other by the Mediterranean Sea (hence, the T shape). More than a thousand T-O maps survive from the Middle Ages, and as a group they are closely linked to encyclopedic texts like the ever-popular *Etymologies* of Isidore of Seville, a seventh-century compilation of knowledge similar to Pliny's *Natural History*.[22] The twelfth-century Worksop Bestiary, for instance, includes an unfinished drawing of just such a map that was intended to illustrate a section on the globe (*De orbe*), extracted from Isidore's encyclopedia (see fig. 19). With their clear concept and simple structure, T-O maps easily lent themselves to additional levels of interpretation. An example can be found in an illuminated commentary on the Apocalypse dated to 1220 and made for a community of nuns at the royal convent of Las Huelgas in Spain.[23] Known as a Beatus manuscript (after the commentary's author), the manuscript features a T-O diagram with an additional set of inscriptions explaining the prevalent medieval understanding of how the three continents were inhabited by different groups of people (fig. 20). According to this theory, Noah divided the continents among his three sons—Shem, Ham, and Japheth—after the great flood described in Genesis (6:5–10:1).

The eldest son, Shem, was given the largest continent, Asia; Japheth was given Europe; and Ham, Noah's cursed son, was given Africa. Prejudiced at its core, this explanation for the origin of humanity's different lineages enabled medieval European scholars to align ancient geography with biblical history, while reinforcing their own sense of superiority.

Although significantly rarer, more detailed pictorial representations of the world were also produced in the Middle Ages. For example, the Las Huelgas Beatus also contains a monumental world map that takes up two facing pages (fig. 21). Fourteen of these large, double-page maps, dating from the tenth to the thirteenth century, survive from various Beatus manuscripts; together they constitute one of the most important and visually impressive sets of maps from the entire Middle Ages. As a group, the Beatus maps place terrestrial paradise (also known as the Garden of Eden) at the very top of the world, with India to the right and Jerusalem close to the center. The inscriptions on these maps regularly describe all sorts of marvelous details, including the Amazons, the mythical Phoenix bird, the precious gems and spices of India and Arabia, or the blazing sun of Ethiopia. One of their most interesting features, however, is the inclusion of a purported fourth part of the world, located at the southernmost (rightmost) edge of the map. Separated from the three known continents by a large body of water, this mysterious land bears an inscription explaining that the region is "unknown to us because of the burning heat of the sun; within its borders are said to live the legendary Antipodeans."[24] The Beatus maps thus hint at the marvels that can be found on the other side of the world.

Another thirteenth-century map, this time from England, features a parade of marvelous beings in precisely the same location described as the realm of the Antipodeans in the Beatus manuscripts (fig. 22). Known as the Psalter Map because of its placement at the beginning of a book of Psalms, this diminutive painting of the world is only about 9 cm across (about 3½ inches).[25] Nonetheless, it features essentially the same information found in the much larger map from the Las Huelgas Beatus, which is more than 76 cm across (30 inches). The Psalter Map, however, takes a slightly different approach to the structure of the world by placing a greater emphasis on the holy city of Jerusalem, which appears in the exact center of the composition, almost like a bull's eye. Throughout the Middle Ages, Jerusalem was indeed regarded as the "navel of the world," a status reflected in many examples of medieval cartography like the Psalter Map.[26] The centrality of the holy city and the density of geographic information surrounding it form a striking contrast with the peripheral status of the legendary beings relegated to the unknown lands at the ends of the world. Scholars have linked this increased focus on Jerusalem to a surge in the related activities of pilgrimage and crusading—that is, the repeated attempts by medieval Christians to conquer the Holy Land.[27]

The understanding of the world represented by these thirteenth-century maps still informed the worldview of the readers of the *Marvels* manuscripts some two hundred years later. Indeed, the example of another map, this time in printed form, demonstrates just how much earlier medieval notions of the world persisted into the fifteenth century. Among the very earliest printed examples to survive from Europe, the so-called Rüst Map (ca. 1480) presents a world that is strikingly similar

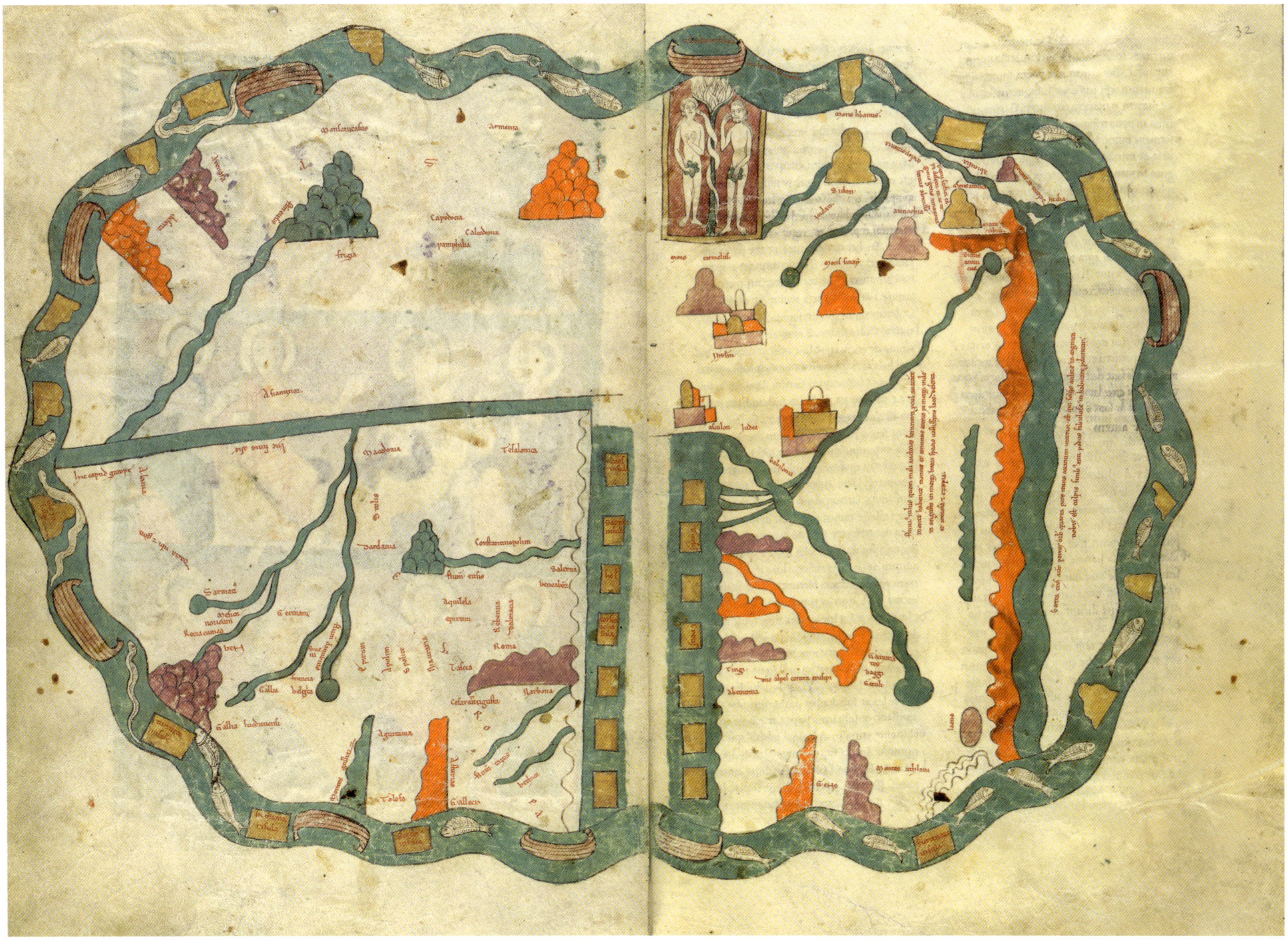

FIGURE 21 *Map of the World*, in the Las Huelgas Beatus. Spain, Burgos, 1220. New York, Morgan Library & Museum, Ms. M.429, fols. 13v–14r

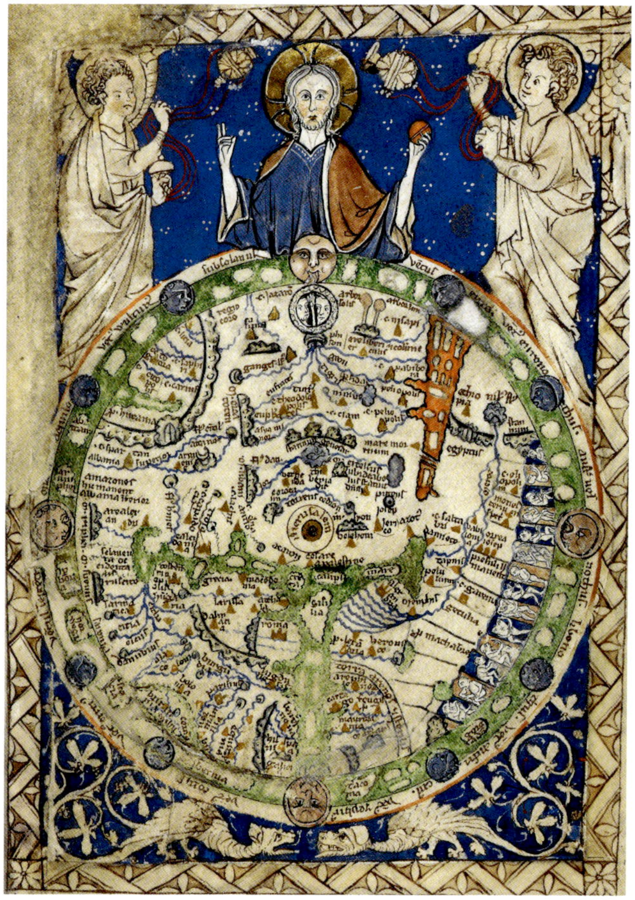

FIGURE 22 *Map of the World*, in the Psalter Map. England, London, ca. 1262. London, British Library, Add. Ms. 28681, fol. 9r

FIGURE 23 Hanns Rüst, *Map of the World*. Germany, Augsburg, ca. 1480. New York, Morgan Library & Museum, PML 19921

to that of the Psalter Map (fig. 23).[28] With the Garden of Eden at the top and Jerusalem prominently occupying the center, the Rüst Map takes its basic composition from the T-O diagrams of medieval encyclopedias. The clarity of the design, however, has been diminished by the map's wildly contorting rivers and its tendency to depict regions erroneously as islands. Additional details include the personifications of the four winds at the edges of the world, aligned with the cardinal directions, as well as two roundels below, depicting the four elements, at left, and a tripartite division

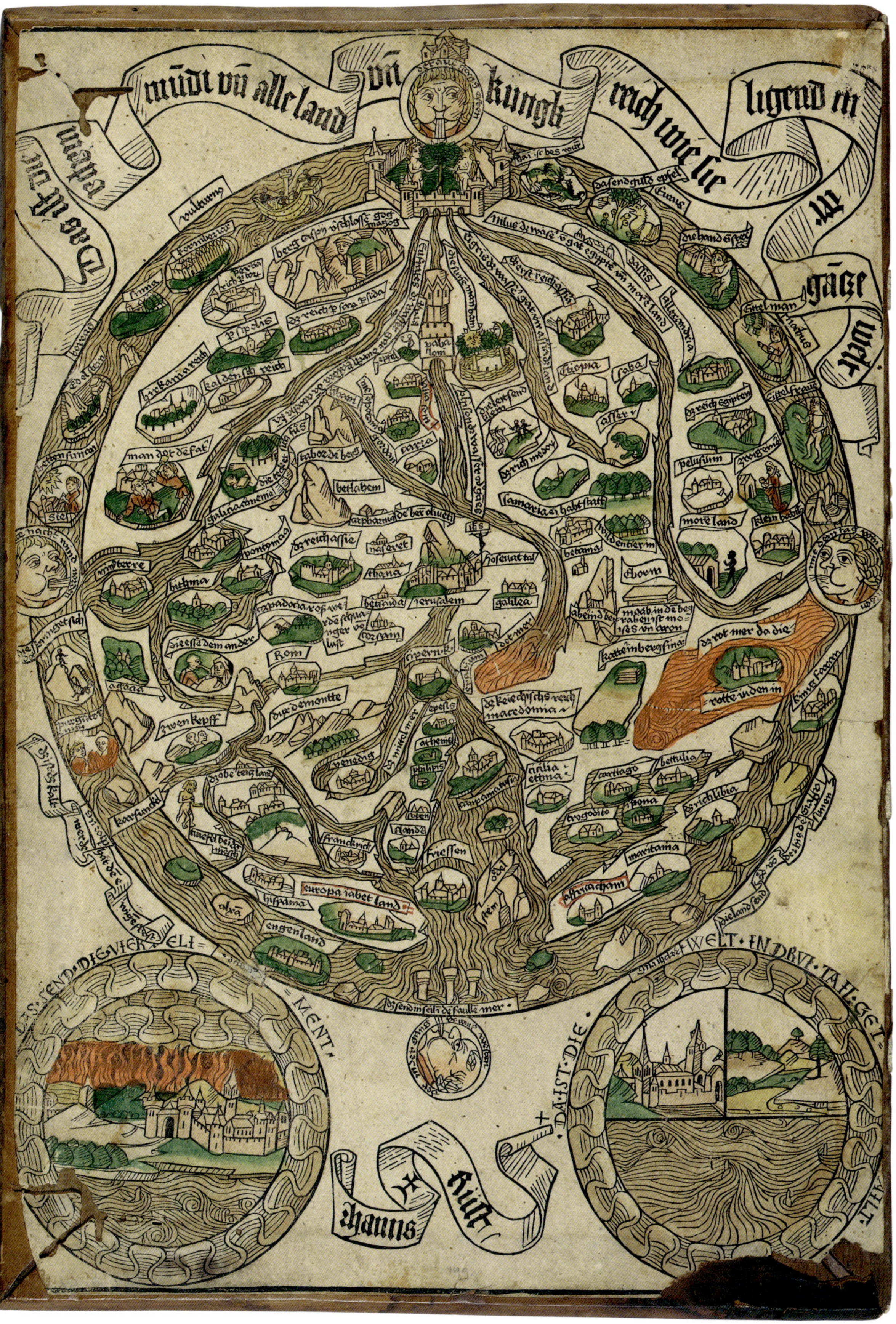
mūdi vñ alle land
ligend in
jerusalem
Rom
hanns
rüst
DA·IST·DIE

of the world, at right. Labels abound, providing the names of various cities, realms, and, in some cases, rudimentary descriptions of a particular region's inhabitants. The prominent banners at the top and bottom of the page feature the map's title as well as the signature of Hanns Rüst (d. 1485), a little-known artist from Augsburg. What is perhaps most unusual about the Rüst Map, however, is how little attention it gives to Europe (lower-left quadrant). Leaving out important cities like Paris or Constantinople, this region contains only about fifteen labeled entries, compared to the many dozens for the regions of Asia and Africa. In line with a greater emphasis on these two continents, Rüst populated his map with a variety of marvelous peoples and wonders, including the Astomi; Sciapods; cannibals; Pygmies battling cranes; sun-worshipers; dragons; dog-headed people, or Cynocephali; and the mythical land of Gog and Magog. The islands near India (upper-right quadrant) are particularly rich in marvels, compared to the islands at lower right, which are described as barren, because of the extreme heat of the sun. This wealth of information is presented in such a shorthand way—due, no doubt, to a lack of available space—that the artist must have presumed that his viewers would have been familiar with the subject matter. Indeed, understanding the contents of Rüst's map requires an encyclopedic knowledge of medieval geography and ethnography much like what one finds in the *Marvels* text.

Traveling the World

In addition to encyclopedias and maps, travel writing was increasingly becoming an important way of encountering the world in the fourteenth and fifteenth centuries.[29] Unlike the related literary genres of pilgrimage reports and itineraries, however, travel literature often blurred the boundaries between fact and fiction. The goal was more to inspire virtual or imaginary travel rather than actual journeys, and in crafting evocative images of the world, medieval travel writers often drew upon traditional understandings of geography and ethnography. Their texts are a fascinating reminder that the later Middle Ages unhesitatingly equated a knowledge of marvels with a knowledge of the world. Indeed, a comparison of the two most famous travel accounts of the period—the travels of Marco Polo and of Sir John Mandeville—reveals just how essential marvels were to their popularity.

As explained in the prologue to his text, Marco Polo composed his travel account in 1298, while a prisoner of war in Genoa.[30] His fellow inmate, Rustichello of Pisa, happened to be an accomplished author of medieval romances, and together they told the now-famous story of how the Venetian merchant had spent the previous twenty-four years traveling throughout Central Asia, China, India, the Arabian Sea, and Russia. Best known to modern English-speaking audiences as the *Travels of Marco Polo*, his text went by several titles in the Middle Ages, most commonly *The Description of the World* (*Le devisement du monde*) or the *Book of the Great Khan* (*Livre de grant Khan*). Two illuminated manuscripts even refer to his text as a book of marvels.[31] An early fifteenth-century copy at the Morgan (Ms. M.723), for example, states: "Here begins the Book of Marco Polo on the Marvels of Great Asia and of India the Greater and Lesser." This emphasis on marvels is puzzling, however, since one of the most remarkable features of Polo's text is how actively it works to dispel deeply entrenched European legends regarding distant lands. For example, Polo famously corrected the traditional medieval conception of unicorns after seeing a rhinoceros in Sumatra—just as he did for griffons.[32] His unorthodox approach to marvels may have posed a challenge for artists, which would explain why his text was so rarely illuminated.[33]

In fact, only four manuscripts with substantial pictorial cycles survive from before 1500. Although their approach to illustration differs substantially, these illuminated manuscripts nevertheless overlap in important ways. Each can be linked—directly or indirectly—to royalty; and in each case Polo's text appears alongside other works related to Asia or the Holy Land, creating what scholars have referred to as "Crusade Compilations."[34] By far the most celebrated example is the magnificent illuminated manuscript commissioned around 1410 by the Burgundian duke John the Fearless, and known as the *Book of Marvels* (*Livre des merveilles*), though it bears no textual relation to the group of *Marvels* manuscripts considered in this publication. In 1396, John suffered a disastrous defeat while battling Ottoman forces at Nicopolis (Bulgaria). He spent much of the next year as a prisoner in various parts of modern-day Turkey, being released only after paying a significant ransom. Scholars have suggested that John's political concerns, as well as his firsthand experience among the Ottomans, informed the commissioning of his *Book of Marvels* to such an extent that he may have even played a role in planning out its visual program.[35] The six travel-related texts (including Marco Polo's) making up the manuscript feature an astonishing 265 miniatures, for which five teams of artists were employed. While not at all accurate or realistic in the modern sense, the 84 miniatures illustrating Marco Polo's text do offer an unusually generous view of the Mongol Empire. For example, the province of Charchan (present-day Qiemo), located along the Silk Road, appears to be an idyllic region where shepherds in tents watch over their flock of camels, sheep, and cattle (fig. 24). The same passage in the Morgan Marco Polo manuscript, however, features a miniature in which three turbaned men worship before the statue of a nude figure, a scene that would have been understood by medieval Christians as representing idolatry (fig. 25). Seen side by side, the miniatures demonstrate how the same text could be illustrated in vastly different ways, depending, perhaps, on either the intentions of the artist or the expectations of the patron. The Morgan illuminator's depiction of Muslim idolatry—repeated several times throughout the manuscript—reflects a common motif in travel writing that informs us more about the anxieties and preconceptions of medieval Christian readers than the actual religious practices of their Muslim counterparts.[36] In its recourse to such stereotypes, the Morgan Marco Polo manuscript relates to the type of imagery one finds in the *Marvels* manuscripts: both showed their medieval European audiences precisely what they expected to see.

The expectation of marvels is perhaps nowhere more evident than in the famous and wildly popular travel account purportedly written by Sir John Mandeville, a knight from St. Albans, England, who claims to have set out on a thirty-four-year journey throughout the known world. Composed in French around 1360, the first half of the book reads like an account of a pilgrimage to Jerusalem, with a description of the holy city occupying the text's very center (as in so many medieval maps).[37] The second half, however, shifts to a description of the marvelous regions of India, China, and Persia, ending with an account of the mythical lands of the fabled Christian emperor Prester John. Often

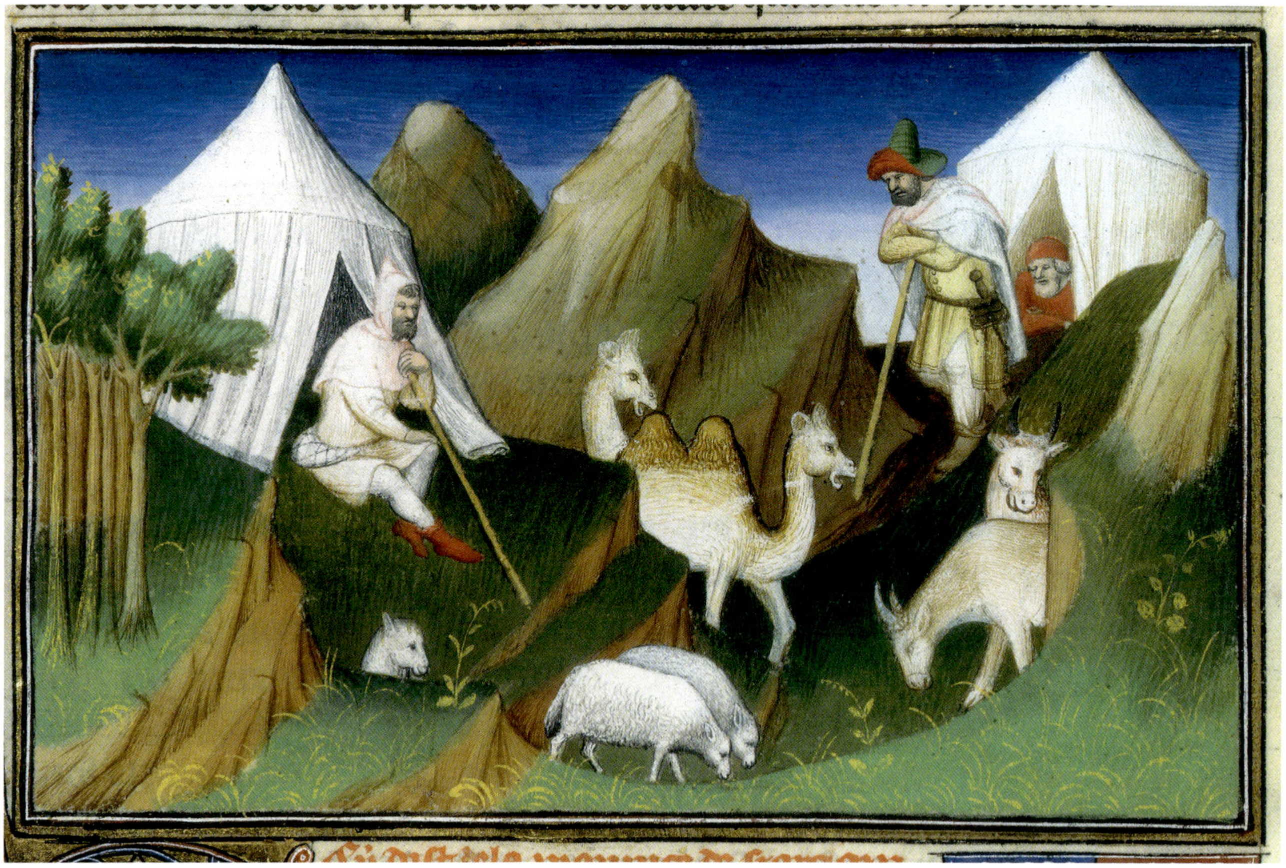

FIGURE 24 Mazarine Master, *The Province of Charchan* (Qiemo), in the *Travels of Marco Polo*. France, Paris, ca. 1410. Paris, Bibliothèque nationale de France, Ms. fr. 2810, fol. 21v (detail)

known simply as the *Book of John Mandeville*, this lively travel account quickly became one of the most widely read texts of the later Middle Ages. More than three hundred manuscript copies, translated into ten languages, survive from before 1500. Astonishingly, it also appeared in more than thirty printed editions within the same timeframe.[38] Marco Polo's text, in contrast, survives in fewer than half as many manuscripts and appeared in only seven printed editions before 1500. The *Book of John Mandeville* was so popular that its purported author became something of a celebrity,

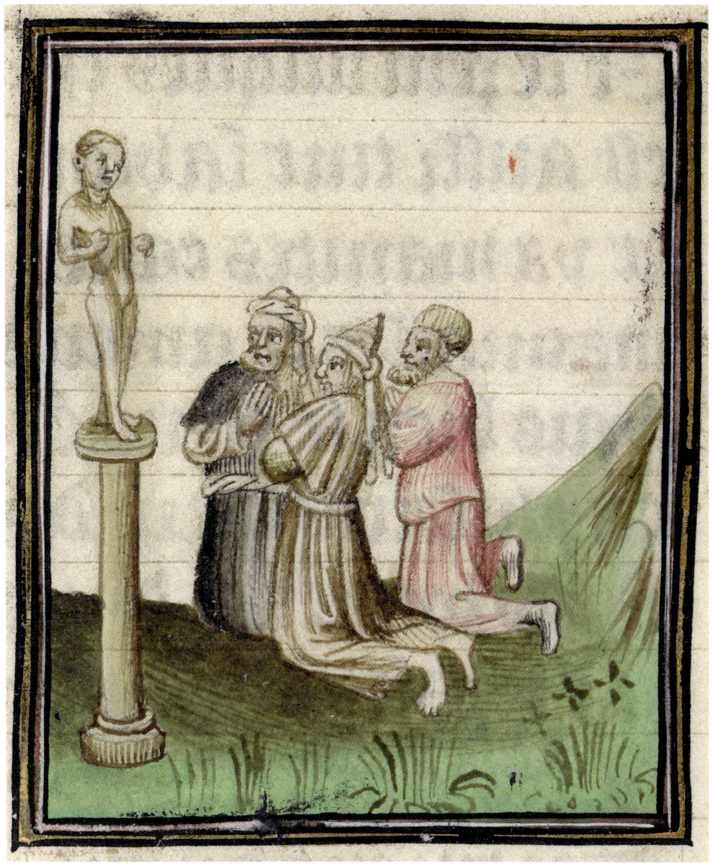

FIGURE 25 Workshop of the Berry Apocalypse Master, *The Province of Charchan* (Qiemo), in the *Travels of Marco Polo*. France, Paris, ca. 1410–12. New York, Morgan Library & Museum, Ms. M.723, fol. 109r (detail)

with both St. Albans and Canterbury claiming to hold relics from his travels.[39] Despite the widespread appeal of his book, however, most scholars maintain that Mandeville never actually existed. Or if he did, he was certainly not the author of the text that bears his name, which is essentially a pastiche of traditional medieval geography transposed into a narrative mode. In contrast to Marco Polo, who based his account at least in part on lived experiences and direct observation, Mandeville's book recycled well-known medieval lore about a world filled with marvels. Far from being disreputable,

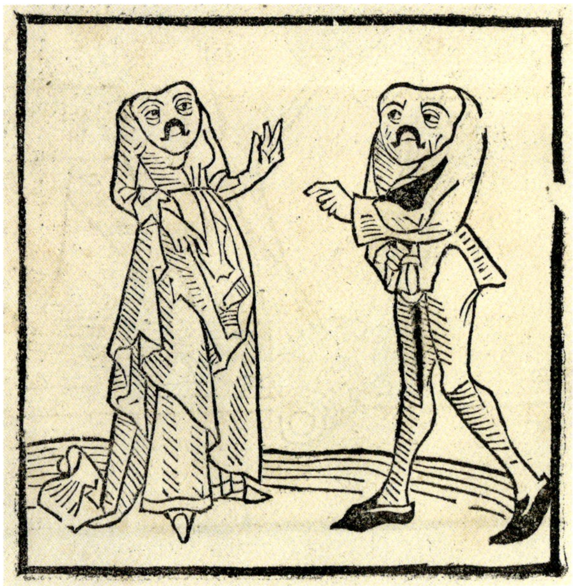

FIGURE 26 *Blemmyes*, in the *Book of Sir John Mandeville*. Switzerland, Basel: Bernhard Richel, 1481. New York, Morgan Library & Museum, PML 42798 (detail)

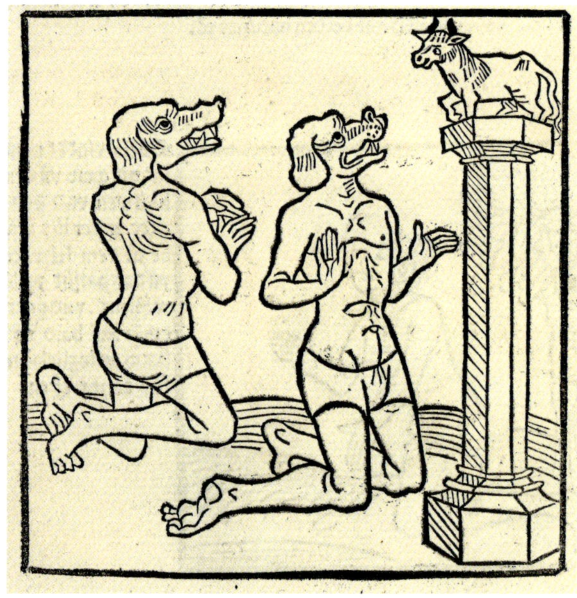

FIGURE 27 *Cynocephali*, in the *Book of Sir John Mandeville*. Switzerland, Basel: Bernhard Richel, 1481. New York, Morgan Library & Museum, PML 42798 (detail)

however, this approach was likely one of the main factors contributing to the text's popularity.

The manner in which fifteenth-century copies of Mandeville's book were illustrated, especially in print, reinforces the idea that marvels were one of its main attractions. Building on the pictorial programs developed for the more than two dozen illuminated manuscripts that survive today, the printed editions of Mandeville's book regularly feature lengthy cycles of woodcuts.[40] The 1481 edition printed in Basel by Bernhard Richel, for example, contains 156 illustrations. About two-thirds of these represent the wonders of India, China, and other marvelous regions, even though these passages make up only about half of the total text. Similar to the image cycle of the *Marvels* manuscripts, the illustrated program of Richel's edition lavishes particular attention on the people said to inhabit these marvelous regions. As one might expect, the section on India includes a multitude of examples, such as Blemmyes and Cynocephali (figs. 26, 27). These woodcuts often feature representative pairs of figures, who are shown either engaging in conversation or performing customs that would have been perceived as unusual by medieval European Christians, like eating unfamiliar food or worshiping idols.

The success of Mandeville's book in both manuscript and print demonstrates that there was a market for medieval marvels well into the fifteenth century. Furthermore, as the comparison with the reception of Marco Polo's text reveals, marvels were a fundamental component of what fifteenth-century audiences expected to hear and see when learning about the world around them. These expectations led to serious consequences. Perhaps the most famous example is that of Christopher Columbus, who traveled with his own annotated copies of Marco Polo and John Mandeville, among other related texts. Despite landing in the present-day Caribbean, Columbus believed instead that he had discovered a more direct route to Asia and the lands of the Great Khan. Based in large part on the information provided by his medieval sources, he and his fellow travelers ruthlessly exploited the local indigenous populations in the search for gold, precious gems, and other marvels, like Terrestrial Paradise and the Fountain of Youth.[41] Stemming from a centuries-long tradition, such assumptions about a world full of marvels inevitably—and, ultimately, dangerously—shaped European perceptions of foreigners at a time when travel, trade, and colonial expansion meant that medieval expectations were increasingly being confronted with global encounters.

NOTES

1 Figg and Friedman 2018, 397.
2 Banks and Binns 2002; Murphy 2004; and Brodersen 2014.
3 Murphy 2004, 33.
4 Murphy 2004, 34–35.
5 Pliny 1938; Murphy 2004, 37–38; and Anguissola and Grüner 2020.
6 For more on Bersuire and the *Marvels* Translator, see the introduction to this volume.
7 Friedman 2000, 5–25; Murphy 2004, 77–128.
8 Olsen 1985, 261–62; Reeve 2007, 131–32.
9 Whalley 1982, 8–9; Armstrong 1983; and McHam 2006, 86–87, 102–4.
10 Akbari 2009, 140–54; Heng 2018.
11 Seymour 1992; Meier 1997.
12 Holbrook 2006.
13 Voelkle and Avril 2006.
14 Franklin-Brown 2012, 96.
15 Chavannes-Mazel 1988; Chavannes-Mazel 1990.
16 Morrison and Hedeman 2010, 147–52.
17 Chavannes-Mazel 1988, 54.
18 Von Euw and Plotzek 1979–1985, 3: 243–49; the miniature is mistakenly identified as India.
19 Cavagna 2017, 322.
20 Clark 2006, 176–77; Morrison and Grollemond 2019, 94–96.
21 Collins 2003, 15–16, 22.
22 Terkla and Millea 2019, xv–xxiv; Mauntel 2021.
23 Sáenz-López Pérez 2014; Williams and Martin 2017, 135–38.
24 Translation modified from Sáenz-López Pérez 2014, 215.
25 Van Duzer 2019.
26 Akbari 2009, 50–66.
27 Harvey 2012, 1–30.
28 Hassinger 1927; Campbell 1987, 79–84.
29 Zumthor 1994; Bale 2016.
30 Polo 1958, 33–34.
31 Cruse 2015a, 175–80, esp. 177 for the title of the Morgan manuscript.
32 Polo 1958, 253, 300; Yeager 2008.
33 Strickland 2005; Strickland 2008.
34 The illustrated manuscripts are London, British Library, Royal Ms. 19 D I; Paris, Bibliothèque nationale de France, Ms. fr. 2810; Oxford, Bodleian Library, Ms. Bodl. 264; New York, Morgan Library & Museum, Ms. M.723. Dutschke 1993, 36–41; Quigley 2009; and Cruse 2015b.
35 Avril 1996, 307–24; Gousset 1996, 363; and Cruse 2020, 223–27.
36 Camille 1989, 151–64; Kosta-Théfaine 2006, 55–56; and Akbari 2009, 200–247; see also the essay by Michael and Morrison in this volume.
37 Mandeville 2012, ix–xxviii.
38 Bennett 1954, 265–385; Seymour 1993, 38–56; and Röhl 2004, 206–13.
39 Röhl 2004, 208.
40 Schramm 1938; Betschart 1996, 250–67.
41 See Flint 1992 and Horodowich and Nagel 2023.

Wonder and Fear in the *Book of Marvels*

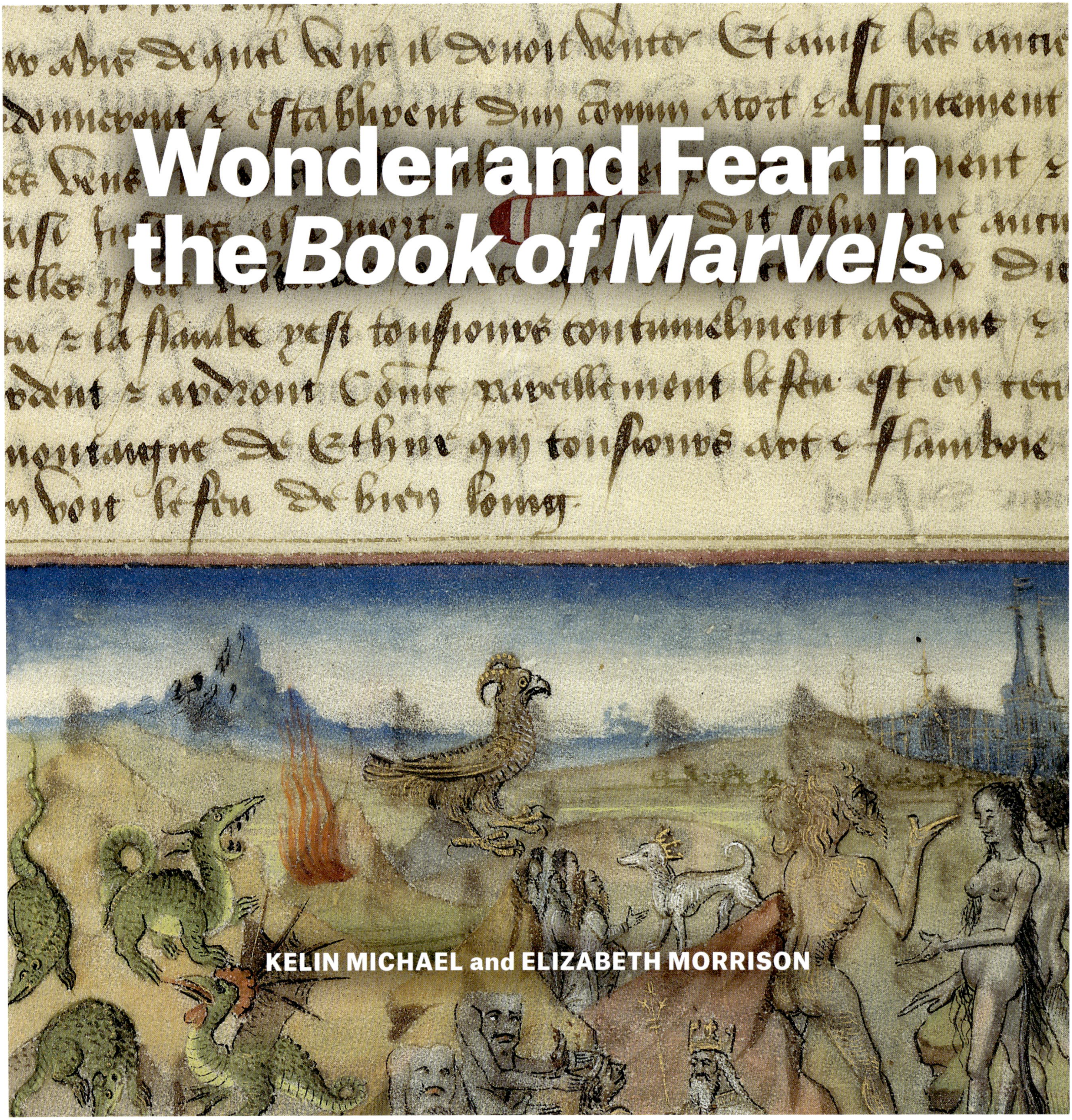

KELIN MICHAEL and ELIZABETH MORRISON

What is the difference between wonder and fear? The *Book of the Marvels of the World* (*Livre des merveilles du monde*, hereafter, *Marvels*) describes strange and inexplicable events, manufactured objects, behaviors, peoples, and natural phenomena meant to induce a sense of wonder in its audience. The medieval European Christian readers for whom the *Marvels* manuscripts were produced perceived some of these tales as captivating, bizarre, or dangerously different, especially those that were far distant from themselves. Just as space-alien and horror movies entertain modern audiences because they offer a thrilling yet vicarious experience of wonder and fear, so too did the compelling text and images of the *Marvels* manuscripts for their intended audience in the Middle Ages.

One aspect that unites many of the descriptions and visualizations found in the *Marvels* manuscripts is the fact that they nurtured an ingrained sense of superiority in their readers. The manuscripts thus actively contributed to an othering in the minds of their intended audience—a process of exclusion, in which individuals and groups are seen primarily in terms of their difference from one's own culture. In the *Marvels* manuscripts, the practice of othering reinforced the dominant position of wealthy, white, able-bodied, heteronormative, European Christian men.[1] Of course, medieval European society was not monolithic, even among the educated class that would have owned a copy of the *Marvels*, and each individual encountering its text and images would have brought personal experiences and responses, including prejudices, to bear. The authors intend, in the discussion that follows, to place the *Marvels* within the larger sociocultural landscape of the period.

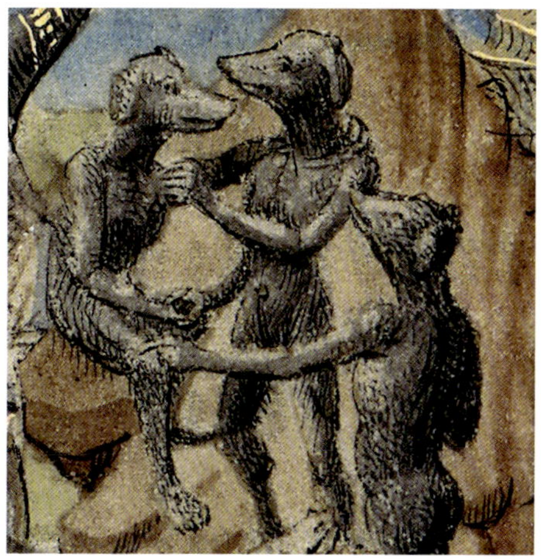
DETAIL, PLATE 12, INDIA (GETTY)

The hundreds of vignettes contained within the images of the *Marvels* cover a vast array of topics and engage the reader by giving the wonders concrete visual form. Marvels range from crane-fighting Pygmies and untamed unicorns (plate 14, no. 1; plate 1, no. 1) to dog-headed men and house-sized snails (plate 12, no. 3; plate 19, no. 2).[2] Although it might be tempting to focus solely on the captivating nature of these accounts and their correspondingly vibrant images, certain recurring themes reveal the biases of the manuscripts' producers and consumers. This essay will explore three of these themes that run like threads throughout the *Marvels*'s imagery: gender and sexual differences, including the dangers of women; divergences in behavior and customs, such as religious practices; and animals as signifiers of foreignness, as well as peoples who exhibit animal-like forms or are shown as occupying a gray area between human and animal. In these ways, the *Marvels* manuscripts provide a powerful example of how the overlapping natures of wonder and fear permeated medieval societies, allowing for a confrontation with the past that helps explain why Western stereotypes of the othered still endure today.[3]

Gender and Sex

A number of entries in the *Marvels* center around the complex relationship between gender, sex, fear, and wonder, concepts that are still interwoven today. In both text and image, viewers encounter regions where one gender is culturally dominant (plate 2), where gender roles are swapped (plate 16, no. 4), and where tales of the dangers of sex and its relationship to violence are prominent (plates 5, 12).[4] These situations are almost always described textually and visually in a way that judges gender and sexuality against the norms created by Christian Europeans. Many regions today still see the effects of these biases, which typically curtail or erase women's rights. The *Marvels* manuscripts show how these embedded norms concerning gender and sexuality have had a long-lasting impact.

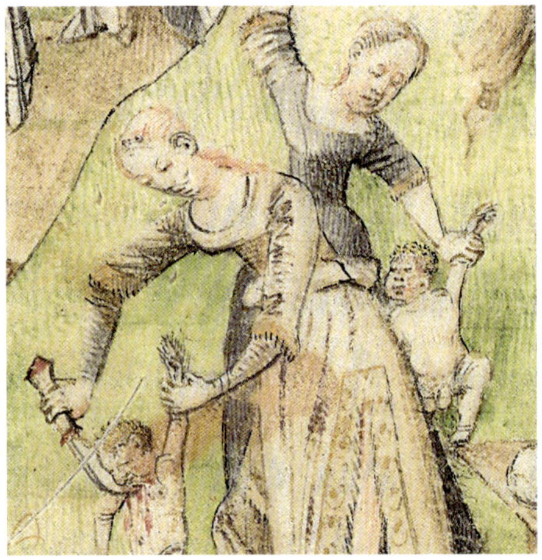

DETAIL, PLATE 2, AMAZONIA

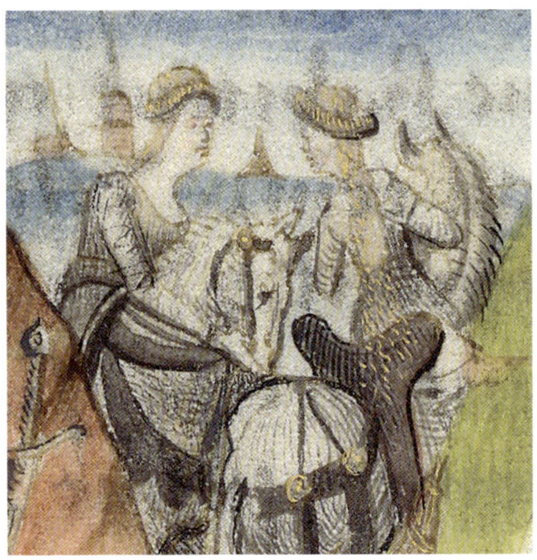

DETAIL, PLATE 16, SCYTHIA (MORGAN)

Amazonia, for example, an imaginary location situated near Scythia, north of the Black Sea, is presented as a region inhabited only by women, women who *do not allow* men to live there (plate 2, no. 1).[5] The text describes them as great warriors with an organized government. The Amazons choose when to have sexual relations with men (plate 2, no. 1), and when they do, it is not to seek pleasure, but expressly to replenish their line. The Amazons thus use their sexuality as a source of power that allows them to control their environment. As an extension of this tradition, when Amazons give birth to a girl, they nurture the child, eventually cutting off one of her breasts so that she might become a better archer. When they give birth to a boy, however, they kill him. A depiction of this practice is shown in the center foreground of the *Amazonia* image, drawing the viewer's attention to acts that must have seemed unfathomable to members of a society that valued male lineage as highly as medieval Europeans did. The historical and fictional writings of male medieval authors typically assigned all these qualities—self-sufficiency, political acumen, and military prowess—to male figures.[6] The Amazons, formidable women who weren't reliant on men, likely both repelled and intrigued readers.

The entry on Scythia describes the women of this region—one that straddles Europe and Asia—in a similar way, saying that they "do all the things that customarily belong to men, such as buying and selling, riding on horseback, and taking arms against their enemies for the defense of their country" (plate 16, no. 4).[7] Men also reside in Scythia, but what makes this region strange for the intended audience is that the men "do and carry out all the tasks that women customarily perform elsewhere, such as spinning, combing wool, and making and washing with lye." This scene is depicted, once again, near the center of the image, drawing the reader's attention to the exchange of standard gender roles, and this time, the women literally hover over their male counterparts, underscoring their superior position in this society. Unlike in Amazonia, both genders are well represented in Scythia, but their stereotypical roles are swapped, portraying a middle ground between the European norm and the fully othered, represented by the Amazons.[8] As Scythia was geographically part of both the intended reader's known world (Europe) and a part of the world less known to most (Asia), its depiction in the *Marvels* presented audiences with the combination of the familiar (the presence of two genders) and the reversal of the familiar (the swapping of gender roles) in a single image.

The section "Wonders of the Human Body" contains several accounts of women turning into men, in both magical and medical contexts (the medical account seems to be of an intersex individual).[9] This unillustrated section emphasizes the veracity of these claims by mentioning several of these individuals by name—Crassus Longis, Aristotle,[10] Isis, Cizisia—and it draws on many different sources for the accounts, including Ovid, Pliny the Elder, Orosius, and Saint Augustine.[11] In these stories, the complete transformations are often confirmed by each individual's ability to produce children with women. Furthermore, the text quotes Solinus and Pliny as saying that "the same thing occurs with animals" and that "when [these animals] come of age, nature overcomes its imperfection."[12] Here, the imperfection is understood by the intended heteronormative audience of the *Marvels* as the state of being female. It is clear through these descriptions that women were seen at the time as the weaker sex, which explains why stories of the Amazons likely incited reactions of awe and fear: these women defied the traditional roles assigned to the female sex. These accounts

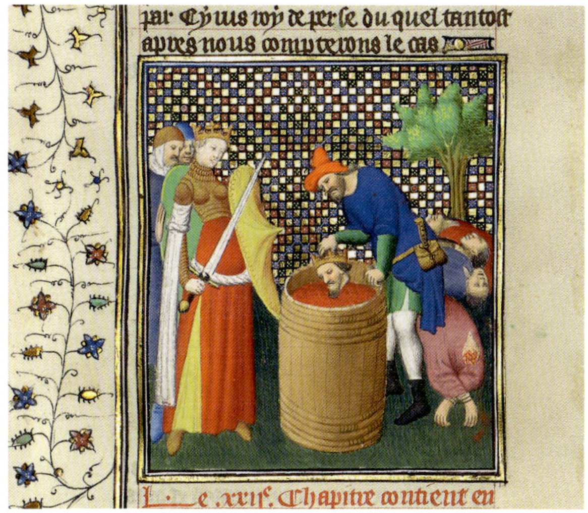

FIGURE 28 Boucicaut Master, *Cyrus the Great, Founder of the Persian Empire, Killed by Thamaris, Queen of the Massagetai*, in Giovanni Boccaccio, *Concerning the Fates of Illustrious Men and Women*. France, Paris, ca. 1413–15. Los Angeles, J. Paul Getty Museum, Ms. 63, fol. 58r (detail)

reflect the discomfort with which medieval people generally reacted to nontraditional gender attributes, whether gender ambiguity, the reversal of gender roles, or a change in gender itself.[13]

Indeed, depictions of women upsetting traditional gender roles appear not only in the *Marvels* manuscripts, but are a common motif in a variety of medieval texts. One example is an image of Thamaris, queen of the Massagetai in the sixth century BCE, killing Cyrus the Great, founder of the Persian Empire (fig. 28), in *Concerning the Fates of Illustrious Men and Women* (*Des cas des nobles hommes et femmes*), originally written in Latin by the Florentine Giovanni Boccaccio in the mid-1300s. In the image, Thamaris of the Massagetai is dressed as a warrior with her blade drawn, standing next to a barrel full of blood that will soon contain the head of her sworn enemy, Cyrus, king of Persia. The Massagetai were an ancient eastern Iranian Saka people, part of the wider Scythian cultures. Once again, a female figure from a region on the outskirts of Western Christian European understanding flips gender roles by taking command of an army and leading it to victory against the Persians, one of the most powerful military forces in recorded history.

In the *Marvels* manuscripts, the representation of female beauty and sexuality is another way in which women are othered. Following a long-standing tradition, beautiful women are used to warn readers away from the temptation of sin and are often portrayed as non-Christians leading men away from expectations associated with Christian doctrine; sexually dangerous women also signified that a region was distant and, hence, "exotic," in comparison to Western Europe. For instance, in India, the text describes "huge women, all naked, who . . . had hair hanging down to the ground. . . . And when they captured a man . . . they forced him to have carnal company with them. For they are so hot, disorderly, and abominable in vile lust that it is a wonder" (plate 12, no. 9). Although these women are not shown actively seducing men, the artist depicts them as temptresses; naked, with small waists, full hips, and long, flowing hair. They display aspects of white, Western European, medieval ideals of beauty, and it is their very beauty that associates them with the qualities of lust and sin. The text on Thrace, which covers portions of Greece, Turkey, and Bulgaria, states that there, a woman's beauty and wealth are more important than her honesty and good name, because women sell themselves to the highest bidder when searching for a husband.[14] The behavior of Thracian men, that is, placing beauty above virtue, is presented here as contrary to the conventional medieval Christian standards for men. The Great Harlot of Babylon, who appears in the biblical Revelation, often cited in medieval texts and images, is another example of a woman's sexuality being used as a metaphor for sin and danger. She is, in fact, a sign of the Apocalypse, the end of days (fig. 29). In this image from the Getty Apocalypse, she is represented as a beautiful young woman, whose vanity is symbolized by the mirror she holds, and she "is full of the abomination and filthiness of her sin" (Revelation 17:4).

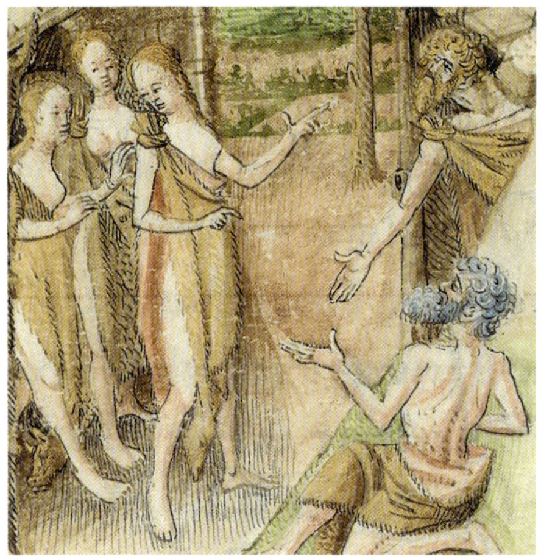

DETAIL, PLATE 5, KEDAR

Women are described as victims of sexual violence in the *Marvels* text, but these acts are never overtly depicted visually. The men of the region of Kedar (a tribe in the Arabian desert), for example, are said to rape women, including virgins.[15] Although there is no explicit violence shown, the divided scene may be suggesting it. On the right, a group made up solely of men gathers in and around rudimentary dwellings, while on the left, three women in such a hut stand in front of two men, two of the women seeming to push the third out toward one of the men, who beckons with his arm (plate 5, no. 2). The textual description and possible visual implication of sexual violence other a distant place and its people from the perspective of Christian

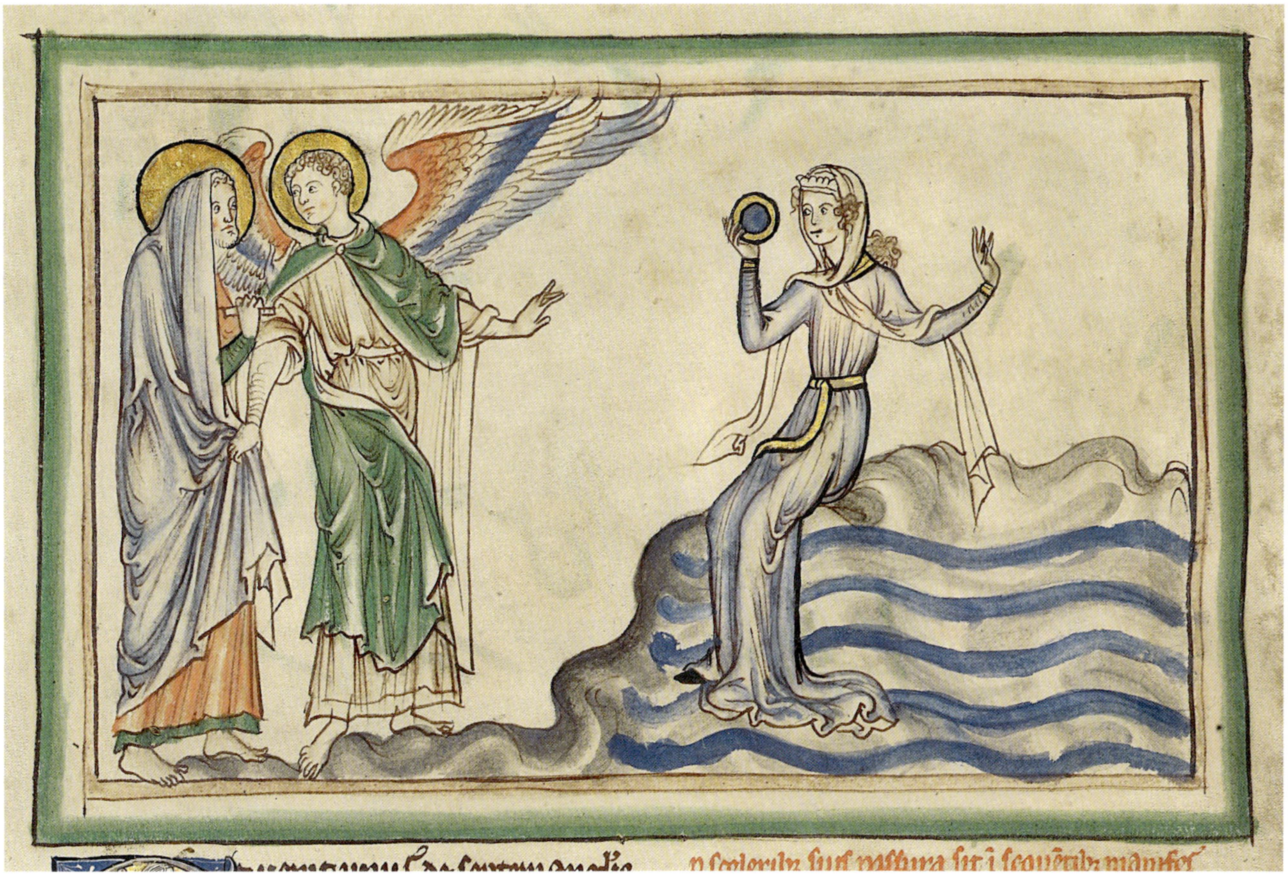

FIGURE 29 *The Great Harlot of Babylon*, in the Getty Apocalypse. England, probably London, ca. 1255–60. Los Angeles, J. Paul Getty Museum, Ms. Ludwig III 1, fol. 35v (detail)

Europeans. The entry labels the behavior of the men of Kedar "inhuman" and calls them "cruel and wild." Likewise, in the entry for Ethiopia (plate 8), one custom that is not depicted, but is described, relates to how men, on their wedding night, leave their new brides to be sexually assaulted by multiple other men. These people, known as Auriges, are said to have the "habit of serving and adoring as their gods the regions of hell."[16] In this case, violent sexual behavior is a basis for othering, along with geographic distance and a form of devil worship.

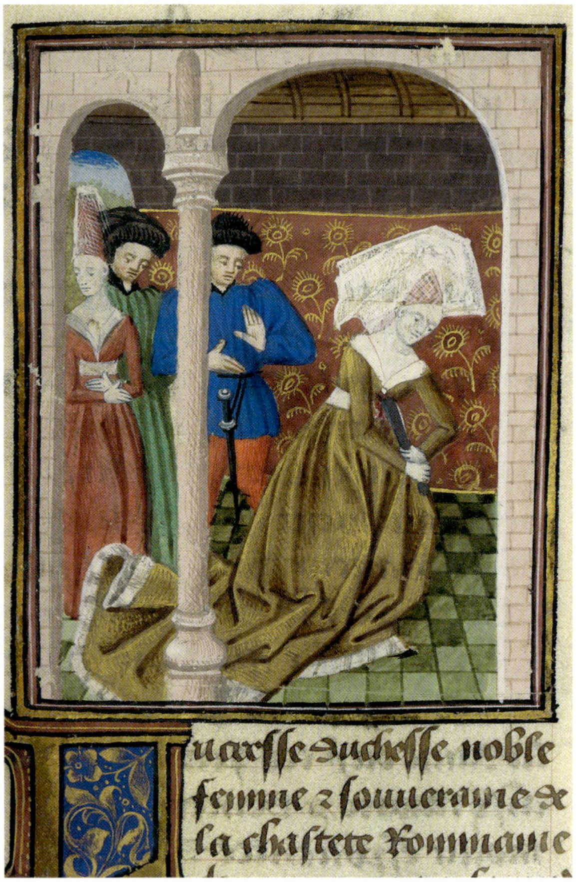

FIGURE 30 Follower of the Bedford Master, *Lucretia Committing Suicide*, in Giovanni Boccaccio, *Concerning Famous Women*. France, probably Paris or possibly the Loire region, ca. 1460. New York, Morgan Library & Museum, Ms. M.381, fol. 25r (detail)

Other medieval artists and authors use violence, both sexual and nonsexual, to draw attention to behaviors that were seen as horrible or inhuman. In the story of the Roman noblewoman Lucretia, she is raped by Sextus Tarquinius. Because Roman society saw a violated woman as immoral, she perceives suicide as the honorable course of action and kills herself. The rape and suicide of Lucretia spur the overthrow of the monarchy, facilitating its shift from kingdom to republic.[17] As shown in a fifteenth-century French manuscript created in this medieval Christian context (fig. 30), sexual assault is seen as a crime to be avenged, as compared to its portrayal in Kedar or Ethiopia, where the text enables othering by presenting sexual violence as an inherent and reprehensible part of these region's cultures.

Behavior, Customs, and Religion

The portrayals of the behavior, customs, and religions of the regions in the *Marvels* manuscripts reflect and likely informed the perspective of the white, Christian, European audience for whom the manuscripts were made. Some of these observations may have been based on kernels of truth, but they are mostly exaggerations or even complete fabrications. Behaviors in the text that were deemed especially strange or abhorrent were the ones most often chosen to be illustrated. Many different customs are shown in the *Marvels* manuscripts, ones that surround death (plates 12, 18), diet (plates 8, 11, 12), governance (plates 4, 8), and most of all, religion (plates 7, 10, 12, 15, 16).[18]

In the *Marvels* text, behaviors and customs surrounding death are often described with a tone of awe. The people of Thule, for instance, are "long-lived and never ill" and because of this, "when the time comes that they are aged and they are very old and decrepit, they throw themselves into the sea and drown" (plate 18, nos. 2, 3). The corresponding image represents this scene not as something sad, but rather as a cause for celebration, with several figures bearing witness to the act. Such practices would have likely been shocking to readers, who, as European medieval Christians, viewed suicide as an irredeemable sin.[19] In India, another custom related to suicide is described, in both image and text. When a married man dies, the *Marvels* tells how the body is placed on a funeral pyre—a practice that would have been abhorrent to medieval European Christians, who, at this time, would not have condoned cremation, believing that the body must be preserved in preparation for the Resurrection. The second part of this Indian custom involves the self-proclaimed most faithful of the deceased's wives throwing herself onto the pyre and dying in order to prove her faithfulness (plate 12, no. 6). This sacrifice, called Sati, was a real practice in India at the time and survives, illegally, today.[20] In the image, this vignette is the only one that has a bright red color, immediately drawing the viewer's attention. The Christian practices associated with death are depicted in images accompanying texts like the Office of the Dead, the prayer cycle said for the souls of the deceased (fig. 31). Having these prayers recited by the clergy and using the occasion to distribute alms to the more unfortunate were important aspects of Christian funerals.

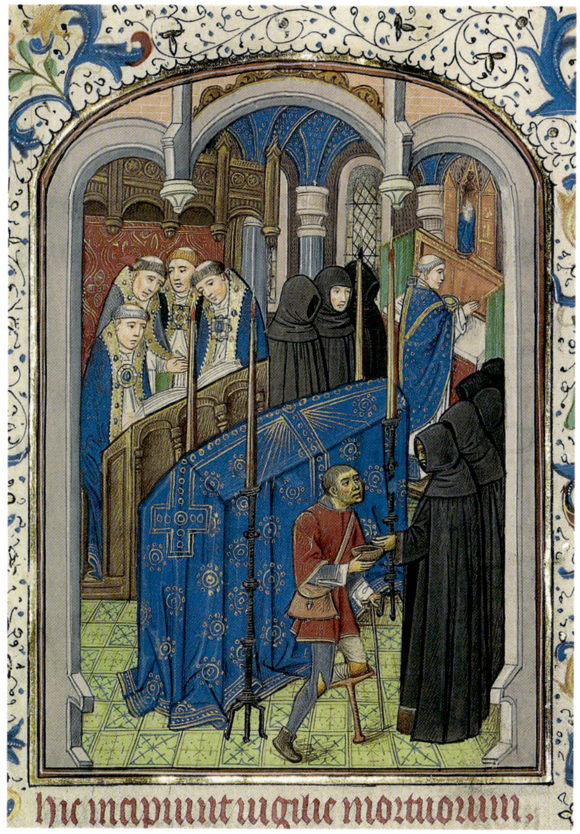

FIGURE 31 Willem Vrelant, *Mass for the Dead*, in the Arenberg Hours. Belgium, Bruges, early 1460s. Los Angeles, J. Paul Getty Museum, Ms. Ludwig IX 8, fol. 189r (detail)

The text and images of the *Marvels* also often feature what people ate in regions outside of France and the broader area of Europe. Typically, the diets described contrast with what would have been familiar to the medieval European reader. The entry on Ethiopia, for example, describes a group of people called Troglodytes who only eat raw flesh, including that of lizards and small snakes, sometimes when they were still alive (plate 8, no. 2). They are pictured prominently in the bottom left corner of the image, consuming multiple reptiles. Similarly, in the region of India, men near a large river are reported as eating only raw fish and are described "as naked and hairy as wild beasts" (plate 12, no. 8). Even though the text describing India is long and contains many anecdotes, the way in which the image depicts these men emphasizes dietary habits as a way of othering. Like the text, the image equates perceived abnormal dietary practices with wildness and inhuman qualities. Similarly, in Ibernia (Ireland), when men vanquish their enemies, they drink their blood (plate 11, no. 3). The image depicts a bloody battle, with one man already drinking from a helmet. While not quite cannibalism, true cannibalism is also portrayed in the *Marvels*. For example, the text on Scythia reports that people in the province of Neutria transform into wolves and "live only on raw flesh" (plate 16, no. 1).[21] Although the text does not explicitly say that the raw flesh is human, the image shows two men hunched over a third, poised to feast. Cannibalism, taboo in Western medieval Europe, was a common accusation associated with othering.[22]

Governmental structuring is yet another way in which the entries draw attention to the differences between the intended audience of the manuscript and peoples in other regions. One example is the account of the region of Ethiopia, where, in the center background of the image, people elect a dog as their king, complete with crown (plate 8, no. 6). A clear manifestation of Islamophobia is present in this depiction. Given the tradition in Europe of representing the Prophet Muhammad and the Egyptian sultan Saladin as dog-headed figures, readers of the *Marvels* might well have associated Ethiopia with Islam.[23] As opposed to representations of a king in a Western European court (fig. 32), featuring a crown on a dog would have belittled the idea of Muslim governance. In this case, the account and its implications were especially fallacious, because, in reality, Ethiopia at the time was ruled by a Christian emperor. Even the entry on Great Britain, a part of Europe close to France, where the *Marvels* manuscripts originated, includes a report that there used to be "beastly barbarians" who "governed themselves according to the state and behaviors of certain animals" (plate 4, no. 2). Presumably, after the advent of Christianity, such beastly barbarians were converted and reigned no more in such an unruly manner. In this case concerning governance, the process of othering was dependent on time rather than geography.

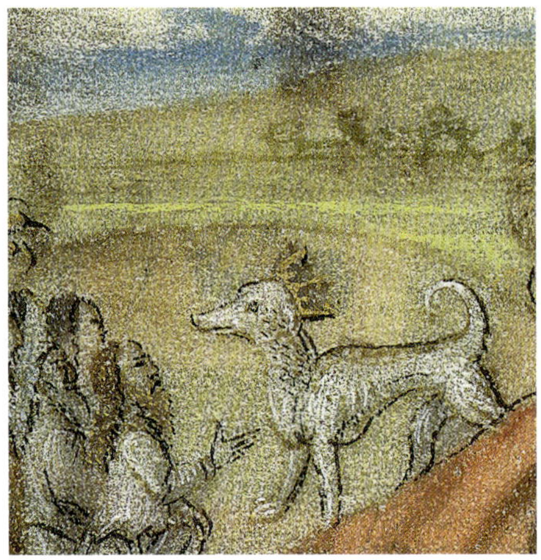

DETAIL, PLATE 8, ETHIOPIA

Religious practices are perhaps the most common type of behavior associated with othering that are found in the text and images of the *Marvels*. Although medieval Europe was home to several religions, it was largely inhabited by a homogenous Christian population who saw Christianity as a key component of their identity. Because of this, much Christian culture othered members of different religions, and in the *Marvels*, this othering is accomplished by defaming non-Abrahamic religions as "pagan."[24] Jewish and Islamic traditions are especially criticized, often for the unfounded notion that they practiced idolatry (plates 7, 10, 15), an invention that likely grew out of the heated discussions within Christian circles of the appropriate use of religious imagery by Christians themselves.[25] The *Marvels* portrays the worship of idols in Egypt, India, and Scythia as part of the customs of the so-called pagans, with the idols taking the form of an ox, a hybrid man-ox, and the Roman god Mars, respectively (plates 7, 12, 16).[26] While the visual depictions

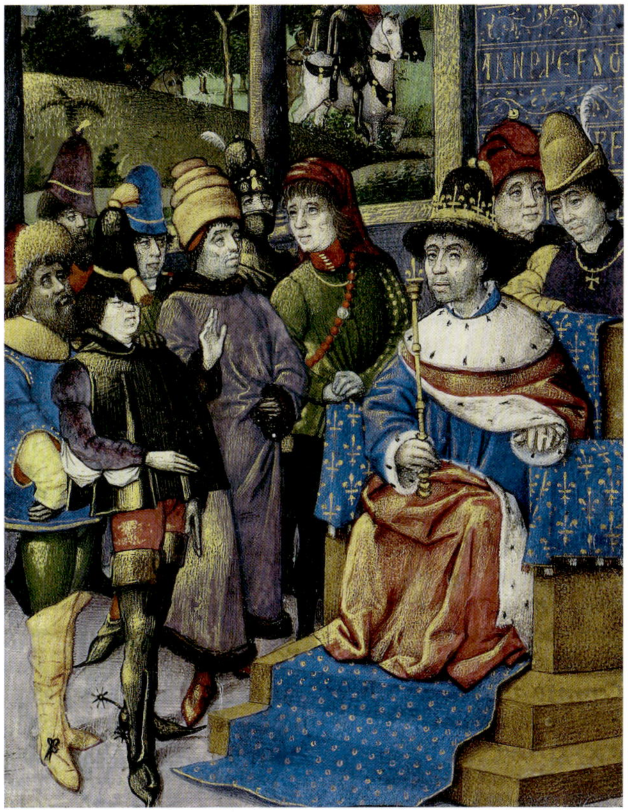

FIGURE 32 *The French King at Court*, in Aeneas Silvius Piccolomini, Letter to Johann van Eich. France, ca. 1460–70. Los Angeles, J. Paul Getty Museum, Ms. 68, fol. 1r (detail)

of idolatry in the *Marvels* are not portrayed as especially threatening (as they are confined to their particular regions), a practitioner of Christianity would have understood them as strange and wondrous to behold. Furthermore, Christian Europeans saw idolatry as a key characteristic that othered non-Christians, one very likely perceived as a threat if such rituals encroached upon the Christian empires of medieval Europe.

Idolatry was not a practice that Christian Europeans saw as limited to distant regions, however. In Spain, an area historically diverse in terms of religion (Christianity, Judaism, and Islam, all of which forbid idolatry, were present there in the

Middle Ages), the text describes one idol that survived destruction by the Holy Roman Emperor Charlemagne in the eighth century (plate 10, no. 5). This idol was said to have been forged by "Mahomet" (Muhammad) himself, who enclosed 6,666 devils within it so that it had the power to kill any Christian who attempted to destroy it.[27] Here, idolatry was understood to be dangerous to both body and soul, even though in the image it appears harmless. In another example, the image of Provence, a region in France, close to where the *Marvels* manuscripts were made, the artist created a terrifying scene of children being sacrificed to an idol (plate 15, no. 1). While the figure carrying out this sacrifice is not explicitly identified, his clothing, particularly his hat, would have suggested to a medieval European Christian audience that he is Jewish. The entry explains that this practice was done for the salvation of the people. While the story is fabricated, Christian Europeans might well have interpreted the practice as an unholy substitute for Christ's sacrifice on the Cross, a particularly insidious example of anti-Semitism.[28]

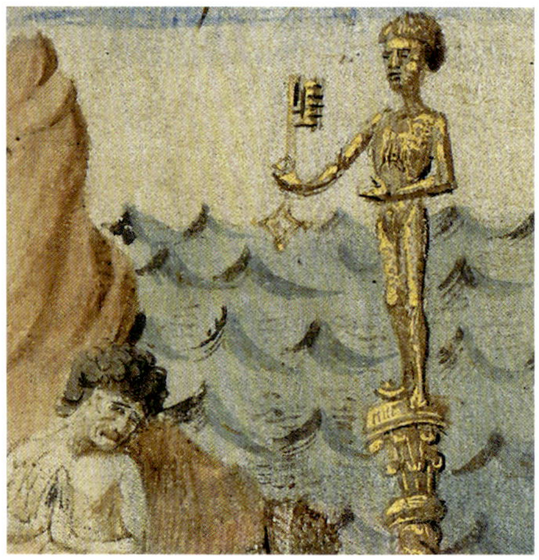

DETAIL, PLATE 10, SPAIN (GETTY)

The Animal/Human Divide

African safaris, *Animal Planet*, and zoos are all manifestations of today's fascination with animals. Animals often stand in as signifiers for place—to many, pandas immediately suggest China, bald eagles are a symbol of the United States, and kangaroos call the Australian outback to mind. In medieval manuscripts, animals that would have been familiar to Europeans, such as dogs, bears, and horses, appear in plenty, but so do lions, unicorns, camels, and dragons, which would have been known to them only through books and images. Although people in the Middle Ages relied on animals as a part of daily agricultural life, and they were fascinated by animals thought to live far from Europe, the didactic or symbolic value animals might hold as evidence of God's creative powers was also an aspect that was celebrated. In addition, in that period, just as now, creatures that slip into the gray area between animal and human seem to have the greatest ability to capture the imagination. Today, zombies, vampires, and sentient aliens in movies, books, and TV shows instill fear and awe with their beastlike behaviors, partly because they also exhibit human qualities. These same characteristics no doubt also made legendary peoples, including headless Blemmyes, giants, and werewolves, captivating to the medieval reader. This section will discuss the creatures found in the *Marvels*, both animal and almost human, whose bestial attributes the authors and artists intended to evoke equal parts fear and wonder in the minds of a medieval European audience, in an effort to create a sense of otherness that seemingly increased the farther one moved away from medieval Europe.

Some of the animals known to inhabit European lands take on unusual behaviors or features in the *Marvels*. Horses, sheep, oxen, and other familiar creatures can be found throughout the text and images of the *Marvels*, even though they often do not look or behave in ways modern audiences

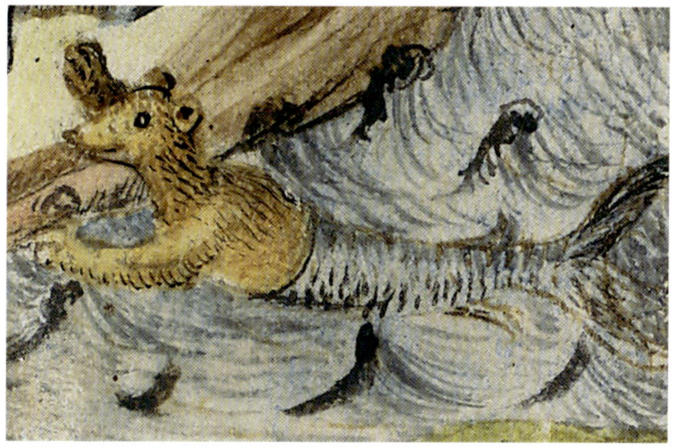

FIGURE 33 *Beaver* (detail, plate 13, no. 6, Getty)

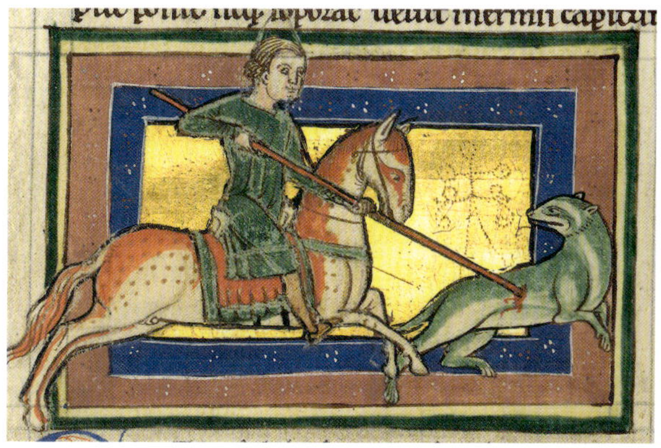

FIGURE 34 *Beaver*, in the Worksop Bestiary. England, Lincoln (?), ca. 1185. New York, Morgan Library & Museum, Ms. M.81, fol. 13v (detail)

might expect. The inclusion of so many animals in the *Marvels* manuscripts indicates that medieval audiences delighted in hearing about them and seeing them depicted. For example, in the entry for Italy, the text talks of "a beast called beaver, that is half animal and half fish" (plate 13, no. 6). Accordingly, the artist has represented just such a creature, resembling a furry bear with a fish tail, jauntily waving as it approaches the shore (fig. 33). The beaver often appeared in medieval manuscripts without its characteristic buck teeth and thick tail (fig. 34), which may be explained by the fact that in the Middle Ages, even common European animals were often discussed and depicted with their Christian symbolic value in mind, rather than with any desire to capture zoological veracity.[29] The beaver, for example, was sought after for the supposed medicinal uses of its testicles. The animal itself was said to willingly tear them off to escape being hunted, a behavior seen as akin to a Christian's willingness to live chastely and throw off sin in defiance of the devil.[30]

Judging by the numbers of animals that appear in manuscripts, church decorations, tapestries, and all other types of artworks of the period, medieval European audiences were also eager to hear about animals from faraway places such as Africa and China, whether animals known to be indigenous to these places or those today considered to be imaginary. Such distinctions were meaningless for medieval Europeans, few of whom would see the animals personally and who embraced a worldview that was largely unconcerned with such categorization.[31] The *Marvels* text for Lower Egypt states that the region features monstrous animals that "like to stay on the seashores and are most dreaded and feared by the inhabitants of the country, the one kind having the name 'hippopotamus.'"[32] The image of this creature also deviates quite significantly from the familiar animal known from scientific renderings and photographs, as it is shown as a hybrid with the head of a fish attached to the rear end of a horse (fig. 35). (The word "hippopotamus" derives from the Greek words for horse and river.) In the *Marvels*, the animal was likely included in the entry for Egypt because of its ferocious nature and was depicted in a way that would have been startling to viewers, enhancing the white, Christian European perspective on Africa as a "foreign"—and hence, dangerous—land.

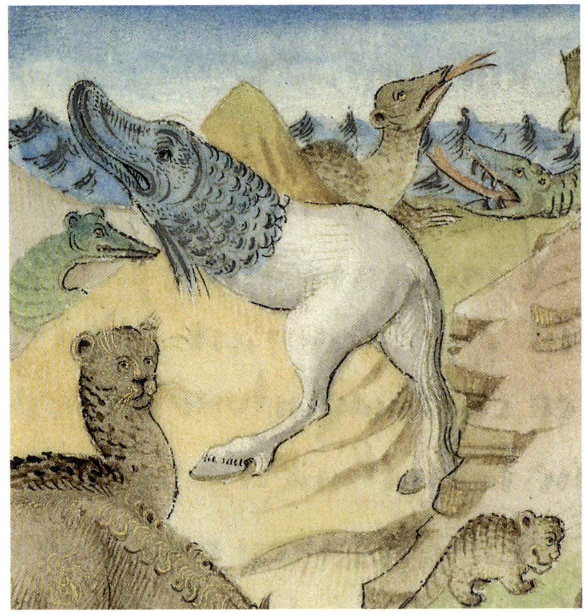

FIGURE 35 Master of the Geneva Boccaccio, *Lower Egypt*, in the *Book of the Marvels of the World*. France, Angers, ca. 1460. New York, Morgan Library & Museum, Ms. M.461, fol. 20v (detail)

In Seres (China), "the deserts there are so great and so terrible and so full of ravenous, wild, venomous beasts like tigers, wolves, serpents, and dragons, that no one would be able to go there in a simple way without being killed" (plate 17, no. 1). Of this list, the artist focused on the dragon in the accompanying image, featuring multiple tongue-lashing specimens, along with another unidentifiable animal. They occupy the sand dunes at the far left, evoking the terrible wastes the viewer was led to believe they would have to brave in order to travel there. Dragons make multiple appearances in the *Marvels*, ranging from Arabia to Seres (China) (plates 1, 3, 8, 12, 17, and 22). Other animals that would have amazed medieval European audiences also make an appearance in the *Marvels*. The text for the island of Traponee (Sri Lanka) contains at the end, almost as an afterthought, the tale of the island's unusually large snails, which serve as both prey for hunters and housing for the inhabitants. These factoids may have driven away any other aspect of the island in the mind of the artist, for the image pictures only these fast-moving, oversized mollusks (plate 19).

For some regions far away from medieval Europe, the entries are accompanied by an image almost entirely composed of the animals said to live there, which most medieval Europeans would probably have deemed exotic.[33] In addition to the individual entries for countries or smaller regions, the *Marvels* also devotes entries to the three divisions of the known world: Africa, Asia, and Europe.[34] The entry for Africa (plate 1) is accompanied by an image focusing almost exclusively on the animals thought to inhabit that continent. At left, a lion and an elephant observe the scene, while a bear lurks in the distance, all three of which are mentioned in the text. A unicorn, while never mentioned in the text, also makes a prominent appearance in the image; both the artist and the audience probably expected a place such as Africa to feature this animal, which typified the exotic in the medieval European imagination.[35] The cows and sheep in the foreground with their heads on backward and horns facing the ground are also explained in the text (plate 1, no. 4). The right side of the image is dominated by the various fantastic serpents (including one with four legs and fur) that were also said to live in Africa, including those that eat illegitimate children offered by fathers unsure of their parentage (plate 1, no. 3). For viewers of the *Marvels* manuscripts, Africa was largely defined by its animals.

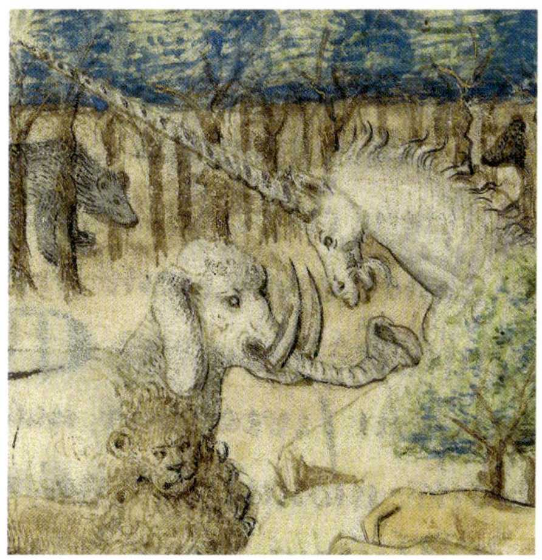

DETAIL, PLATE 1, AFRICA

Beyond the animals of land, sea, and air that inhabit the *Marvels*, there are also those creatures that appear to verge on the human, often identified in the text and portrayed in the images as "savage" or "beastly" (plates 4, 7, 8, 9, 12, 16). They were perhaps even more frightening than the animals included, due to the uncertainty of their nature.[36] For Christians in the Middle Ages, the theological distinction between animal and human was an absolute and important one: according to Christian dogma, humans have souls and animals do not. And, if there were creatures who were human, however animal-like in appearance or behavior, then they still had the capability of Christian salvation. It was, partly, this very difficulty in deciding whether these beings were animal or human that led to a fascination with them. They were often thought to live literally at the edges of the earth, as seen in the Psalter Map discussed by Joshua O'Driscoll in this volume (see fig. 22), but whether these ambiguous beings lived within Europe or outside its boundaries, they may have attracted special attention due to the readers' need to determine the creatures' place in the Christian worldview.

The entry for Great Britain states that "there used to be certain people that were called beastly barbarians, who under the shadow and color of penitence changed their appearance by adopting bestial manners and qualities. And . . . they painted their faces and hands and various parts of their bodies with diverse colors in order better to resemble animals" (plate 4, no. 2). The artist has represented them as spotted, naked people, some of them shown in odd bodily positions suggestive of crawling on all fours, and, significantly, they surround a Christian church, but do not enter (although the presence of a church implies the possibility of conversion and salvation). These characteristics would have reinforced a sense of their otherness for a medieval Christian viewer.

In the *Marvels*, the farther from Europe, the more forms of creatures seem to fall outside of a stark definition of animal or human. In the entry for Scythia, the text describes people who, on certain days when they cross a river, transform into wolves, feed on raw human flesh, and then turn back into people again (plate 16, no. 1). The artist shows the river on the upper left. On the near side are a wolf and a wolf with a human head, mid-transformation. On the far side of the river, two people crouching on all fours like animals eat the body of a third. The artist thus shows the various stages of the werewolf, as well as the bestial behavior that the conversion entails. The scene is balanced at the far upper right with images of two other types of beings, grouped together with a griffon in the corner, perhaps to suggest that they are less than human: a man with horse hooves and another with only one eye in the center of his head (plate 16, nos. 6, 8).

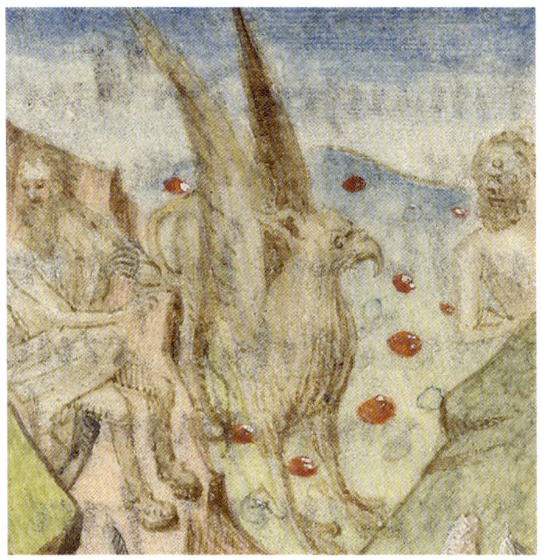

DETAIL, PLATE 16, SCYTHIA (MORGAN)

Perhaps the most complex images found in the *Marvels* are the ones depicting two regions that encapsulated the othered for white, Christian, medieval Europeans: India and Ethiopia (plates 12, 8). In fact, there was often little difference between these two places in the medieval imagination, because both were so far distant for the vast majority of Europeans that they were virtually unknowable. Medieval texts would often refer to "Ethiopia or India" as if they were interchangeable, frequently in circumstances where the text was simply trying to denote the exotic or foreign for their audience.[37] The images accompanying India and Ethiopia in the *Marvels* are crammed full of animals that would have struck European audiences as unusual, as well as a variety of beings whose animal or human nature is difficult to discern. The artist dwells on all these types of creatures. While India features elephants, unicorns, and two-headed ducks, Ethiopia is home to dragons, tragoppa birds, and a crowned dog king (see the discussion above about the layered meanings of the dog king). Meanwhile, the various peoples of India are depicted with their feet on backward, are said to live solely on smells instead of food (Astomi), or are shown with dog heads (Cynocephali). Ethiopia features an even greater variety of beings who might fall outside of the fully human category: Blemmyes (faces on their chests), Sabarines (hairy and without ears), and

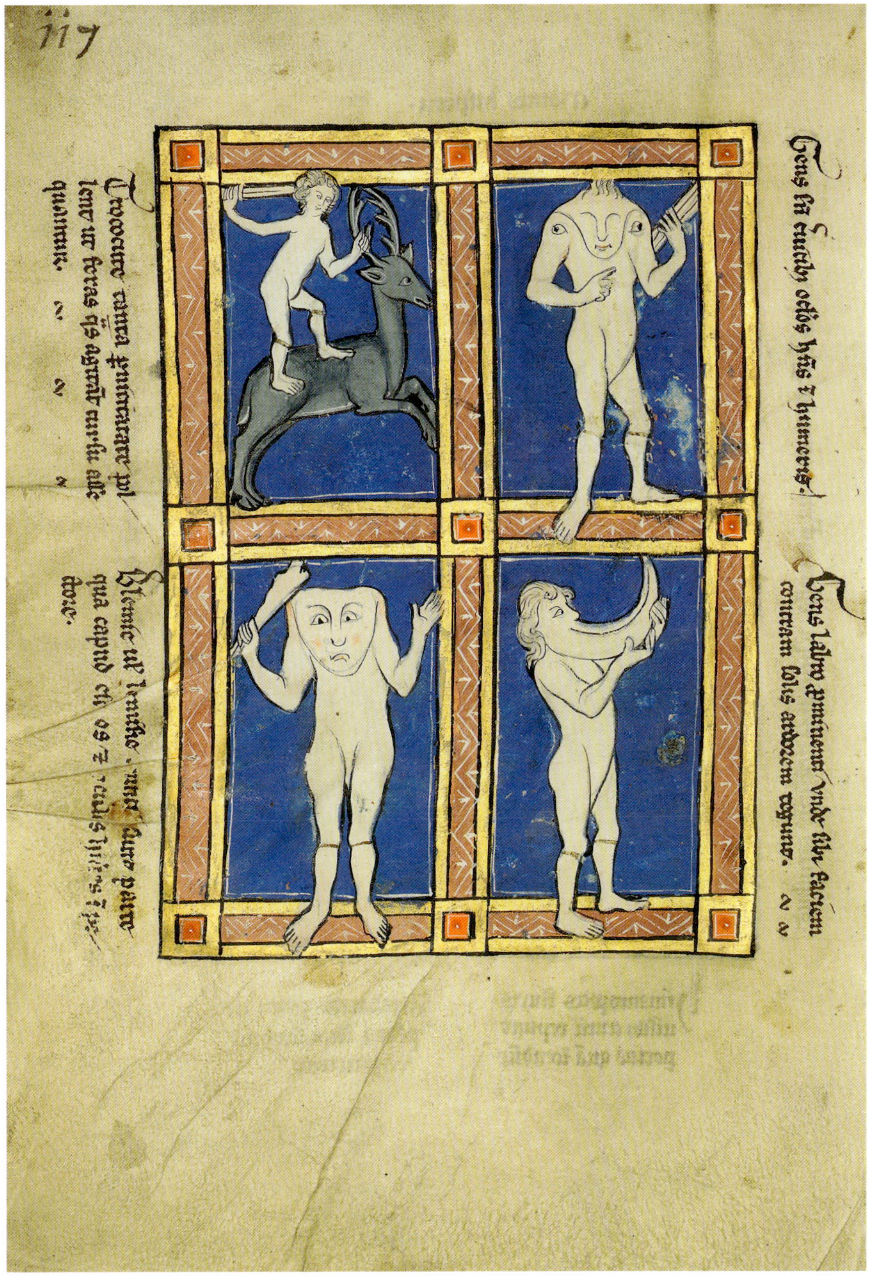

FIGURE 36 *Legendary Peoples*, in the *Wonders of the World*. France, Thérouanne, after 1277. Los Angeles, J. Paul Getty Museum, Ms. Ludwig XV 4, fol. 117v

Cinophages (one eye on their foreheads), as well as women with beards or tails, and giants galore. Medieval images often grouped these legendary peoples together to emphasize their otherness (fig. 36).

The combination of fascination with and fear of the unknown lies at the heart of the *Marvels* manuscripts. Othering appears to be an inherent aspect of the human condition, radiating out from what each society considers to be the norm. A powerful example of this is the fact that although the United States touts itself as a melting pot of diverse cultures, a systemic fear of difference that is rooted in an enduring Eurocentric mindset still exists among white people of Christian European descent, which, in extreme cases, has resulted in organized and individual violence.[38] The *Marvels* manuscripts reveal themselves to be complex, nuanced representations of the world that provide a historical lens for understanding how white, Christian Europeans positioned themselves as the standard by which to judge all those they deemed outsiders. This type of persistent fixation on difference underscores how people, both historically and today, continually portray those whom they have othered as marvels.

NOTES

1 Although the *Marvels* manuscripts do not often discuss or depict those who are differently abled, the very fact of their absence reinforces able-bodied dominance. Similarly, most peoples in the manuscripts are depicted with light skin, no matter their geographical origin, but this does not mean that racism did not influence the content or experience of the manuscript (see "Note to the Reader" and the introduction to this volume).

2 For a discussion of what constituted a marvel in the Middle Ages, see the introduction to this volume.

3 Much has been written about otherness and marginalized groups in the Middle Ages. See "Suggested Further Reading," at the end of this volume, as well as Blanks and Frassetto 1999; Bynum 1999; Fleck 2000; Stråth 2004; Eisenbeiss and Saurma-Jeltsch 2012; Rowe 2012; Goetz and Wood 2021; and Thomson 2022.

4 See Bullough and Brundage 1999 and Nirenberg 1996, esp. chap. 5.

5 The region of Amazonia in the *Marvels* has no relation to the modern region of the Amazon rainforest in South America.

6 Cohen and Wheeler 1997.

7 Figg and Friedman 2018, 282. For quotations in this essay, when taken from one of the entries featured in the "Plates with Translations" section, the plate number and the number of the excerpt are given. For quotations taken from entries not featured in the plates, the translation is directly cited.

8 The opening text of the entry for Scythia reads, "Scythia is a very great and powerful province that is partly in Asia and partly in Europe. For Upper Scythia is located in Asia. . . . And Lower Scythia is situated in Europe." Figg and Friedman 2018, 281.

9 Figg and Friedman 2018, 299–301.

10 The Aristotle mentioned in the text shares a name with the famed ancient Greek philosopher, but was a medieval individual.

11 Figg and Friedman 2018, 299–301.

12 Figg and Friedman 2018, 300.

13 For further reading on this subject, see DeVun 2021, esp. chap. 2. The modern use of the word "transgender" refers to an individual whose gender identity is different from the gender they were assigned at birth. Due to the fact that in this section of the *Marvels* the individuals do not speak for themselves, the authors do not use the term "trans."

14 Figg and Friedman 2018, 292.

15 The men forced to have sex with the lustful women of India, mentioned above, are also not shown as the victims of sexual violence. It was relatively rare for manuscripts to depict rape scenes; usually, the woman, fully clothed, is being forcefully grasped by the hand as a signifier or shown disheveled after the attack. For a discussion of how the imagery of rape in the Middle Ages reflected societal changes in attitude toward the act, see Wolfthal 1993.

16 Figg and Friedman 2018, 220.

17 For an insightful interpretation of the meaning of the rape of Lucretia, see Glendinning 2013.

18 For more on these issues, see Phillips 2014 and Thomson 2022.

19 Cusack 2018.

20 Medieval readers of the *Marvels* manuscripts would not have made distinctions between imaginary and factual accounts, both of which circulated orally and in written form. Practiced since the Middle Ages, Sati was not outlawed by the British governor-general of India until 1929, but it was still performed in the twentieth century often enough to merit being

criminalized by the Indian government in 1987. Brick 2018.
21 Figg and Friedman 2018, 281.
22 At services, Christians may elect to consume the Eucharist, the bread and (sometimes) wine that, according to Catholic doctrine, become the body and blood of Christ. Christians have never associated this practice with cannibalism.
23 Strickland 2003, esp. 203–7 and 222–26, and Cohen 2001.
24 The Abrahamic religions are Judaism, Christianity, and Islam.
25 See Strickland 2003 for more on this topic.
26 See Akbari 2009 and Arjana 2015.
27 This idol is portrayed as a man in the Getty *Marvels* and as a woman in the Morgan *Marvels*. Although the gender change of this idol is intriguing, previous scholarship and the authors of this essay have no explanation or interpretation to offer.
28 For more on the history of blood libel and anti-Semitism in Europe, see Rose 2015, 1, and Teter 2020.
29 One of the most common medieval sources for information about animals, especially their symbolic meaning, was the bestiary. See Clark 2006 and Morrison and Grollemond 2019.
30 Beavers are native to all of Europe but were largely hunted to extinction in the early Middle Ages, except in Germany and Scandinavia, which exported their pelts. Beaver fur was a sought-after commodity; Spriggs 1998.
31 Gravestock 1999.
32 Figg and Friedman 2018, 202.
33 Besides the image for Africa discussed in this essay, others include those illustrating Libya and Lower Egypt. The illustrations for Germany and Saxony also feature only animals, just as the corresponding entries contain little else besides descriptions of animals; even though the animals are often purported to have unusual qualities, the animals look like those that would have been familiar to the readers of the *Marvels* manuscripts.
34 See the essay in this volume by Joshua O'Driscoll for the medieval understanding of the map of the world, as well as the discussion of the depiction of Europe found in the Introduction.
35 See the essay by Joshua O'Driscoll in this volume for a discussion of European expectations that places far from Europe would be home to exotic animals such as unicorns, a vision shared by authors, artists, and readers alike.
36 These creatures have been referred to by some scholars as the "Monstrous Races," while others, such as Asa Mittman, question the use of the term; see Mittman 2015. This volume uses the term "legendary peoples." On the theme of legendary peoples, see Bynum 2001; Friedman 2000; Jones and Sprunger 2002; Strickland 2003; Mittman 2015; Lindquist and Mittman 2018.
37 Strickland 2003, 85–86.
38 The practice of othering is certainly not limited to any particular group of people, but because of the nature of the *Marvels* manuscripts as products of a white, Christian, medieval Europe, the authors have chosen to focus on this case of inherited othering.

Copying, Creation, and Collaboration in the *Book of Marvels*

LARISA GROLLEMOND

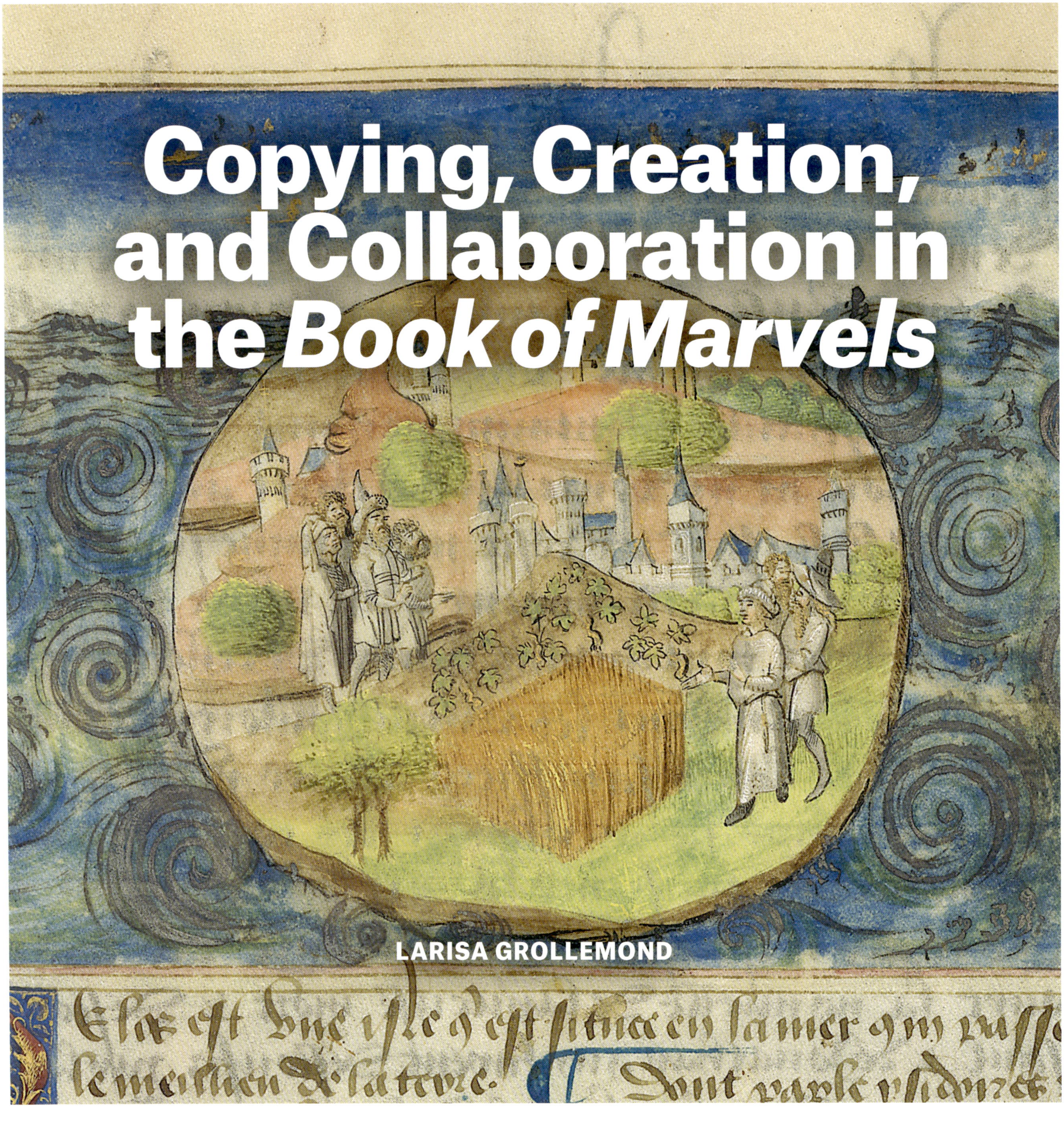

The idea of copying today perhaps has some negative connotations, signifying a certain lack of artistic originality and a reliance on imitation or simple reproduction of an existing work.[1] In the medieval world, though, the practices and processes of copying in manuscript culture not only were necessary components to the dissemination of texts and images but were also far less laden with the baggage of expectation surrounding artistic innovation. Medieval notions of authenticity and value in some cases depended on the reproduction of texts and images in ways that run counter to modern ideas about the inherent value of artistic creativity. In the medieval world, the nature of copying manually not only meant reproducing a text, and in some cases a set of images, but it was also understood to inherently introduce variation.

The surviving group of fifteenth-century manuscripts of the *Book of the Marvels of the World* (*Livre des merveilles du monde*, hereafter *Marvels*) is remarkable in that it presents a cohesive comparative case study of this kind of copying in both text and image, with the core of the known surviving examples produced over around three decades of the fifteenth century. Five *Marvels* manuscripts or manuscript fragments exist with images illustrating the French translation of the Latin text: the earliest copy of the group, in the Bibliothèque nationale de France, Paris, hereafter, the BnF *Marvels*; the Angers *Marvels*, a fragmentary copy of only two images preserved together in the Bibliothèque municipale d'Angers; New York's Morgan *Marvels*; the Getty *Marvels*, in Los Angeles; and the final and latest iteration also preserved at the Bibliothèque nationale de France.[2] The first four form a distinct group with close visual relationships in terms of book design and layout and the images' content and style. Because they are so close, they introduce questions about the order in which they were made, and how they were created and copied, who had them made, and who used the manuscripts and their contents and in what ways.

The variations among them allow a glimpse into the ways in which knowledge was not only reproduced but reimagined over time.[3] Because the French text had been relatively recently translated when it was reconceived to include images, the group of *Marvels* manuscripts forms a fascinating opportunity for thinking through the nature of artistic creation in the Middle Ages, especially as it responded to the tastes, desires, and expectations of particular audiences. The manuscripts' image program could only have been devised in fifteenth-century France, in terms of both content and artistic approach.

Understanding the order in which the manuscripts were produced allows for greater insight into the development and expression of the worldview contained within the images and the crucial role that artists played in shaping the contents of the text for its readers, deciding what to copy and take forward, and which details to change. By casting light on these aspects, the surviving *Marvels* broaden the view of modes of artistic creation in the Middle Ages.

The Earliest Marvels Manuscript

The oldest surviving copy is the BnF *Marvels*, preserved in three volumes (a modern modification), the illuminations of which have been attributed to an anonymous painter known by the name of convenience the "Master of Marguerite d'Orléans."[4] Marguerite d'Orléans (1406–1466), countess of Vertus and granddaughter of King Charles V of France (d. 1380), owned a prayer book whose many rich illustrations are attributed, on the basis of style, to the *Marvels*'s artist.[5] When no name can be gleaned from archival sources or otherwise located in history, modern scholars often use this kind of nomenclature to delineate the bodies of work of artists with particularly recognizable styles—artistic personalities—who can be identified as participating in individual works and traced through time.[6] However, this naming practice also carries assumptions about the nature of artistic creation and the ways in which it is credited. The desire to assign names of convenience despite the often slippery and subjective process of judging artistic style is perhaps driven by a modern attachment to the idea of artist as a singular creative genius. It has, sometimes unnecessarily, complicated the study of medieval manuscript copies because such naming assumes that it is possible to identify the "hands" of individual artists through time and across geography, based on the surviving visual evidence.[7] Nearly all the artists associated with the production of *Marvels* manuscripts are known by such names of convenience. They are a useful shorthand when discussing these artistic personalities, but it is far more productive to see them as flexible designations that may encompass groups of illuminators, often working collaboratively on image programs.

The version of the *Marvels* created by the Master of Marguerite d'Orléans can be dated to 1428, based on an effaced ex-libris. The year fits with the likely date in the late fourteenth or early fifteenth century when the French translation of the text from Pierre Bersuire's Latin *Moral Reduction* (*Reductorium morale*) was finished.[8] With its richness of details that can seem fantastical to a twenty-first-century reader, and information about a variety of places, the *Marvels* was particularly well-suited for an image program of the type that the Master of Marguerite d'Orléans executed. Though it is now the earliest surviving version of the image program, it may not have been the first created from Bersuire's newly translated text. Whether the illuminator copied an image program from a now-lost earlier example or fashioned a new set of images, the artist(s) succeeded in adapting the text to suit a new, wider, French-speaking audience, where Bersuire, and the surviving corpus of Latin versions of his text, had been oriented toward an ecclesiastical audience and a Christian interpretation and application of its contents.[9] The "armchair traveler" aspect of the *Marvels* provided ample fodder for an artist charged with its illustration.

A text as densely packed with detail as the *Marvels* necessitated an equally complex set of images. The illuminator(s) of the BnF *Marvels* filled dozens of rectangular spaces spanning the width of the folios—fifty-six illuminations total—with narrative vignettes described in the text, visually embellishing them with stories from the text, covering the globe from Africa to Scandinavia.[10] A single illumination is dedicated to each successive location, but all teem with features from the text, inviting the reader's attention and contemplation. The overall approach to narrative and composition can be seen in the illumination for Crete (fig. 37). The image divides the landscape into diagonal wedges, with the green and brown triangle of mountains, trees, and land bisecting it. Meanwhile, a ship floats on undulating blue water on the left; on the right are a cobblestone street, intersecting rooftops, and cutaway peeks into the town's architecture. Sections of crenelated walls and a distant castle in the left background complete the image of the advanced civilization

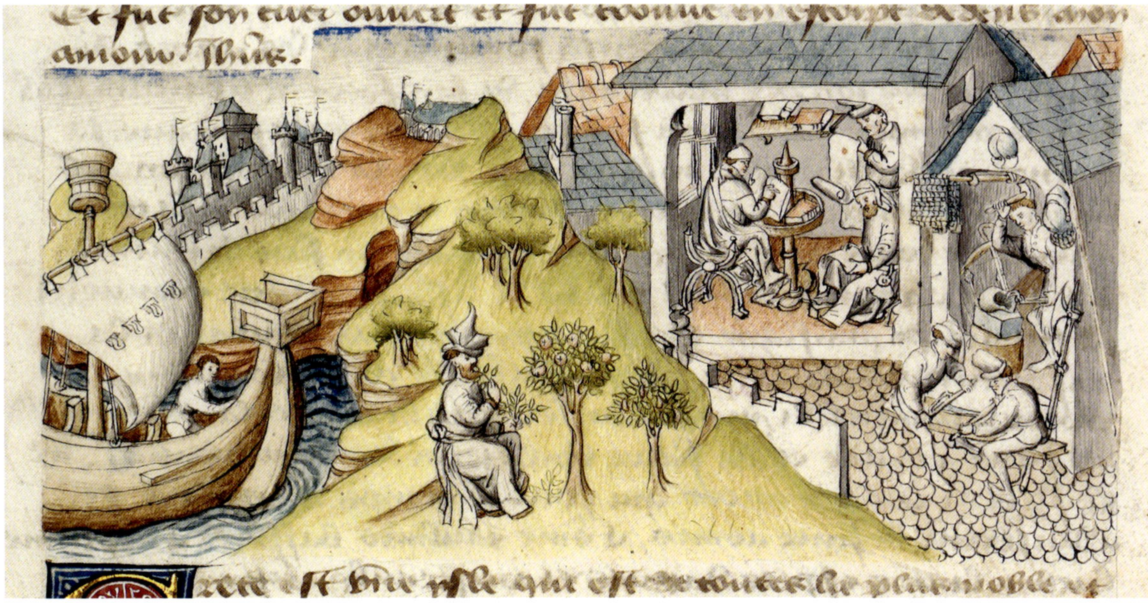

FIGURE 37 Master of Marguerite d'Orléans, *Crete*, in the *Book of the Marvels of the World*. France, Bourges, 1428. Paris, Bibliothèque nationale de France, Ms. fr. 1377, fol. 19r (detail)

that the text describes.[11] The impression of bustling action permeates the image, with all the figures at different tasks and engaged in various intellectual pursuits, each carefully differentiated.

Certain features in this early copy of the *Marvels*—the use of grisaille and the narrative vignette-packing in each location—appear in all the other surviving manuscripts in the group. The overall style of the images in the BnF *Marvels* is strongly graphic, even planar, an effect achieved with relatively heavy black outlines of ink containing a restrained color palette heightened with white. This treatment is largely confined to the landscapes, while the figures remain mostly in grisaille. Grisaille—painting entirely in tones of gray to create a monochrome, often sculptural quality—was used by many French and Flemish illuminators in the fifteenth century for a variety of types of illustrated texts, though it was a preferred technique in luxury manuscripts created for high-ranking patrons.[12] The artists associated with all the *Marvels* used this approach, which characterizes the illumination of this group of manuscripts; colored grisaille, the sensitive mixing of grisaille with color wash, distinguishes the Morgan and Getty *Marvels*.

The body of work by the illuminator associated with the 1428 copy, the so-called Master of Marguerite d'Orléans, remains somewhat of a mystery, illustrating the many challenges involved in attempting to follow these anonymous artists through time. According to several scholars, the artist worked in a number of major French cities that were centers of illuminators and patrons: Paris, Bourges, Rennes, Angers, and Poitiers, from the 1420s to around 1460.[13] Some scholars have identified the Master's "hand" in several ambitious nonreligious texts, as well as in many private prayer books, all of which were probably created for prestigious patrons, often in conjunction with other artists from prominent workshops across France. In a conception of artistic identity based on style, the BnF *Marvels* would be one of the Master's earliest works, along with frontispieces in the *Great Chronicles of France* (*Grand chroniques de France*), intended for the king of France himself, Charles VII,[14] and in a copy of Giovanni Boccaccio's *Concerning the Fates of Illustrious Men and Women* (*De casibus virorum illustrium*),[15] both also from the mid- to late 1420s.[16] This rough sketch of a career would require a single artist to have moved around quite a bit, and to have collaborated frequently with different groups of artists.

The BnF *Marvels* is an outlier from the rest of the oeuvre attributed to this artist in its use of grisaille, while the other works mentioned above are executed in highly saturated color.[17] One of these is Marguerite d'Orléans's Hours, a prayer book dated contemporaneously to the BnF *Marvels*.[18] Its margins teem with detailed depictions of historical events, aspects of medieval daily life, and scenes of mercantile trade and travel.[19] The extensive marginal illumination on folio 174v provides the viewer with a glimpse of the wide world: the upper margin contains a hair-covered pair, a monkey perched high in a tree, and a turbaned man guiding a group of camels along a path (fig. 38). The path continues down the right side of the page, with interludes of agricultural harvest in progress; the path becomes a waterway in which ships move. In the lower right corner, goods are being unloaded from a ship and piled onto a waiting cart, with a group of merchants standing nearby. The folio's more static principal miniature of Mary Magdalene recedes beside the bustling activity in the margin, which evokes a wide and complex world connected via trade routes, a world in which the farther the place, the stranger the peoples.

While it is, of course, possible that a single artist employed different styles depending on the book, the internal inconsistency of this attributed group of manuscripts based on tiny aspects of execution already begins to illustrate the trouble with identifying these anonymous hands. The BnF *Marvels* itself shows evidence of internal collaboration, indicating that the question of artistic authorship is more complex than simply assigning a name of convenience to a single illuminator. Two miniatures in the BnF *Marvels*, *Kedar*, illustrating a tribe in the Arabian desert (fig. 39), and *Lower Egypt* (fig. 40), exhibit clearly different approaches to the illuminations. The *Kedar* artist applies black penwork outlines much more, in figures and landscape alike, resulting in much crisper and strongly defined edges. The artist of *Lower Egypt*, on the other hand, has a more delicate approach to the execution of the grisaille tones of the figures' clothing and applies pigment to the landscape with a lighter hand, giving the effect of watercolor.

Based on the inscription in the manuscript, the production of the BnF *Marvels* can be localized to the French city of Bourges, a center of political gravity as the frequent residence of the French royal court. However, the remaining copies in the group (the Angers, Morgan, and Getty *Marvels*) have been associated with the nearby city of Angers and with the Angevin artistic context and its patrons in the circle of Duke René of Anjou.[20]

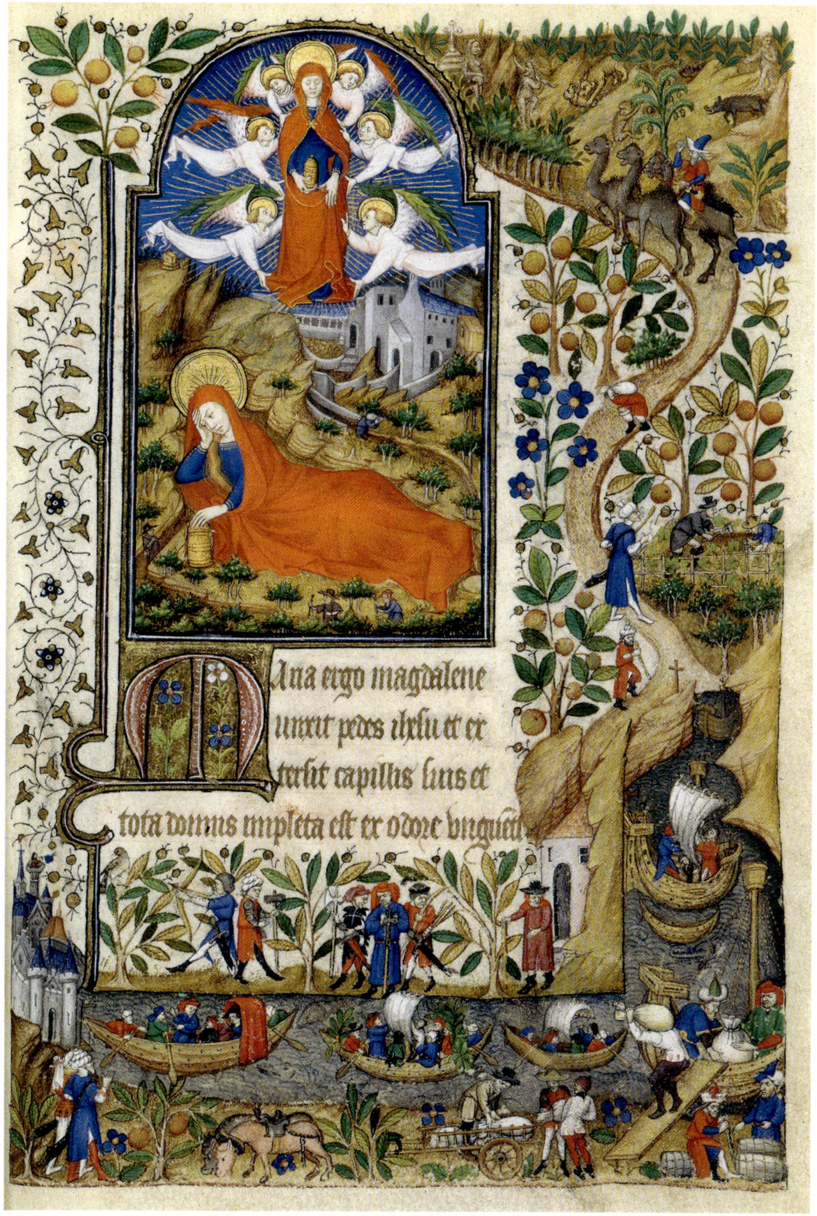

FIGURE 38 Master of Marguerite d'Orléans, *Mary Magdalene Surrounded by Scenes of Travel and Trade*, in the Hours of Marguerite d'Orleans. France, Rennes and Paris, ca. 1430. Paris, Bibliothèque nationale de France, Ms. lat. 1156B, fol. 174v

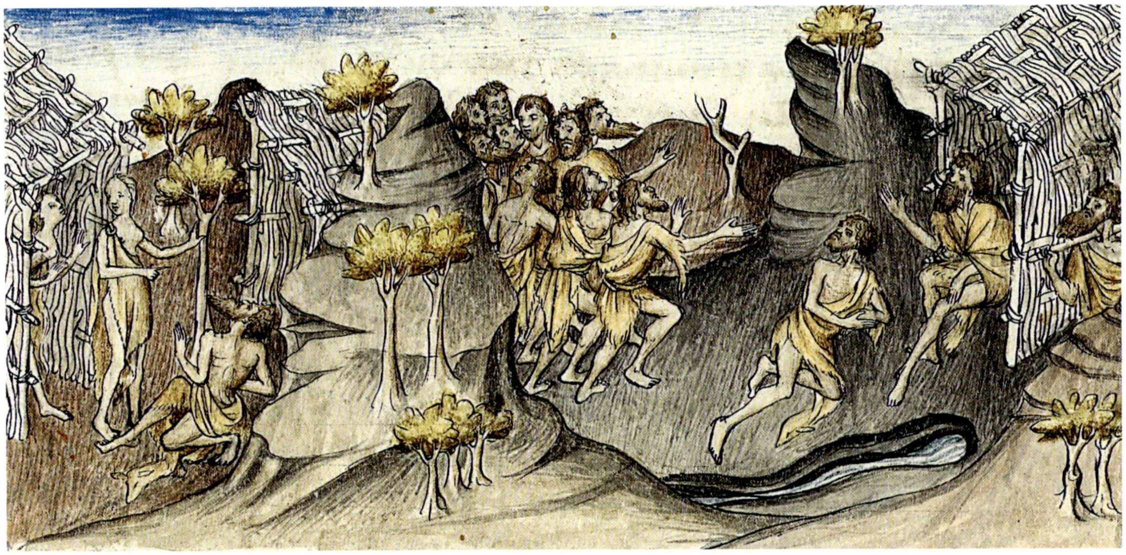

FIGURE 39 Master of Marguerite d'Orléans, *Kedar* [tribe in the Arabian desert], in the *Book of the Marvels of the World*. France, Bourges, 1428. Paris, Bibliothèque nationale de France, Ms. fr. 1377, fol. 17r (detail)

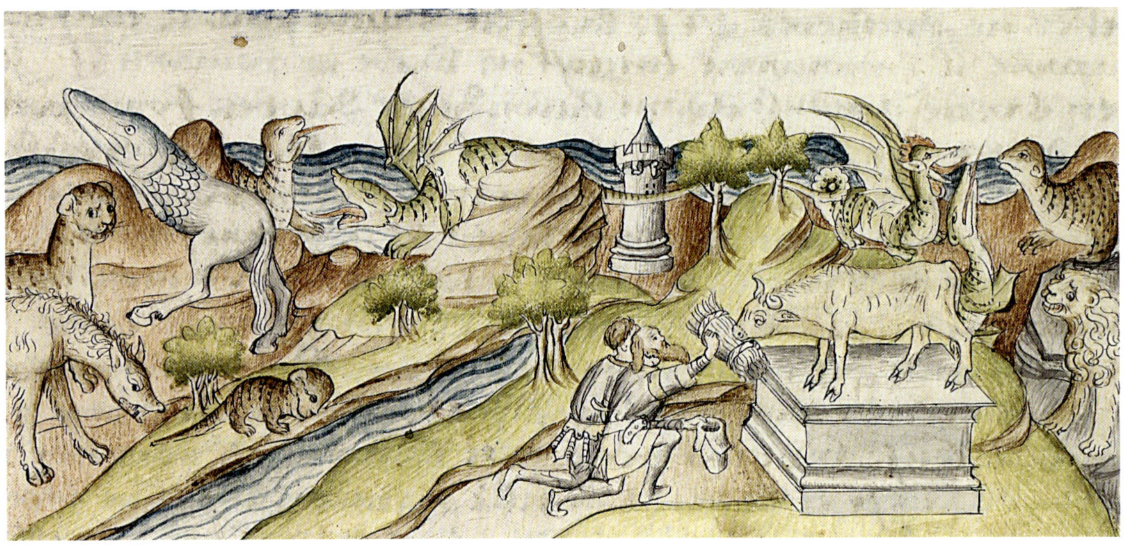

FIGURE 40 Master of Marguerite d'Orléans, *Lower Egypt*, in the *Book of the Marvels of the World*. France, Bourges, 1428. Paris, Bibliothèque nationale de France, Ms. fr. 1377, fol. 20r (detail)

Regardless of the location of production, the artists of the subsequent copies of the *Marvels* follow the same approach as the illuminators of the BnF *Marvels*, suggesting that the image program and certain aspects of the style retained their appeal for both the artists and the reader-viewers.

Subsequent Copies: The Angers, Morgan, and Getty Marvels

The copy of the *Marvels* likely produced next is a version that now exists in only two surviving miniatures. These leaves, the Angers *Marvels*, provide tantalizing but limited evidence, given their condition and highly fragmentary state. Scholars have dated these images to sometime between about 1430 and 1450 and have suggested that they are also the work of the artist(s) known as the Master of Marguerite d'Orléans, although it is difficult to make a firm artistic attribution.[21] The two later surviving copies, the Morgan and Getty *Marvels*, were produced around 1460–65 and are both attributed to another anonymous artist, known as the Master of the Geneva Boccaccio. Scholars have long recognized that the Morgan and Getty *Marvels* are similar enough to be considered siblings, quite closely related in their composition, style, size, attentiveness to narrative detail, and overall quality.[22] The Getty copy has unfortunately lost a number of its narrative miniatures, but, unlike the Morgan copy, it includes a series of historiated initials, in addition to its suite of miniatures.[23] The possible relationships between these manuscripts can best be determined by comparing miniatures of subjects common to the four manuscripts in the group.

The most fragmentary copy, the Angers *Marvels*, is composed of only two images, *Melos* (a Greek island) and *Media* (in Persia). Similar images of both appear in all three of the other copies. In each case, the *Melos* and *Media* illuminations appear on the same folio (though the Angers example has been cut down to just the images), separated by a brief text. The iterations of *Media* in particular contain sensitively executed narrative details that are very close to the contents of the accompanying text (figs. 41–44).[24] The region is described as having a particularly high mountain, great caverns with openings like doors, and many "snakes and other poisonous beasts."[25] The entry for Media also discusses a native tree covered in sharp thorns, whose fruit protects against poison and immediately regenerates on the tree when plucked off.[26] Each of these central narrative elements is included in all of the examples, with the artists responding to the text by including minor pictorial details. One such is the depiction of a precious stone called "elloseopetra," which is in the shape of a human tongue and falls from the sky; it appears as a series of red teardrops in the sky between the tree and the mountaintop.[27]

Although the compositional elements of all four images are quite similar, stylistically the images fall into two groups. The close relationship between the BnF and Angers *Marvels* is clear in the illumination of Media. Both lack a frame separating image from text, and they feature nearly identical compositions: a green hill with a craggy cavern opening and a whipped-cream spiral mountain, sets of trees dotting the landscape in the same places, and a waiting ship floating in the wavy blue lines of a striated ocean. The wondrous tree is the same shape in both images, and a similar figure appears at left, with a long piece of fabric tied around his head and a curved sword at his hip, as he reaches both hands up to gather the marvelous fruit. The reptilian creature making its way out of the cavern

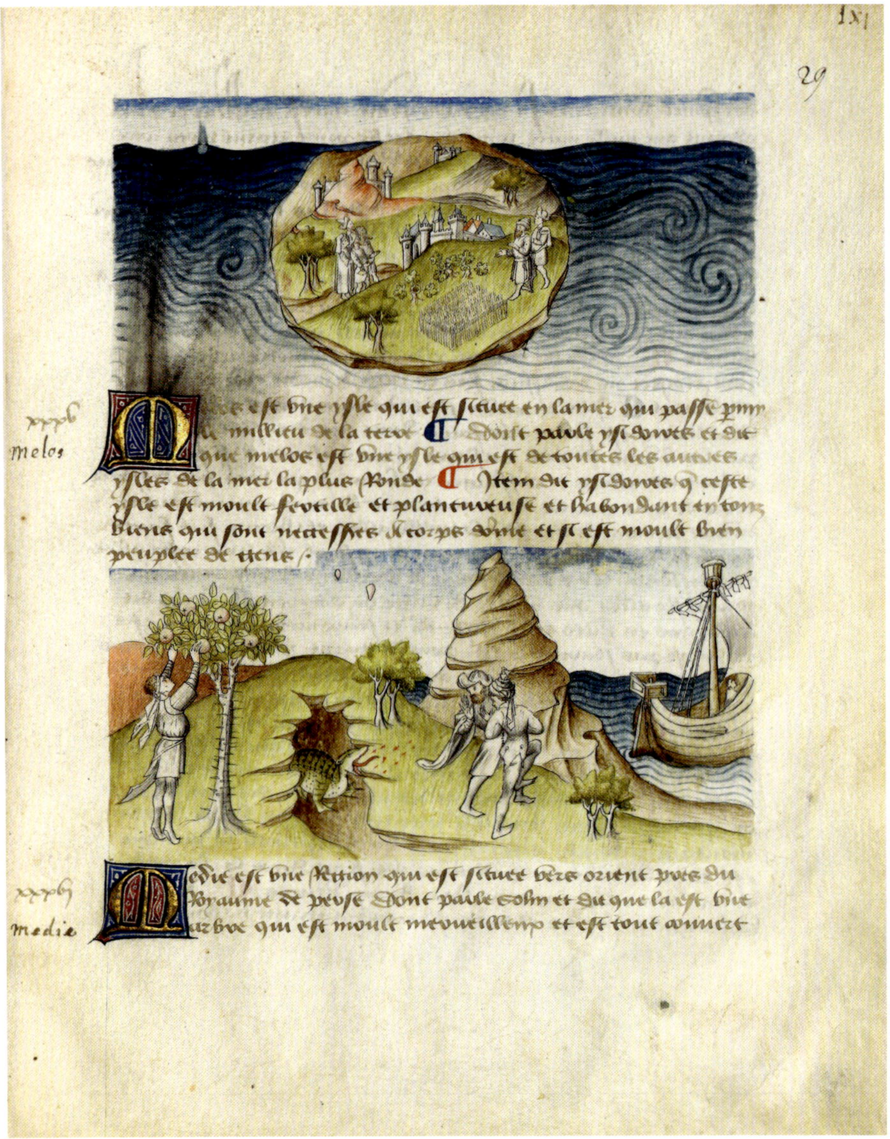

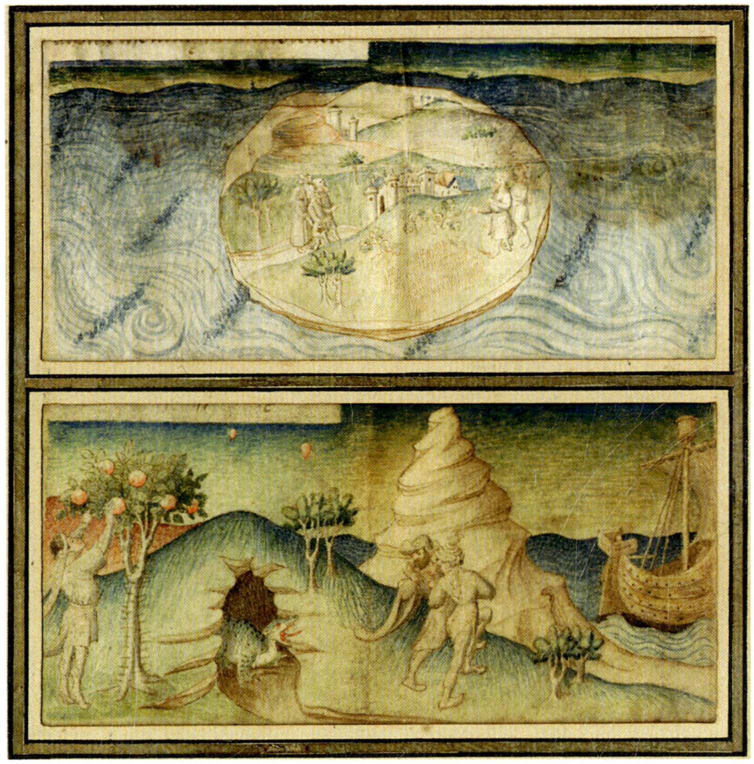

FIGURE 41 Master of Marguerite d'Orléans, *Melos* and *Media*, in the *Book of the Marvels of the World*. France, Bourges, 1428. Bibliothèque nationale de France, Ms. fr. 1378, fol. 29r

FIGURE 42 Circle of the Master of Marguerite d'Orléans, *Melos* and *Media*, in the *Book of the Marvels of the World*. France, Angers, ca. 1428–50. Bibliothèque municipale d'Angers, Rés. Ms. 2850

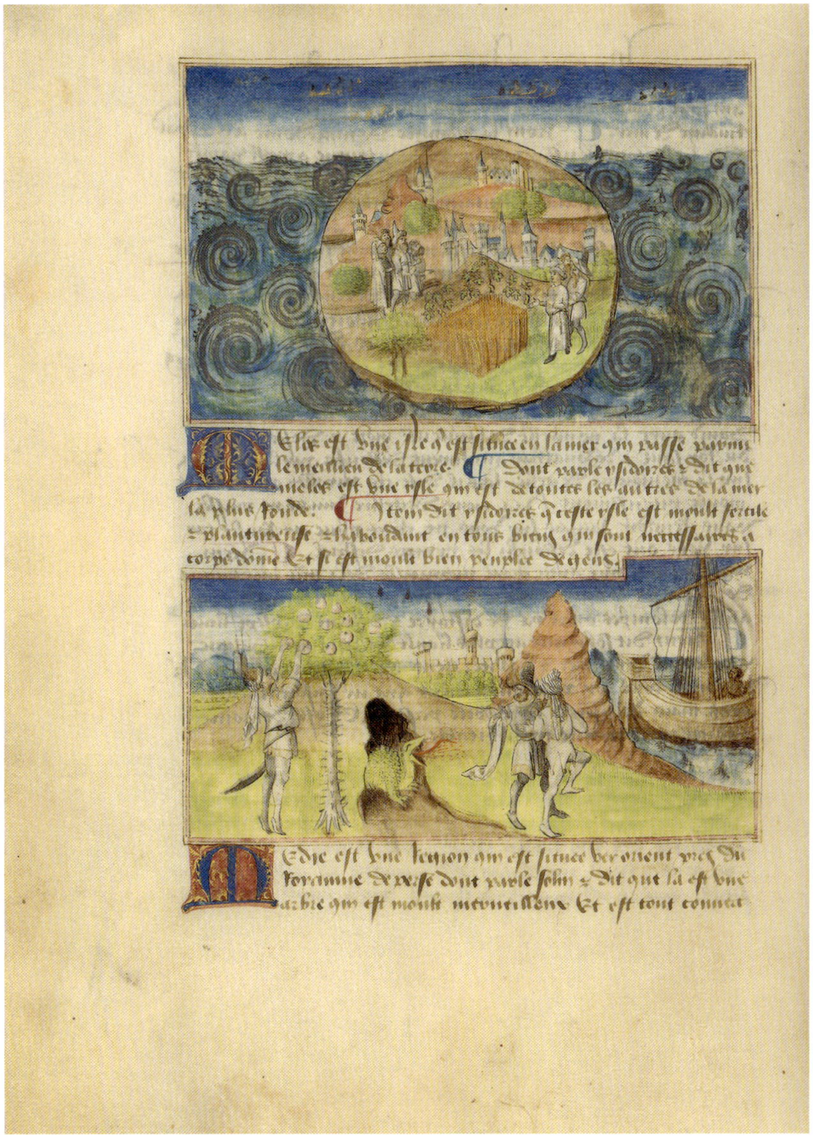

FIGURE 43 Master of the Geneva Boccaccio, *Melos* and *Media*, in the *Book of the Marvels of the World*. France, Angers, ca. 1460. New York, Morgan Library & Museum, Ms. M.461, fol. 57v

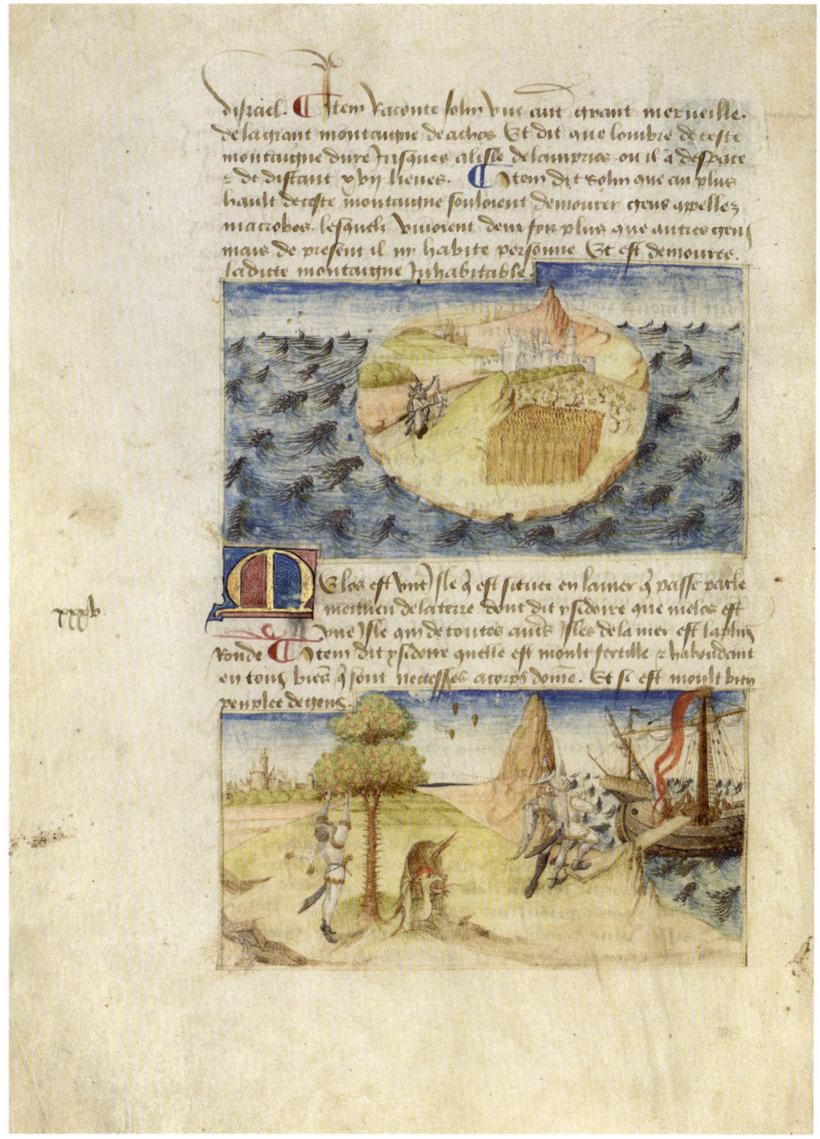

FIGURE 44 Master of the Geneva Boccaccio, *Melos* and *Media*, in the *Book of the Marvels of the World*. France, Angers, ca. 1460–65. Los Angeles, The J. Paul Getty Museum, Ms. 124, fol. 17v

has the same webbed front feet, alligator-like scales on its back, and red tongue protruding from its open mouth. It menaces two figures walking hurriedly away from it, both of whom look back at the creature, their hands raised in surprise or fear. Even the small, barely articulated figure in the ship, seemingly raising the sail, appears in both images. While the Angers artist takes a similar stylistic approach, he does not exactly reproduce the BnF *Marvels* images. The figures in both are executed in semigrisaille, with color washes denoting gradations in the landscape, but the Angers artist has used more highly saturated color and added darker shading in the sky and landscape, the wood of the ship, the floating stones, and the fruit on the tree. The result is a less graphic, highly contrasted image that relies less on the use of heavy lines and more on color. While these two manuscripts may indeed have been painted by the same artist, perhaps within the same few years, it is impossible to be certain, given the fragmentary state of the Angers *Marvels*.[28]

What seems clear, however, is that the Angers *Marvels* represents a kind of midpoint between the BnF *Marvels* and the remaining two very closely related copies, the Morgan and Getty *Marvels*. These latter two versions present a greater variety of pictorial techniques, both in relation to the earlier copies and between each other. The artist(s) of the Morgan and Getty copies introduce a greater range of color, and create a deeper, more dynamic sense of space than the artist(s) of the BnF *Marvels*, while still relying heavily on the iconography, that is, the specific imagery, and the sense of narrative in that early copy. In general, the layouts of the pages for Melos and Media in the Morgan and Getty *Marvels* are remarkably similar, with some small variations: the arrangement of the illuminations for Melos and Media on the folio in the Morgan *Marvels* has been carried over from the BnF *Marvels*, but the Getty *Marvels*'s format is different. There, the first quarter of the page is taken up by the end of the text from the previous folio (fol. 17r), rather than by the image of Melos, as in the BnF and Morgan *Marvels*. The text describing Media in the Getty *Marvels* begins on the facing folio (fol. 18r), rather than at the bottom of the page, under the image. Similarly, the Morgan *Marvels* image for Media follows much more closely the example set by the BnF *Marvels*. The artist of both images maintains the general composition: the thorned tree at the left, towering mountain at the center, waiting ship in blue waves to the right, and even the same general arrangement of the figures and the presence of the reptilian creature in the cave opening. In the Morgan *Marvels*, the appearance of the mouth of the cave is different, rounded out and with smooth edges; the artist adds some faraway landscape elements and a distant castle in the center background of the image. The artist keeps the rounded, swirl-shaped mountain; the single figure in the waiting ship; and the narrative relationship between the green creature with red tongue and the pair of men turning to meet its gaze, one man's elaborate sleeve fluttering out behind him. The painter of this image in the Getty *Marvels*, though, makes several additional adjustments: the tree has been made taller; the creature given a more avian look, with hooked beak and red comb; the mountain made more vertical and craggier; and the hill at the far left given a rocky profile.

Further modifications to the details of *Media* suggest that the Getty copy was made after the Morgan copy, perhaps even with the Morgan copy to hand: the distant architecture that the Morgan artist had added in is now confined to the left edge, and a gangplank has been added at the sea's shore. Although certain details are maintained, including the costumes and poses of the two men fleeing the cavern creature, the addition of the gangplank changes the narrative weight of the image. Rather than encountering the creature at the mouth of the cave and quickly making their exit, the men in the Getty copy step on to the gangplank, boarding a ship already full of waiting passengers. The ship is also more elaborate, with a more prominent prow and a red banner unfurling in the sea breeze. These changes, though relatively small and largely irrelevant to the relationship of the image to the text, suggest an artist more willing to modify and adapt the earlier images, or one who was even perhaps working with a different model. A similar willingness to change is evident in the approach to the image of the island of Melos. The Getty artist has modified the composition of the island in the Morgan *Marvels* significantly, moving and consolidating the castle architecture, deleting some of the figures, and making more prominent the field of wheat that is evidence of the island's prosperity, described in the text. Other changes, including the shift from the round, spiral-shaped waves surrounding the island of Melos in the BnF, Angers, and Morgan *Marvels* to peaked, pointed waves in the Getty *Marvels*, differentiate the approach of the artist from the other manuscripts.

Similar patterns of pictorial adjustments to the examples of *Media* and *Melos* are apparent in other comparative sequences from the BnF to the Getty *Marvels*. In the Getty version, the artist(s) makes more significant changes to the details of the composition in the BnF copy than the Morgan artist(s) do. In the image for Provence, in France, for example, the Morgan copy keeps the elements of the BnF *Marvels*: the image bisected by a rounded rock formation, the outdoor location of the gruesome sacrifice of children and the drinking of their blood at left, and the skeletal appearance of the giant figure in the center, described in the text as a "body . . . that was complete in the flesh and bones and in no way was abased" (plate 15, no. 2).[29] The Getty artist, though, attempts to integrate the narrative by connecting the architecture of the castle gate to the scene of sacrifice, moving the altar and the assembled crowd indoors, and bridging the scenes with a pulled-back curtain. The giant himself has been transformed from a skeleton into a fleshier corpse with flowing hair, arguably corresponding slightly more closely to the text. However, the manner of execution in both the Morgan and Getty *Marvels*—the color wash for the landscape, with the details in dark ink—is consistent between the two manuscripts.

The brief comparison above is applicable to many other correspondences between the Morgan and Getty manuscripts. It is not that the Getty artist(s) were more innovative, simply that they were willing to make more significant modifications to the image program. Although the Morgan manuscript is closer to the BnF *Marvels* in layout and composition, there are clear resemblances in execution between the images in the Morgan and Getty manuscripts. In the shift from the early approach of the artist(s) of the BnF *Marvels* to the more diverse color palette and deeper, more detailed landscapes of the Morgan *Marvels*, we can see the illuminators changing the style of the image program, while retaining its hallmarks of grisaille, choice of iconography, and packed compositions. The case of the Morgan and Getty *Marvels* indicates that even copies that were probably intended to be very close, if not identical, could change slightly with each iteration. The Morgan artist(s) modified the style from the BnF *Marvels*, and the Getty artist(s) exhibited even greater freedom in adjusting aspects of the images and their composition. The close similarities between the various copies of the *Marvels* in both composition and style of execution is not accidental: the illuminators chose or perhaps patrons instructed them to create copies that looked like existing examples. Rather than create a new image program in a different style, the illuminators of the *Marvels* consistently returned to and recreated a particular look and feel, despite the lapse of several decades between the illumination of the BnF *Marvels* in 1428 and the completion of the Getty *Marvels* in 1460–65. The comparison of these three manuscripts and the Angers *Marvels* fragments illustrates the nature of the demand for these texts: patrons desired copies.

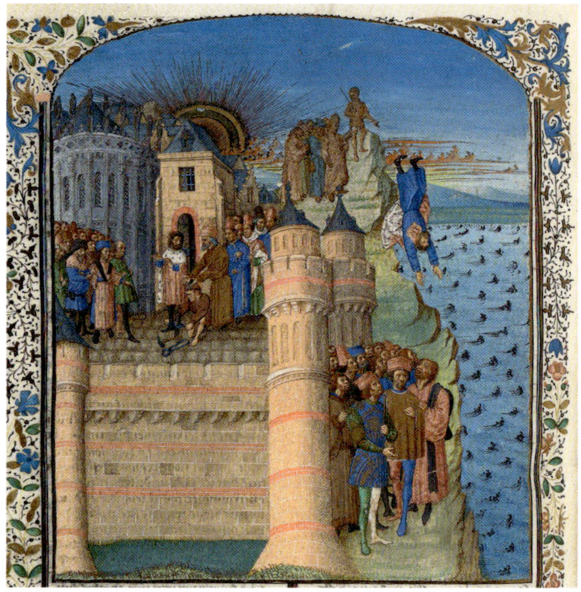

FIGURE 45 Master of the Geneva Boccaccio, *Manlius Capitolinus Thrown from the Tarpeian Rock*, in Giovanni Boccaccio, *Concerning the Fates of Illustrious Men and Women*. France, probably Angers, around 1460. Geneva, Bibliothèque municipale de Genève, Ms. fr. 191, fol. 110v (detail)

Artists and Collaborations

Scholars have traditionally attributed both the Morgan and Getty *Marvels* manuscripts to the same anonymous illuminator, known as the "Master of the Geneva Boccaccio," after a luxury manuscript copy of Laurent de Premierfait's French translation of Giovanni Boccaccio's *Concerning the Fates of Illustrious Men and Women* (*De casibus virorum illustrium*), now in Geneva (fig. 45).[30] As with the Master of Marguerite d'Orléans, an entire career for this artist has been constructed from stylistic identification. Supposedly, this illuminator was active in France from around 1445 to 1470, and got his start working with the "Jouvenel Master," yet another anonymous artist, this one linked to a manuscript produced in around 1447–50 for the chancellor of France, Guillaume Jouvenel des Ursins.[31] The artists associated with the Jouvenel Master have proven so difficult to identify individually that they are often identified as a famously collaborative group working in and around Angers during the mid-fifteenth century.[32] Authors of the most recent studies of the Master of the Geneva Boccaccio have concluded that the artist, a particularly prominent member of the Jouvenel Group, was probably responsible for several works associated with the court at Angers beginning around 1460, and many other individual miniatures have also been attributed to him in large, collaborative projects.[33] Indeed, the name of convenience assigned to the Master of the Geneva Boccaccio has been modified several times over the last century of scholarship, just as the work of the Jouvenel Master and his associates has been defined and redefined in ever more granular ways.[34]

The curious differences in the compositions of the Morgan and Getty *Marvels*, as outlined above, and the tellingly different approaches to mundane details—the shift from spiral to peaked waves and from whipped cream–shaped to rockier, craggy mountains, for example—raise a fundamental question. If the goal was to create a straightforward copy, why would the same artist introduce these relatively minor changes, which are stylistic rather than content-related? The most likely explanation is that the Morgan and Getty *Marvels* were produced quite closely together, perhaps even simultaneously, by different, but connected artists or, more probably, groups of artists. Given what is known about the working methods of the artist(s) known as the Master of the Geneva Boccaccio, and the other illuminators who have come to be known under the heading of the Jouvenel Group, it seems far more reasonable to believe that none of the copies of the Marvels were produced by a singular artist working in isolation, but rather by a group or groups of illuminators working in collaboration.

As in the case of the BnF *Marvels*, these two later copies display internal stylistic differences that may reveal the inherently collaborative endeavor of illuminating such ambitious productions. In the Morgan *Marvels*, a close comparative analysis reveals some minor differences in the approaches to color and composition. Comparing *Amazonia* (fig. 46) to both *Boeotia* and *Bohemia*, the latter two found on facing folios (fig. 47), provides some insight. The scene of Amazonia, located near Scythia, is highly refined, using the grisaille technique to maximum effect in the figures, while setting them into different pockets of a delicately color-washed landscape. The images of Boeotia, in Greece, and Bohemia, in the Czech Republic, in contrast, evince an artist with a slightly different approach to compositional construction, with a relatively simple, more horizontally divided landscape, large figures set in the foreground, and a blockier application of more intensely saturated colors.

The manuscript's incomplete state makes a full assessment of the artists active in the Getty *Marvels* impossible. Still, given that the complement of images in its complete state was probably very similar to the Morgan *Marvels*'s, it is reasonable to assume that there was a similar division of labor in the manuscript. This resulted in slight variations to the compositions and styles of figures and landscapes, but a general visual consistency, as the reader moved through the manuscript. Although close looking and comparison detect these small differences in approach and execution, overall, the illuminations work together and appear to be a stylistically cohesive program. The theory that different artists were at work in these manuscripts in the same copies reveals each production of the *Marvels* as a complex and necessarily collaborative effort. This is in keeping with the surviving evidence for prominent fifteenth-century French illuminators working together on high-profile commissions.[35] It is necessary, therefore, to think of the Master of the Geneva Boccaccio as encompassing at least a few different individuals. We should perhaps use "Masters of the Geneva Boccaccio" as a more useful shorthand for thinking about this artistic sensibility, instead of using the term "workshop," in which are embedded many assumptions about a hierarchical organization of labor in which there is an accomplished master

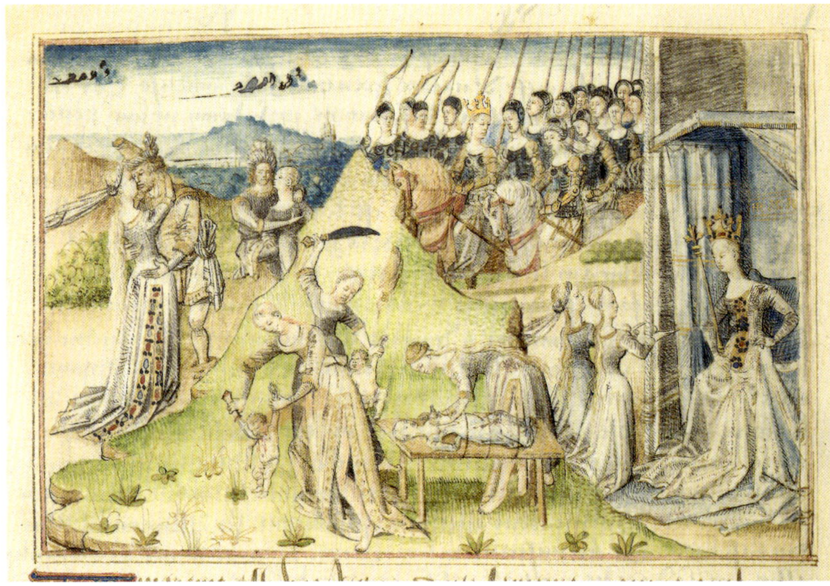

FIGURE 46 Master of the Geneva Boccaccio, *Amazonia*, in the *Book of the Marvels of the World*. France, Angers, ca. 1460. New York, Morgan Library & Museum, Ms. M.461, fol. 5v (detail)

and less-experienced assistants. Trying to force the collaborative model that emerges from the *Marvels* manuscripts into that of the traditional conception of a workshop may well prevent a full consideration of the complex social relationships that conditioned the making of books in medieval France.[36]

It seems clear that the scale of the *Marvels* projects required the work of several hands. The size of the surviving group of manuscripts and the imprecise relationships among them suggest that there were perhaps even more copies produced for an even wider audience than has previously been imagined. The stylistic approach that characterizes the Morgan and Getty *Marvels*—their attentiveness to narrative details and the style defined by the subtle shading of drapery, individualized facial features, meticulously detailed and lush landscapes, and lithe, elegant figures—seems both inspired by and tailor made for the content of the *Marvels* text. Just as the bustling scenes and packed narrative spaces attributed to the Master of Marguerite d'Orléans translated the contents of the *Marvels* text into visual expression, so, too, do the images in the Morgan and Getty manuscripts give a sense of a global adventure, through an organized list of locations with brief peeks into the various wonders of the world.

The colored-grisaille technique that appears in both the Morgan and Getty *Marvels* allows for dynamic compositions that complement the subject matter perfectly. It is absent from other known manuscripts, save one: a prayer book

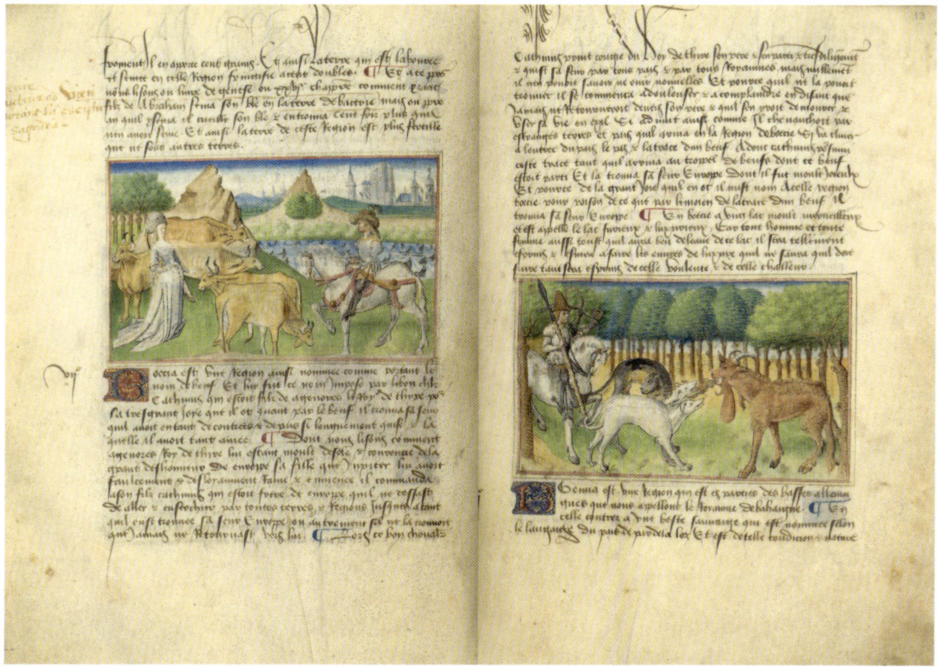

FIGURE 47 Master of the Geneva Boccaccio, *Boeotia* and *Bohemia*, in the *Book of the Marvels of the World*. France, Angers, ca. 1460. New York, Morgan Library & Museum, Ms. M.461, fols. 12v–13r

that has also been attributed to the Master of the Geneva Boccaccio.[37] If this small volume was made around 1470, as is likely, it is later than both the Morgan and Getty *Marvels*. Likely produced for a high-ranking member of the Angevin court, Philippa of Guelders, the wife of Duke René II of Anjou, it also displays the colored-grisaille technique.[38] Philippa was the granddaughter-in-law of Duke René of Anjou, the probable patron of the Morgan *Marvels*.[39] Her prayer book's images are as densely packed and complex in terms of their compositions as the images in the Morgan and Getty *Marvels* even though the folios are smaller. In a representative example, the central miniature of the kiss of Judas and the arrest of Christ (fig. 48) is surrounded by complex borders that feature several additional narratives connected by landscape elements, but with the figures at different scales. The result is a visually continuous journey around the page, filled with figures and scenes for the viewer to peruse, offset by some moments of confusion. For example, the right margin shows Christ confounding a group of soldiers, who appear to be upside down, but they are simply lying on the ground at Christ's feet, packed into the thin marginal space. Like the Morgan and Getty *Marvels*, this artist constructs complicated images and combines colored grisaille

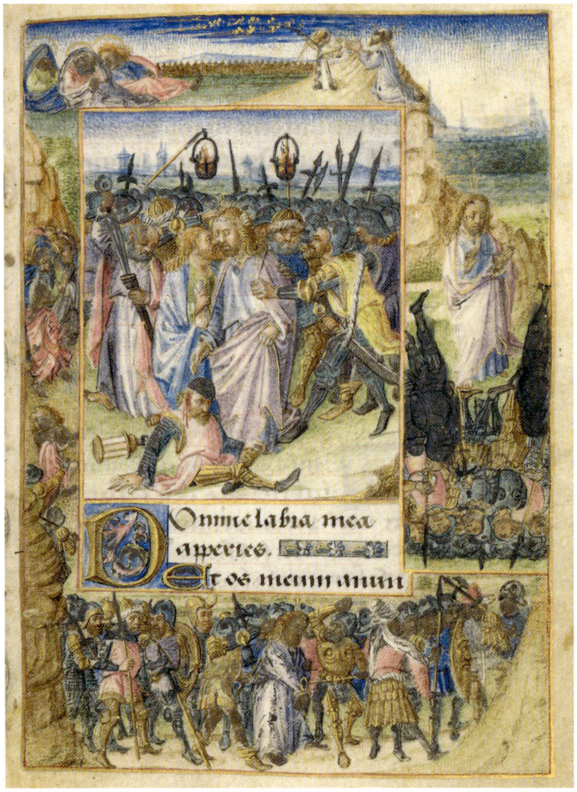

FIGURE 48 Master of the Geneva Boccaccio, *The Kiss of Judas and the Arrest of Christ*, in the Hours of Philippa of Guelders. France, probably Angers, ca. 1470. New York, Morgan Library & Museum, Ms. M.263, fol. 1r

and black penwork detailing.[40] Although many other illuminated manuscripts are attributed to the Master of the Geneva Boccaccio and close associates, none feature quite the same colored-grisaille and ink-detailing style as the Morgan and Getty *Marvels*. Perhaps the technique had a limited audience or was considered more appropriate for a text like the *Marvels* than for more traditional devotional texts.

The group of *Marvels* manuscripts discussed here, completed in Bourges and Angers from the period between around 1428 and 1465, is a case study in the medieval practice of copying images and the transmission of visual information. The standard art-historical practice of creating names of convenience to define artistic personalities has been and still can be useful in some respects but has its own barriers to understanding. The as-yet-anonymous masters responsible for the *Marvels* manuscripts likely worked within collaborative systems of production outside the traditional workshop system, catering to the tastes of patrons in French cities, encountering one another, sharing commissions, and absorbing stylistic influences as they went. The surviving visual evidence of the *Marvels* manuscripts suggests copyists recreating existing models, but not mimetically, introducing degrees of variation between and within the known examples. In this way, the *Marvels* text and its inventive image program traveled from a merchant in Bourges to the Angevin court of Duke René and beyond.[41] The fifteenth-century group of the *Marvels*, with their lively and complex images, provides a glimpse into the demand among wealthy medieval Europeans for richly presented information about the world and its, to them, often mysterious inhabitants, strange customs, and exotic creatures, visualized in a dynamic and lively way. Artists met these demands through the creation of images that conveyed a huge amount of information in visually efficient, interesting new ways.

NOTES

1 Foundational modern works investigating copying as a concept include Benjamin 1935 (2008) and Schwartz 1996 (2014).

2 Paris, BnF, Ms. fr. 1377–1379; Angers, Bibliothèque municipale d'Angers, Res. ms. 2850; New York, Morgan Library & Museum, Ms. M.461; Los Angeles, Getty Museum, Ms. 124; and Paris, BnF, Ms. fr. 22971.

3 Pairs or sets of sibling manuscripts, especially of large-scale nonreligious texts, seem to have been relatively common, but the survival of such a cohesive group as the *Marvels* is rare. See Alexander 1992, 138 and Elizabeth Morrison's essay in Morrison and Grollemond 2019, 51–66.
4 König 1991, 83–86, 97–98; König 2002, 80–82.
5 Paris, BnF Ms. lat. 1156B. For a summary of the artistic personality of the Master of Marguerite d'Orléans and a consideration of works with which the artist is credited, see König 1991; Avril and Reynaud 1993, 28–29; König 2002; Booton 2010, 50–53; Seidel 2017, 173–79; and Friedman, Giogoli, and Figg 2018, 45–48.
6 Lorentz 2017.
7 Camille 1994, 835.
8 Friedman, Giogoli, and Figg 2018, 24. For more on the influence on the *Marvels* text, see the essay by Joshua O'Driscoll in this volume.
9 See the essay by Joshua O'Driscoll in this volume.
10 Friedman, Giogoli, and Figg 2018, 42–43. See the "Descriptions of the Getty and Morgan Manuscripts" in this volume for more detail about the physical structure and arrangement of images in each of the copies.
11 Figg and Friedman 2018, 200–201.
12 See Morgan and Moodey 2016.
13 Avril and Reynaud 1993, 28; and Booton 2010, 50–53.
14 Paris, BnF Ms. fr. 2605.
15 Chantilly, Musée Condé, Ms. 858.
16 König 1991; Avril and Reynaud 1993, 28–29; König 2002; and Booton 2010, 50–53.
17 For the list of eleven works with which this artist is currently credited, see Friedman, Gigoli, and Figg 2018, 45.
18 The Hours of Marguerite d'Orléans has been dated to ca. 1430, though this is based on payment records in documentary sources spanning at least two decades. König 1982, 64–66, 122–24; and Booton 2010, 320. For the most comprehensive studies of the manuscript, see König 1991 and König 2002.
19 Kathrin Giogoli argues for other features from Marguerite's prayer book that were excerpted for use in the BnF *Marvels*, including some specific animal forms. Friedman, Giogoli, and Figg 2018, 44.
20 Friedman, Giogoli, and Figg 2018, 48. Scholars have also localized other manuscripts attributed to the Master of Marguerite d'Orléans to Angers, offering a possible connection between the artist(s) of the early copy of the *Marvels* and the later manuscripts in the group. König 1982, 189–90; König 2002, 100–106; and Booton 2010, 52.
21 Gautier 2017.
22 Friedman, Giogoli and Figg 2018, 49–53.
23 See the "List of Locations in the *Book of Marvels*" and their images in this volume for a full accounting of the manuscripts' contents.
24 Figg and Friedman 2018, 262–63.
25 Figg and Friedman 2018, 262.
26 Figg and Friedman 2018, 262.
27 Figg and Friedman 2018, 262.
28 The Angers fragments were attributed to the Jouvenel Group, of which the proposed artist of the Morgan and Getty *Marvels* (the Master of the Geneva Boccaccio) was a member, in the 2017 Sotheby's sale and given a proposed date of ca. 1450. The artist's identification was later revised to the Master of Marguerite d'Orléans, and the date stretched to ca. 1430–50, when the fragments entered the collection of the municipal library in Angers in 2017. Sotheby's 2017 and Gautier 2017.
29 Figg and Friedman 2018, 271–72.
30 Geneva, Bibliothèque de Genève, Ms. fr. 191. König 2009, 134–37.
31 Paris, BnF, Ms. lat. 4915. Avril and Reynaud 1993, 112–13; König 2009, 136–37. It should also be noted that while cases of women (both secular and religious) as manuscript illuminators do exist from the medieval period, the majority of such artists were men.
32 König 1982, 27–51; Avril and Reynaud 1993, 109–10; König 2009, 134–35.
33 König 2009, 140–41; Friedman, Giogoli, and Figg 2018, 63.
34 König 1982; Avril and Reynaud 1993, 109–10.
35 Alexander 1992, 130. See also the discussion of the five teams of artists at work in BnF ms. fr. 2810 in the essay by Joshua O'Driscoll in this volume.
36 Camille 1994, 834, briefly discusses the need to consider artistic "networks." Farquhar 1996, 135, 144–45, discusses a similar "web" model of manuscript production in the fifteenth-century southern Netherlands, in which nonhierarchical collaboration is central, and which provides a useful case study in acknowledging multiple artistic personalities in a single manuscript.
37 New York, Morgan Library, Ms. M.263. See the most updated catalogue information here: https://www.themorgan.org/manuscript/76863.
38 König 1982, 134; König 2009, 142; and Seidel 2017, 37.
39 See the introduction to this volume.
40 Avril and Reynaud 1993, 119; and König 2009, cat. no. 37.
41 The latest copy of the *Marvels* (BnF Ms. fr. 22971) was made for Count Charles of Angoulême with an extensive and imaginative program of illuminations by Robinet Testard. Testard's work is distinctive and idiosyncratic, and his images are not related stylistically to the earlier group, though they do bear some iconographic resemblance to the earlier copies of the *Marvels*, building upon what had become an image tradition. The image program is similar enough to suggest that Testard may have known an earlier copy, perhaps even the Morgan *Marvels,* but a direct connection is difficult to establish. Friedman, Giogoli, and Figg 2018, 68.

Epilogue

Imagining Otherness in a Marvelous World

NOEL B. SALAZAR

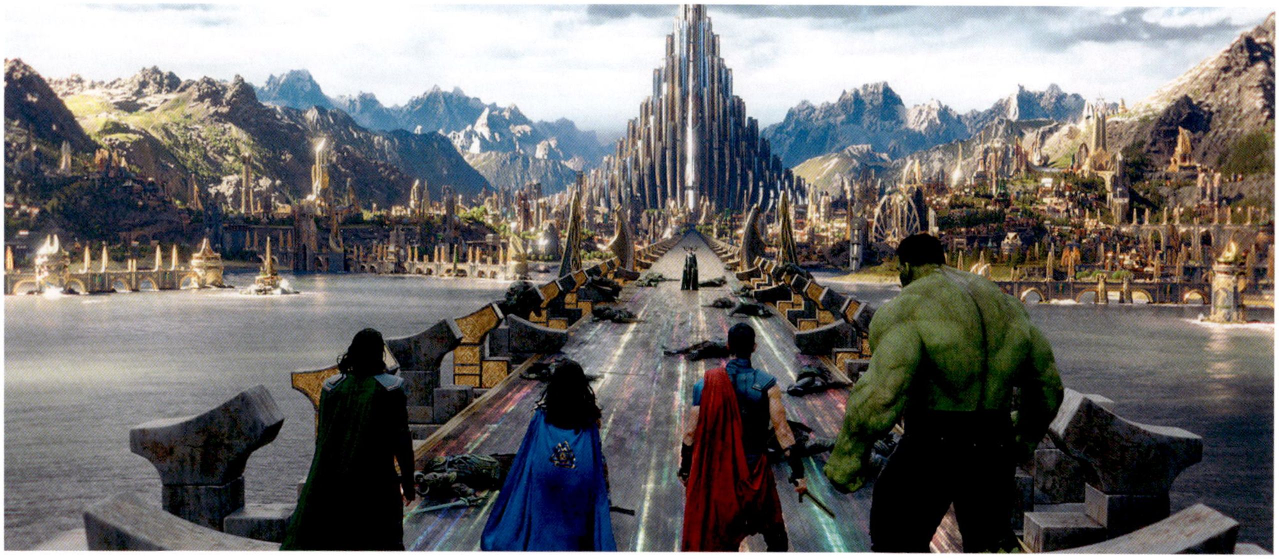

FIGURE 49 Still showing an imagined landscape from the Marvel Universe. In *Thor: Ragnarok* (Marvel Studios, 2017)

Why should we bother talking about medieval manuscripts in the twenty-first century? Works like the *Book of the Marvels of the World* continue to influence beliefs and practices in the contemporary world in ways that are frequently neglected or unappreciated. Medieval imaginaries, or the contents of people's imaginations in the Middle Ages, continue to dominate the Western worldview today, affecting writing, the visual arts, and popular culture. Many of the tales, legends, and myths that have molded our imagination have their origins in the Middle Ages. The adventures of King Arthur and Robin Hood, the love songs of the troubadours, and the nine circles of Hell from Dante's *Inferno* have inspired works of literature, cinema, and other media, and they continue to captivate people around the globe.

Today, many people across the world identify the term "marvel" with Marvel Entertainment, the American company best known for its comic books, blockbuster films, and television series (fig. 49). Most of Marvel's fictional characters live in the so-called Marvel Universe, an alternate reality in which some places are duplicates of real-world locations but are populated by superhero characters with various marvelous abilities. This kind of imaginative "mirroring" is at the heart of all representational processes, including storytelling, playing games, and (day)dreaming. As such, it is a crucial characteristic of how people's imagination works.

As a sociocultural anthropologist, I have devoted most of my time and energy to studying how people rely on their imagination to make sense of their lives and the world in which they live. This forms part of the larger anthropological endeavor to provide a deeper understanding of humankind (how people are similar) and human diversity (how people are different). Imaginaries are powerful in part because they are culturally shared and socially transmitted. Geographic imaginaries, for example, refer to how places are pictured, how meanings are assigned to physical spaces, how knowledge about these places is produced, and how these representations affect people's actions. This last is important because imaginaries influence social practices, beliefs, and behaviors. In other words, they not only make meaning but also act as world-shaping devices. Migration imaginaries may determine where migrants end up moving to, while tourism imaginaries may shape the expectations of tourists in terms of what their travel destinations—the next "wonder of the world" to discover—should look like. Importantly, there is often a considerable gap between these imaginaries and the reality on the ground.

In addition to evoking wonder, admiration, delight, and surprise, imaginaries of marvels can also contradict, unsettle, and frighten. In the medieval manuscripts at the heart of this publication, marvels include what the perceiver may view as exotic locales, imposing architecture, extreme natural events, uncommon customs and traditions, strange animals, and monsters. The overarching concern when imaginatively enjoying marvels is not so much to learn about distant places and peoples, but rather to exercise some kind of control over them, starting from the premise of difference. This has been described as "othering," the process of excluding individuals or groups identified primarily as different from one's own culture—in the case of the *Marvels*, from that of the reader-viewers' culture. Because othering creates a sense of belonging and in-group status for one's own group ("us"), while denying that same sense of belonging to those imagined as "other" ("them"), it is closely tied to conceptions of self and identity. Stated differently, othering engenders otherness, which is less about any actual or perceived difference than about the point of view and the discourse of the one who does the othering.

Anthropologists study practices of othering by analyzing the contexts in which they occur. We examine how groups and societies construct and understand differences between individuals and groups, and how these differences, as they are imagined, shape actual social relationships, cultural practices, and unequal power dynamics. For example, the ways in which today's global popular media and tourism have imagined the Maasai people of East Africa stay remarkably close to the first colonial descriptions of the Maasai during the nineteenth century (figs. 50, 51), including in the movie *Black Panther* (2018), in which the Dora Milaje appeared in the Marvel Universe (fig. 52). Apart from the intentional gender reversal, these spear-fighting female warriors in their bright red outfits are clearly inspired by the stereotypical image of the male Maasai warrior. Outsiders may have created a monolithic romanticized, distorted, and exoticized imaginary of the Maasai people, but what is crucial to acknowledge is how these iconic discourses and images influence how both outsiders and the Maasai people themselves now understand Maasai culture and identity.

This approach is useful when trying to grasp historical examples of othering such as the *Marvels*. As an encyclopedia of the known—and

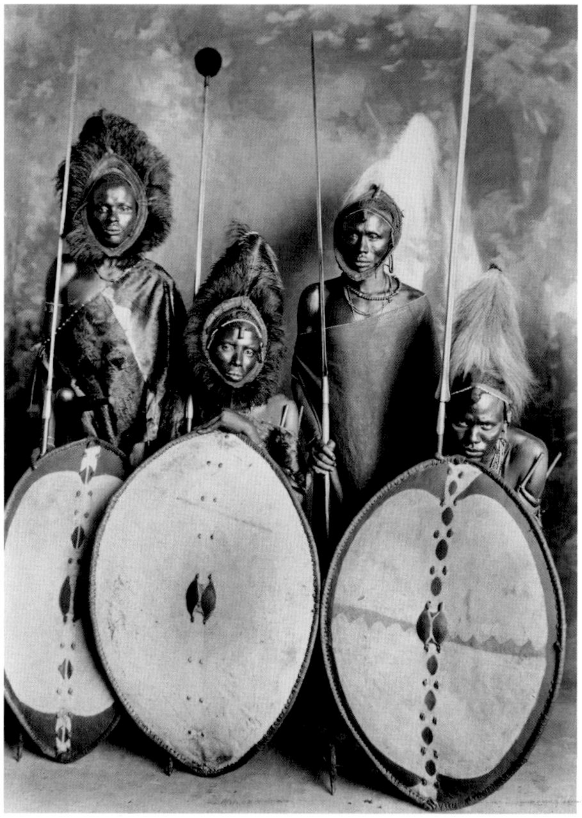

FIGURE 50 Four Maasai Warriors in Full War Dress, Kenya, 1900

imagined—world, this medieval text reflects not just how the fifteenth-century, predominantly Christian, European elite perceived otherness, but also how they viewed themselves in relation to imagined "others." The *Marvels* thus provides insight into how these people thought about and interacted with the wider world around them. As such, it is a fascinating illustration of how imaginaries of the world go hand in hand with imaginaries of oneself, whether as individuals or as members of society.

The visuals and descriptions of "other" peoples and places in texts like the *Marvels* have the potential to (re)activate fear and rejection of those imagined others, leading to ethnic and gender prejudice, national stereotypes, and other kinds of intolerance. Intolerance feeds directly on imaginaries of otherness. Even a seemingly innocuous phrase such as "These folks are not like us" hides an enormous collection of biases in the underlying imaginaries. As explained above, being "different" often comes to mean being "less than." It should come as no surprise that portraying and categorizing othered people—whether they are represented as humans with strange and exotic behaviors, or as monsters and animals—is a longstanding practice. Indeed, no civilization or society has existed without such conceptions, so that these classifications tell us as much about the classifiers as about the classified. Exaggerated distinctions between the self and the othered, whether these are genuine or invented, very often lead to exclusionary processes. Historically, they have been the starting point for systemic hierarchization and social, religious, racial, sexual, and gender oppression, at times leading to armed conflict and even genocide. While the European continent is certainly not the only place where such processes have been historically documented, it has played an important role in the development of narratives of exclusion and xenophobia across global history. This is mainly due to Europe's colonial expansion and imperialism, its role in global power dynamics, and its cultural influence (including the presentation of Western norms and values as superior and universal).

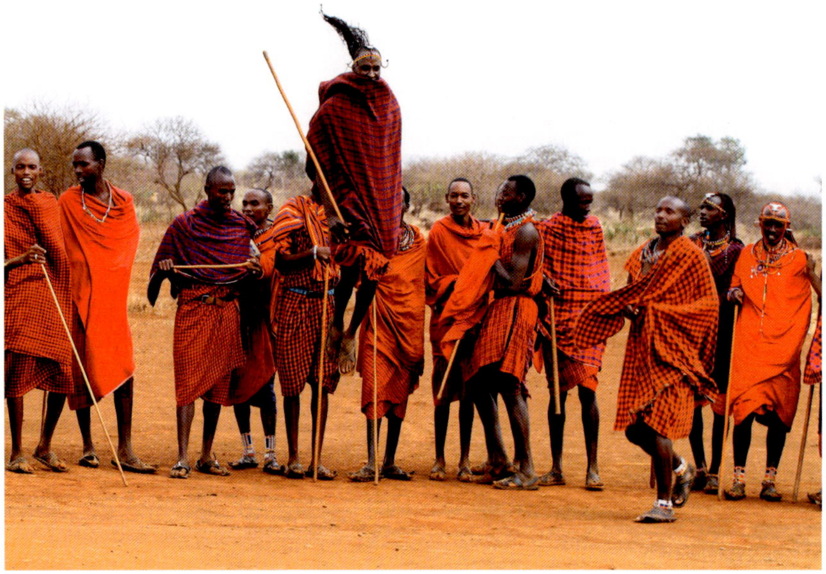

FIGURE 51 *Maasai Tribe*. Photograph. Kenya, 2013

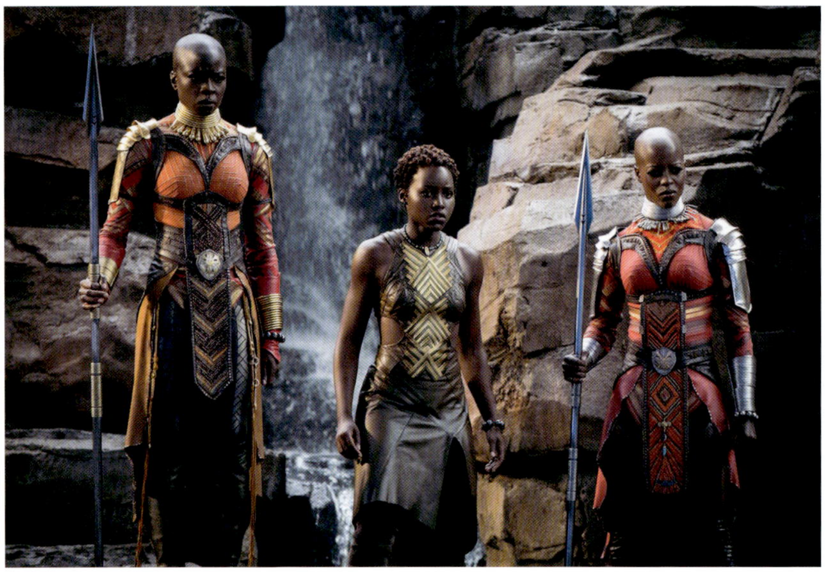

FIGURE 52 The Dora Milaje. Foreground, left to right: Okoye (Danai Gurira), Nakia (a former Dora Milaje, played by Lupita Nyong'o), and Ayo (Florence Kasumba). In *Black Panther* (Marvel Studios, 2018)

Imaginaries of otherness elevate inaccurate cultural constructions above biological and social realities. It is paradoxical that over time negative imaginaries of otherness have taken root, spread, and become stronger, despite an increase in travel that theoretically should have diminished or obliterated them. However, as my research on contemporary tourism shows, physically traveling to remote regions certainly does not eliminate a state of mind that revels in the so-called "exotic." On the contrary, tourists are often looking for evidence at their destination that confirms their exoticized imaginaries about peoples and places. They expect the Maasai to be warrior-like—dancing or charging across the open plains with spears and shields—and are disappointed when this is not the case. While some non-Maasai end up pretending to be Maasai for economic gain, many Maasai people, for the same reason, are also forced to play an imagined version of themselves. This ultimately serves to reinforce that fictional image.

The case of the Maasai people demonstrates how difficult it is to modify imaginaries once they have been established. Imaginaries of radical difference may be a psychological mechanism deployed for various reasons. They appealed to people in the Middle Ages and still appeal to people today, for positive experiences such as fantasy, escapism, joy in the mere exercise of the imagination, but also often for a sense of "control" of the (dreaded) unknown. People in the Middle Ages created monsters because they were attractive to the medieval imagination, as much for their potential for moral instruction as for the delight and curiosity they evoke. Both the past and the present have an equivalent imaginative dimension, depending on a wide variety of assumptions, premises, prior beliefs, and expectations. The "foreign" world can be imagined as frightening, mysterious, confused, or simply weird, but it is also immensely demanding, interesting, and exhilarating.

Even though the *Marvels* was produced centuries ago, the imaginaries it contains continue to shape modern ways of imagining otherness. Indeed, imaginaries, aided by contemporary mass media, have gone global, altering how people collectively view the world and their own positions and perspectives within it. We must remember to approach imaginaries, like those in the *Marvels* and others, with a critical eye.

⁊ nont autre habitation.

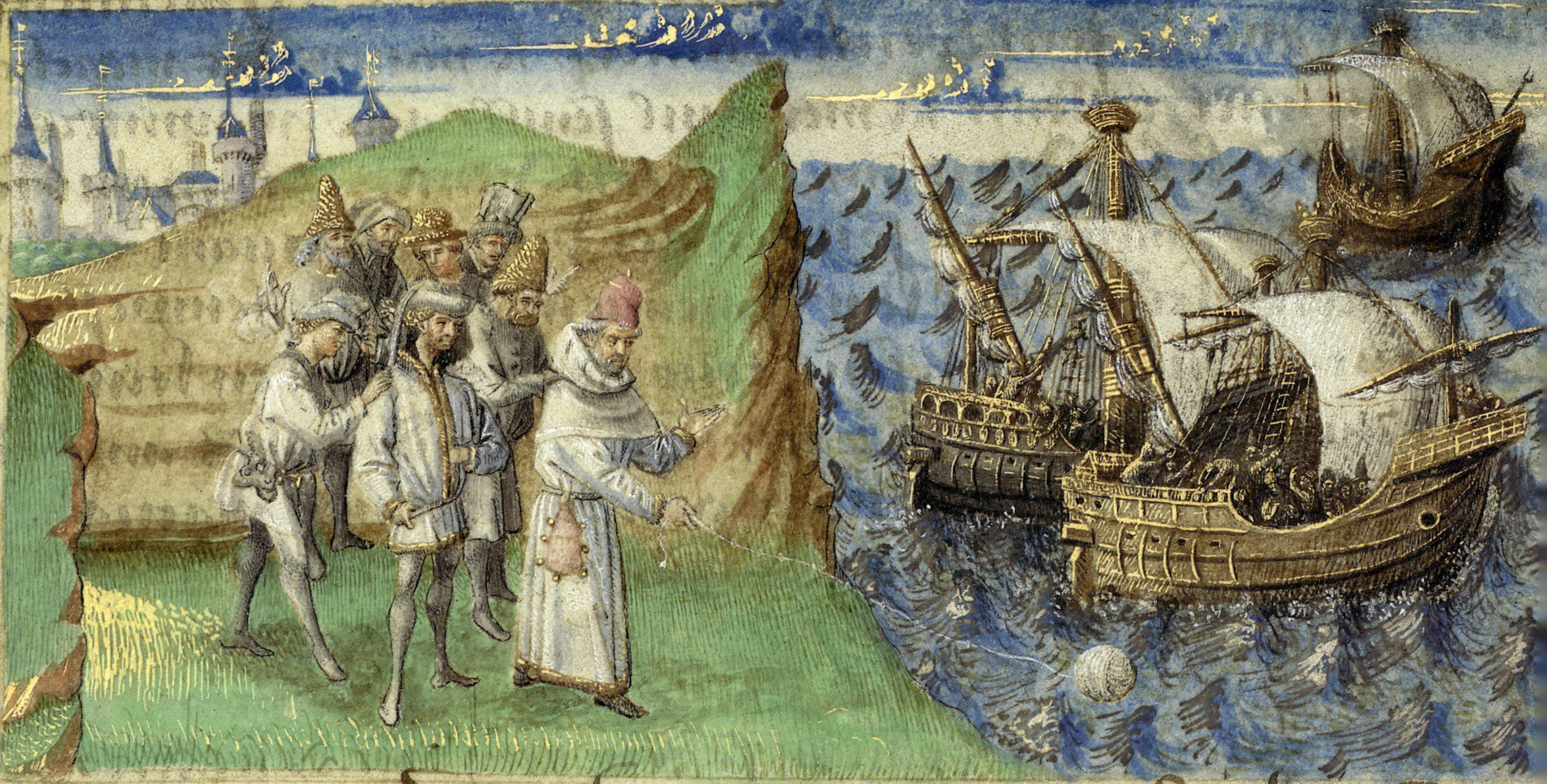

Vlulande est vne region situee es haultes motan
de norvegue dont les habitans sont gent barba
⁊ plains de grant cruaulte Car ceste gent m
toute leur estudie a aprendre ⁊ savoir les invocation
dyaboliques selon lart ⁊ science magique Et quant
marchans marinners viennet ⁊ arrivent en celle terr
par fortune de vent Et ne sen peuent partir par fau
de vent . lors les magiciens de vlulande cest assavoir ce
qui scevent user de lart ⁊ science magique viennen
par devers yceulx marchans ⁊ marinners ⁊ les offren

Descriptions of the Morgan and Getty Manuscripts

New York, Morgan Library & Museum, Ms. M.461
Purchased by J. Pierpont Morgan (1837–1913) in 1911
https://www.themorgan.org/manuscript/76918
France, probably Angers, ca. 1460
Book of the Marvels of the World (*Livre des merveilles du monde*);
57 miniatures by the Master of the Geneva Boccaccio

Colored washes, gold, and ink on parchment, bound in red gilt Morocco; 129 folios. Page: 28.1 × 22 cm (11 ⅛ × 8 ¹¹⁄₁₆ in.); text area justification: 21.1 × 14 cm (8 ⁵⁄₁₆ × 5 ½ in.); one column of 35–37 lines of *bastarda* in French; continuous foliation in pencil in upper right corner of rectos

Provenance: Possibly René of Anjou; Spain, around 1600; no. 1236 in an old catalogue; J. Barrois Collection (no. 148); sold in 1849 to the Earl of Ashburnham; his sale (London, 1901, no. 397) to Quaritch; Octave Gallice Collection, Épernay; purchased by J. Pierpont Morgan (1837–1913) from Léon Gruel in 1911

Gathering structure (by Joshua O'Driscoll, Associate Curator of Medieval & Renaissance Manuscripts, Morgan Library & Museum):

1^{8+1}, $2–15^{8}$, 16^{10-2}

The Morgan copy is complete.

Los Angeles, J. Paul Getty Museum, Ms. 124 (2022.15)
https://www.getty.edu/art/collection/object/10A38V
France, probably Angers, ca. 1460–65
Book of the Marvels of the World (*Livre des merveilles du monde*);
23 miniatures and 16 historiated initials by the Master of the Geneva Boccaccio

Colored washes, gold, silver, and ink on parchment, bound in red velvet over wood boards; 60 folios. Page: 30.2 × 22.5 cm (11 ⅞ × 8 ⅞ in.); text area justification: 21.5 × 14 cm (8 ½ × 5 ½ in.); one column of 37 lines of *bastarda* in French; continuous foliation in pencil in far upper right corner of rectos (older foliation in pen at upper right corner of rectos)

Provenance: Jean Bregerault, 1500s, Brittany; member of Le Fruglaye family, 1600s, Brittany; Charles Stein (1840–1899) –1886, Paris [sold, "Collection Stein," Galerie Georges Petit, Paris, May 10–14, 1886, lot 125, to M. Esnault]; M. Esnault, 1886– ; Pierre Gélis-Didot (1853–1933), Paris [sold, "Catalogue de manuscrits et miniatures . . . composant la collection de M. P. Gélis-Didot," Théophile Belin Libraire, Paris, April 12–13, 1897, lot 14]; Librairie Théophile Belin, Paris, no. 6, 1906; Comte Paul Durrieu (1855–1925), ca. 1906–25, Paris; Private collection 1925–2022, Paris; J. Paul Getty Museum, Los Angeles, 2022

Gathering structure (by Nancy Turner, Conservator of Manuscripts, J. Paul Getty Museum):

1^{6}, 2^{8+1}, 3^{8-5}, 4^{8}, 5^{8-1}, 6^{8}, 7^{8}, 8^{8}, $9^{8-5?}$

The Getty copy is missing around half of its original text and illuminations. It begins near the end of the description of Gaul, with the first extant image illustrating Germany. It ends in the middle of "Wonders of the Earth." It is also missing a number of folios between "Germany" and "Wonders of the Earth." All missing images are indicated in the "List of Locations in the *Book of Marvels*."

estes femes sont coustumieres de prier les homes z les sui
ussi ardanment pour avoir leur compaignie come ho
rodera les femes. mais les homes en sont estant reffu
nt aux femes aussi estranges come sont rodera les pr
ux homes. C Et a ce propos nous lisons ung exemple
ible ou livre de genesis ou chappitre que la fe
de putifar pria Joseph de coucher avecqs elle. Mais le
a reffusa en disant que jamais ne feroit ne ne vou
avoir telle trahison ne desloyaulte a son maistre qui en
moult se fioit.

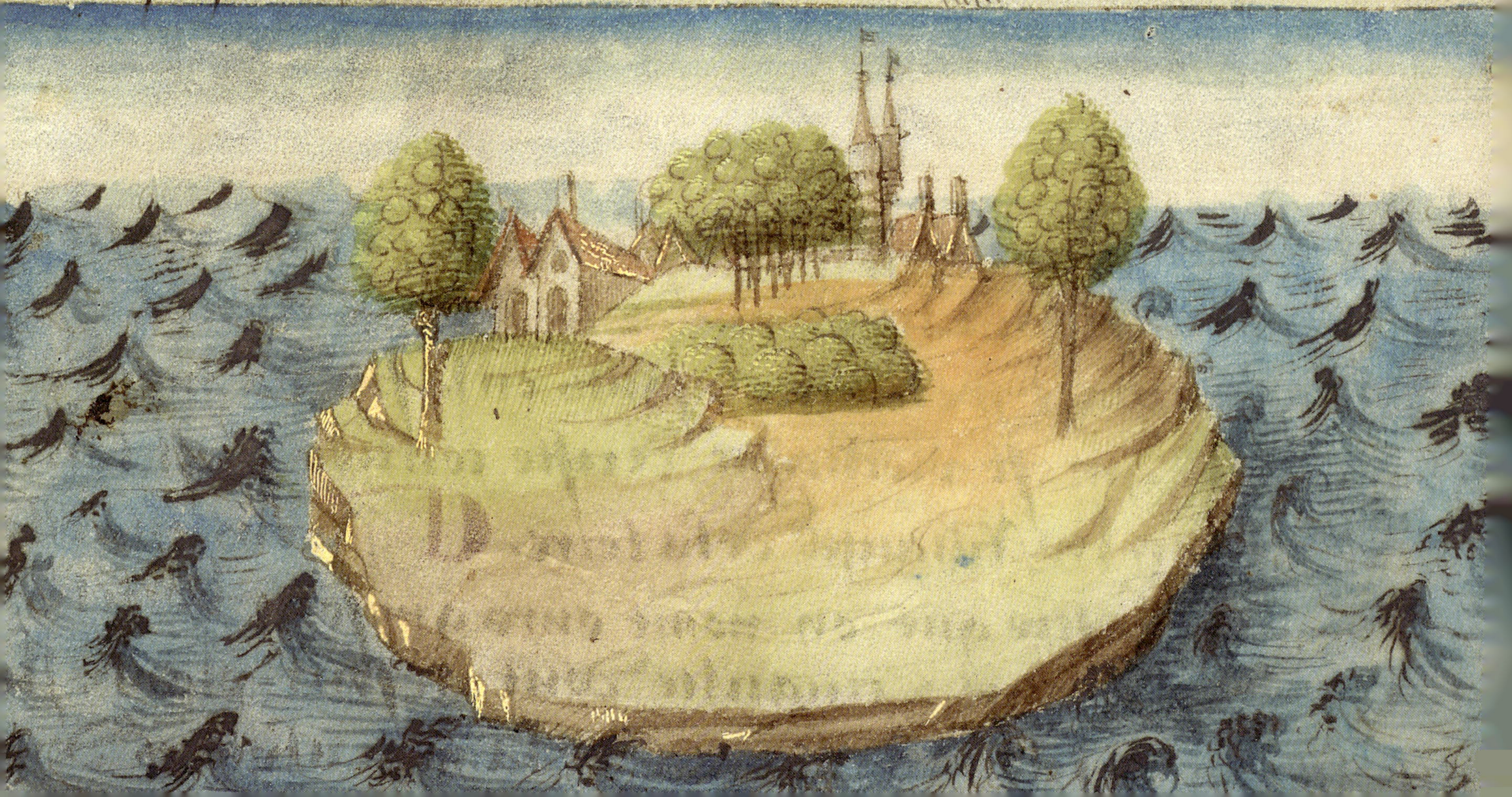

List of Locations in the *Book of Marvels*

The following lists the locations found in the Morgan and Getty copies of the *Book of Marvels* in the order in which they are found in the manuscripts, which is alphabetical in the original French.

Locations that are illustrated in the "Plates with Translations" section are underlined.

The modern equivalents of locations that may not be known to readers are given in brackets in light red. Place names in brackets in light blue are geographical indications given within the text of the *Marvels* itself.

1. <u>Africa</u> (Morgan, fol. 4r; Getty, missing)
2. <u>Amazonia</u> [near Scythia] (Morgan, fol. 5v; Getty, missing)
3. England (Morgan, fol. 6v; Getty, missing)
4. <u>Arabia</u> (Morgan, fol. 10r; Getty, missing)
5. Asia (Morgan, fol. 11v; Getty, missing)
6. Bactria [in Persia] (Morgan, fol. 12r; Getty, missing)
7. Boeotia [in Greece] (Morgan, fol. 12v; Getty, missing)
8. Bohemia [in the Czech Republic] (Morgan, fol. 13r; Getty, missing)
9. <u>Great Britain</u> (Morgan, fol. 13v; Getty, missing)
10. Campania [in Italy] (Morgan, fol. 15v; Getty, missing)
11. <u>Kedar</u> [tribe in the Arabian desert] (Morgan, fol. 17v; Getty, missing)
12. Cyprus (Morgan, fol. 18v; Getty, missing)
13. <u>Crete</u> (Morgan, fol. 19v; Getty, missing)
14. Lower Egypt (Morgan, fol. 20v; Getty, missing)
15. <u>Upper Egypt</u> (Morgan, fol. 22v; Getty, missing)
16. Hellespont [in Byzantium] (Morgan, fol. 25r; Getty, missing)
17. Aeolians [islands north of Sicily] (Morgan, fol. 26r; Getty, missing)
18. <u>Ethiopia</u> (Morgan, fol. 26v; Getty, missing)
19. Europe (Morgan, fol. 31v; Getty, missing)
20. Frisia [northwestern Europe] (Morgan, fol. 32r; Getty, missing)
21. Fortunate Isles [Canary Islands] (Morgan, fol. 32v; Getty, missing)
22. <u>Gaul</u> [France] (Morgan, fol. 33r; Getty, missing)
23. Germany (Morgan, fol. 37r; Getty, fol. 1r)
24. <u>Spain</u> (Morgan, fol. 38r; Getty, fol. 1v)
25. <u>Ibernia</u> [Ireland] (Morgan, fol. 40r; Getty, fol. 4r)
26. <u>India</u> (Morgan, fol. 41v; Getty, fol. 5r)
27. Isle (Morgan, fol. 50r; Getty, fol. 13r)
28. Ireland [Iceland] (Morgan, fol. 50v; Getty, fol. 13v)
29. <u>Italy</u> (Morgan, fol. 51r; Getty, fol. 14r)
30. Judea (Morgan, fol. 53v; Getty, fol. 16v)
31. Libya (Morgan, fol, 55r; Getty, missing)
32. Lydonie [east of the Baltic Sea] (Morgan, fol. 55v; Getty, missing)
33. Lytonie [Latvia] (Morgan, fol. 56r; Getty, missing)
34. Macedonia (Morgan, fol. 56v; Getty, missing)
35. Melos [Greek island] (Morgan, fol. 57v; Getty, fol. 17v)
36. Media [in Persia] (Morgan, fol. 57v; Getty, fol. 17v)
37. Moesia [in the Balkans] (Morgan, fol. 58v; Getty, fol. 18v)
38. Norway (Morgan, fol. 59r; Getty, missing)
39. Offir [in India] (Morgan, fol. 59v; Getty, missing)
40. Terrestrial paradise (Morgan, fol. 60v; Getty, missing)
41. <u>Pygmy</u> [in Judea] (Morgan, fol. 61v; Getty, missing)

42. Poitou [in France] (Morgan, fol. 62r; Getty, missing)

43. Provence [in France] (Morgan, fol. 64r; Getty, fol. 20r)

44. Saba [in Arabia] (Morgan, fol. 68v; Getty, fol. 24v)

45. Saxony [in Germany] (Morgan, fol. 69r; Getty, fol. 25r)

46. Sardinia [island in Italy] (Morgan, fol. 69v; Getty, fol. 25v)

47. Scythia [north of the Black Sea] (Morgan, fol. 70r; Getty, fol. 26r)

48. Scotland (Morgan, fol. 73v; Getty, fol. 29v)

49. Syria (Morgan, fol. 74v; Getty, fol. 30r)

50. Seres [China] (Morgan, fol. 75r; Getty, fol. 30v)

51. Trapo [Sri Lanka] (Morgan, fol. 76r; Getty, missing)

52. Tuscany [in Italy] (Morgan, fol. 76r; Getty, missing)

53. Thule [possibly Orkney, Hebrides, Shetland, or Iceland] (Morgan, fol. 76v; Getty, fol. 31r)

54. Thrace [portions of Greece, Turkey, and Bulgaria] (Morgan, fol. 77v; Getty, fol. 31v)

55. Traponee [Sri Lanka] (Morgan, fol. 78r; Getty, fol. 32r)

56. Ululand [in Norway] (Morgan, fol. 79r; Getty, fol. 33r)

57. Wonders of the Human Body (Morgan, fol. 79v; Getty, fol. 33v)

58. Wonders of the Animal World (Morgan, fol. 89v; Getty, fol. 40v)

59. Wonders of the Heavens (Morgan, fol. 95v; Getty, fol. 47v)

60. Wonders of Fire (Morgan, fol. 99r; Getty, fol. 51r)

61. Wonders of Birds (Morgan, fol. 100r; Getty, fol. 52v)

62. Wonders of the Sea (Morgan, fol. 102r; Getty, fol. 54r)

63. Wonders of Fresh Waters (Morgan, fol. 103r; Getty, fol. 56r)

64. Wonders of Fish (Morgan, fol. 105v; Getty, fol. 57v)

65. Wonders of the Earth (Morgan, fol. 107r; Getty, fol. 59r)

66. Wonders of Trees (Morgan, fol. 110v; Getty, missing)

67. Wonders of Plants (Morgan, fol. 113r; Getty, missing)

68. Wonders of Stones (Morgan, fol. 116r; Getty, missing)

69. Wonders of Human Industry (Morgan, fol. 116v; Getty, missing)

70. Wonders of Buildings (Morgan, fol. 117v; Getty, missing)

71. Marvels of Poison (Morgan, fol. 121r; Getty, missing)

72. On Monstrosity (Morgan, fol. 124r; Getty, missing)

73. Wonders of Portents (Morgan, fol. 126v; Getty, missing)

stroumera mais quil ne quiere point la fontaine qui
pense autrement il trouuera les enseignes mais se les
enseignes jamais ne les trouuera. Et tout ainsi est
deles fontaines dont cy deuant a este parle. Item d
naise q en prouince pres du chastel de Berlem a une fo
t leaue est moult medicinable a ceulx qui ont les gout
tes et ont communement ceulx du pais de pymont et ceu
vallees de pireneus et gascoingne et plus autres pour la ri
ut froidure des eaues dont ilz usent en leurs beuurag
pour estre guariz viennent des pais dessus diz boire de le
este fontaine qui leur est vrai et souuerain remede.

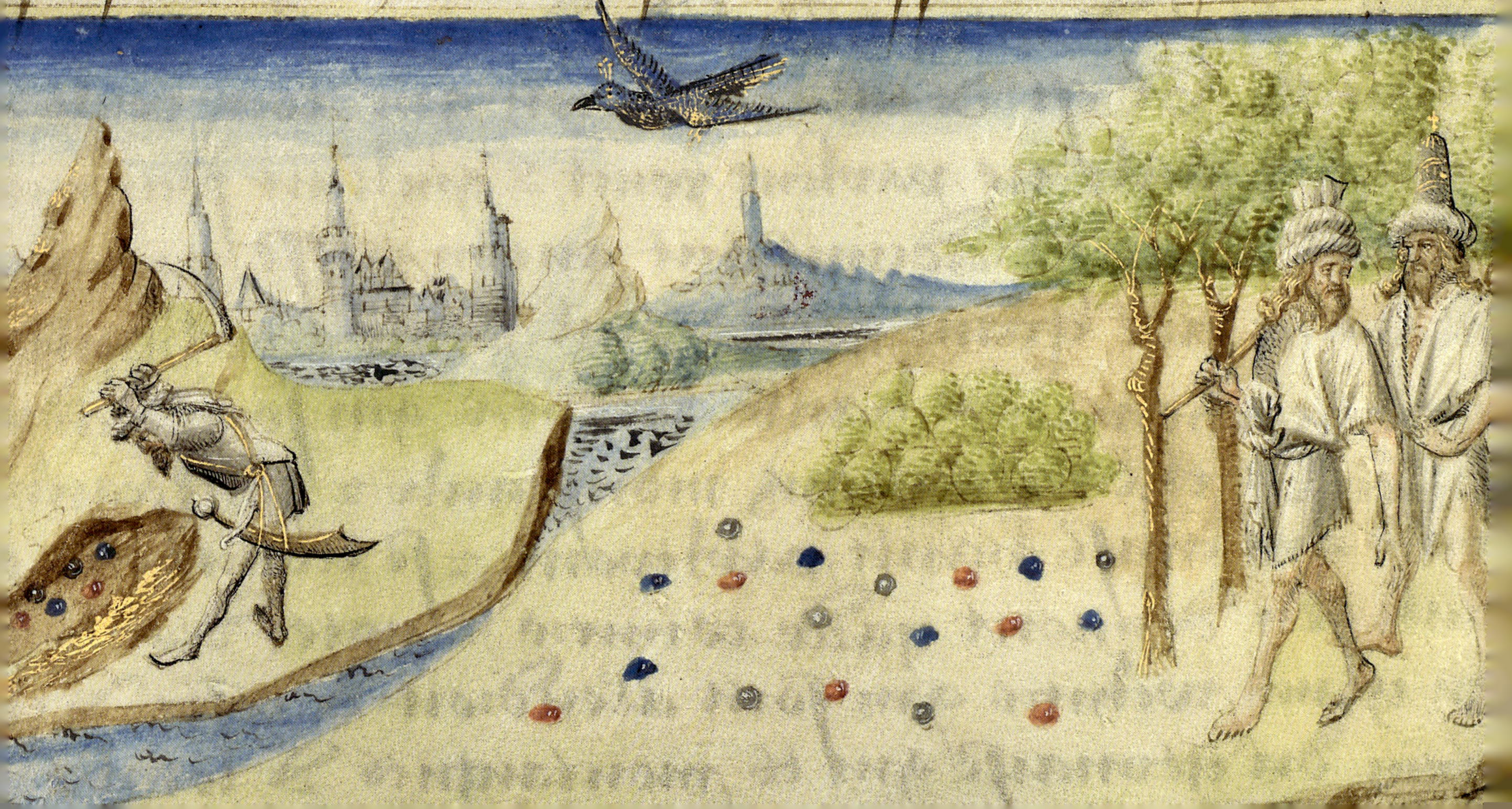

Plates with Translations

The following excerpts translated from the *Book of Marvels* are keyed to the images. The first occurrence of a theme is the one cited (the text often quotes Pliny, Solinus, Gervase, and others on the same topics in quite similar terms). Occasionally, it was difficult to match a visual motif to a particular excerpt; these cases are indicated by an asterisk. All black-and-white renderings with portions synchronized to the matching text are taken from the Morgan *Marvels*. Regarding the plates containing initials (plates 21–25), some of the initials do not include images directly related to the text; in those cases, a short description of the image is given in brackets, followed by the beginning of the text for that section. All illuminations from both manuscripts are available online in high resolution; links to each manuscript are given on page 79.

All the texts in the plates as well as the chapter and page numbers are from Kristen M. Figg and John Block Friedman, "Transcription and Translation," in *Book of Wonders of the World, Secrets of Natural History: MS fr. 22971: Original Held in the National Library of France, Paris: Studies and Translation*. Burgos: Siloé, 2018.

PLATE 1

AFRICA

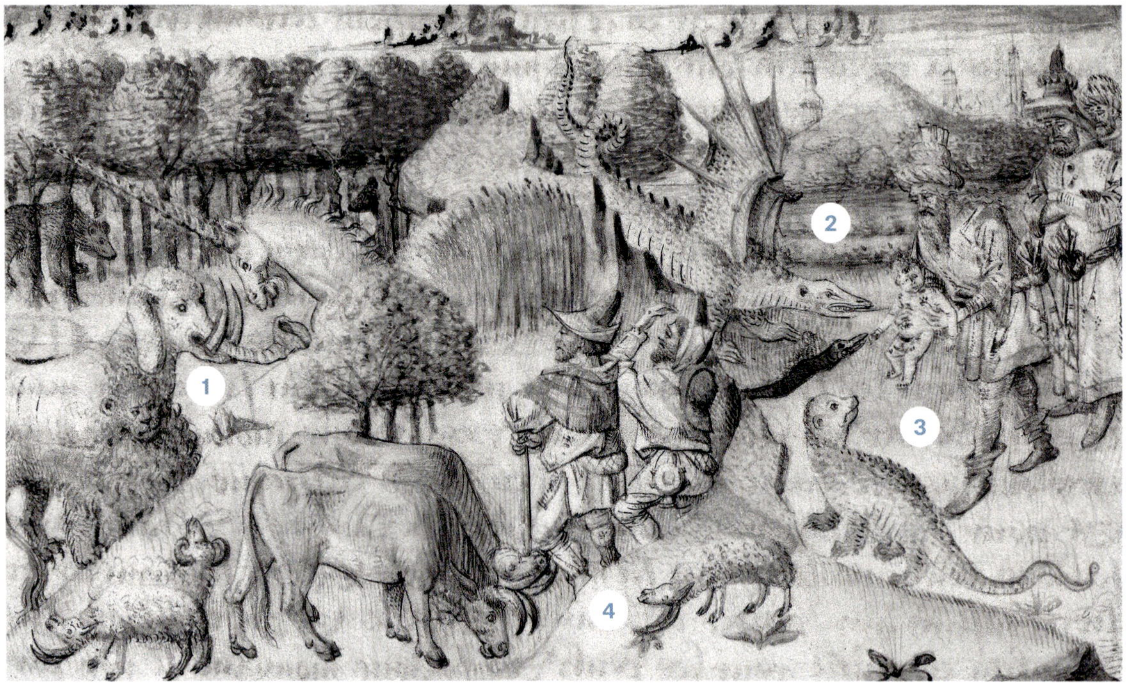

1 *And here too are an abundance of elephants and all sorts of wild animals such as bears, lions, hyenas, wild asses, onagers, and serpents of many different kinds.*

2 *[T]hese people and their offspring live among serpents in a very confident, firm, and constant manner, and also among venomous beasts.*

3 *And Pliny says that when any man of this country has a newborn child and he doubts or has any suspicion regarding the mother's fidelity, in order to determine if the child is legitimate or not, he exposes it and lays it before serpents, and if the child is truly by nature and blood the offspring of the man who delivers it to the serpents, the serpents will not harm it. But if the child was fathered by another and is put before the serpents, it is immediately eaten and devoured.*

4 *Solinus says that livestock there such as steers and cows graze in the field with the head turned to the side, one eye towards the ground and the other towards the sky. Thus they hold their throats sideways. The reason is that their horns are bent backwards and stretched out towards the earth and thus their horns prevent them from grazing on the grass with their heads right to the ground. And it is necessary for them to turn their heads to graze or else they could not eat and they would have to die of hunger; and it is exactly the same for the sheep and lambs that live in that country.*

—Figg and Friedman, pp. 175–77 (chap. 1)

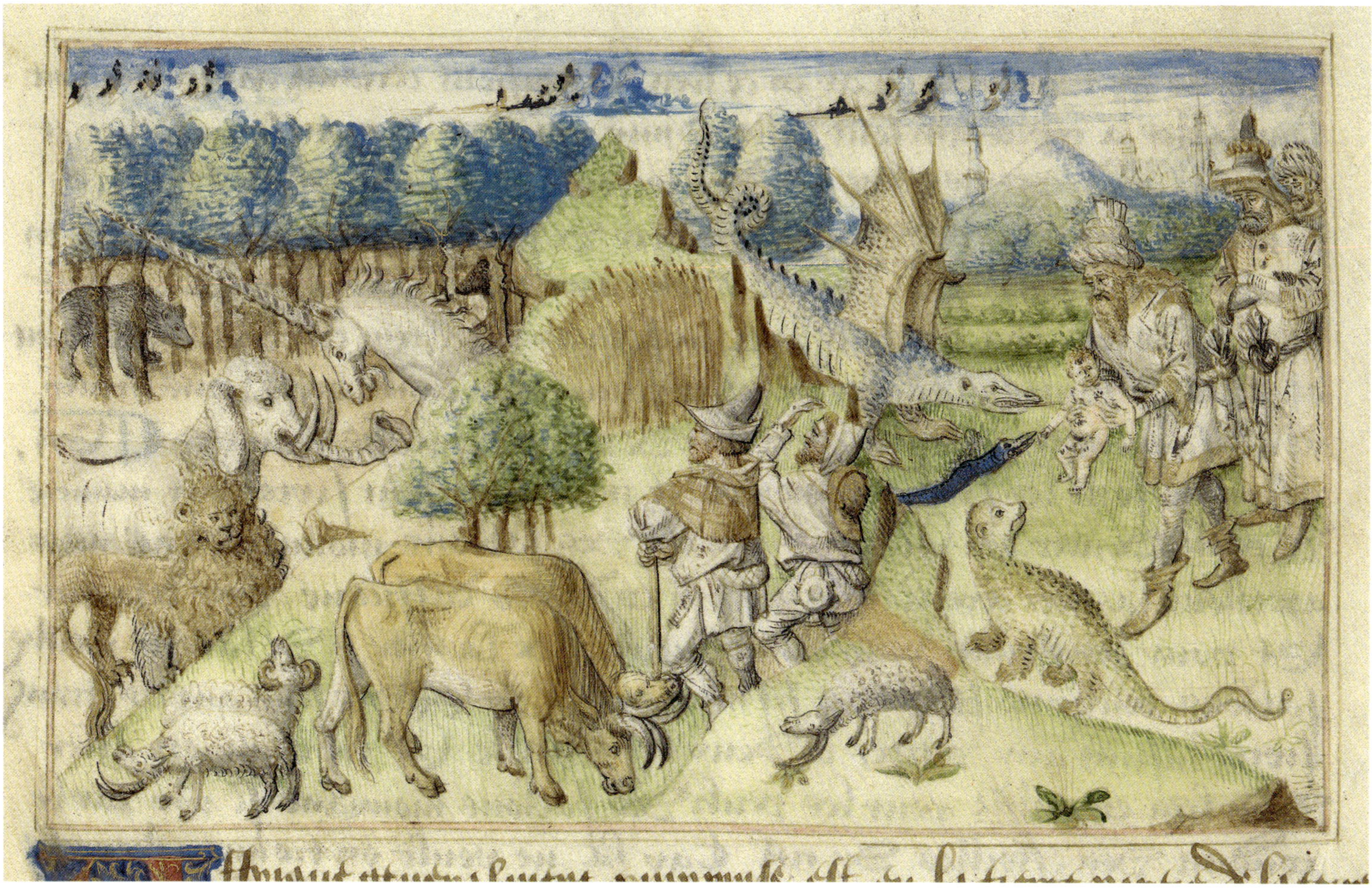

MORGAN, FOL. 4R
(GETTY, MISSING)

PLATE 2

AMAZONIA [NEAR SCYTHIA]

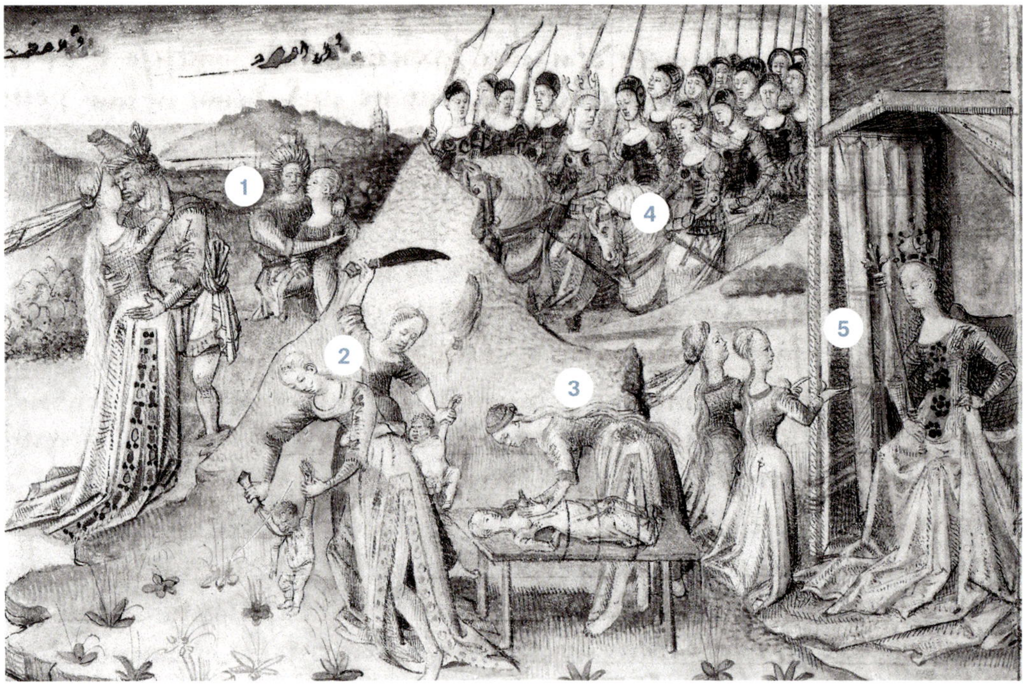

1 *Amazonia is a region called Feminie because only women dwell there. And they allow no men to dwell or live among them, save at a certain time when they have sexual relations with men in order to replenish their line, but they do only that, and otherwise the women always stay away from the men.*

2 *And when it comes time for the delivery of the child, if they have a male child, they kill and dispose of him.*

3 *The women of this land have a custom of cutting off the right breasts of their daughters at the age of eight in order that they not be impeded from shooting the bow and also in order that they be more skillful at defending themselves against their enemies.*

4 *Of their government and political practices, Solinus says that they have two queens they obey, of whom one is the mistress and leader of the army and is responsible for making war in defense of their country against all nations and for assaults and battles both outside their land and within, whether they be near or far.*

5 *The other queen dwells in the realm as sovereign lady of the land, serving both as judge and as the one responsible for governance of public affairs.*

—Figg and Friedman, pp. 177–79 (chap. 2)

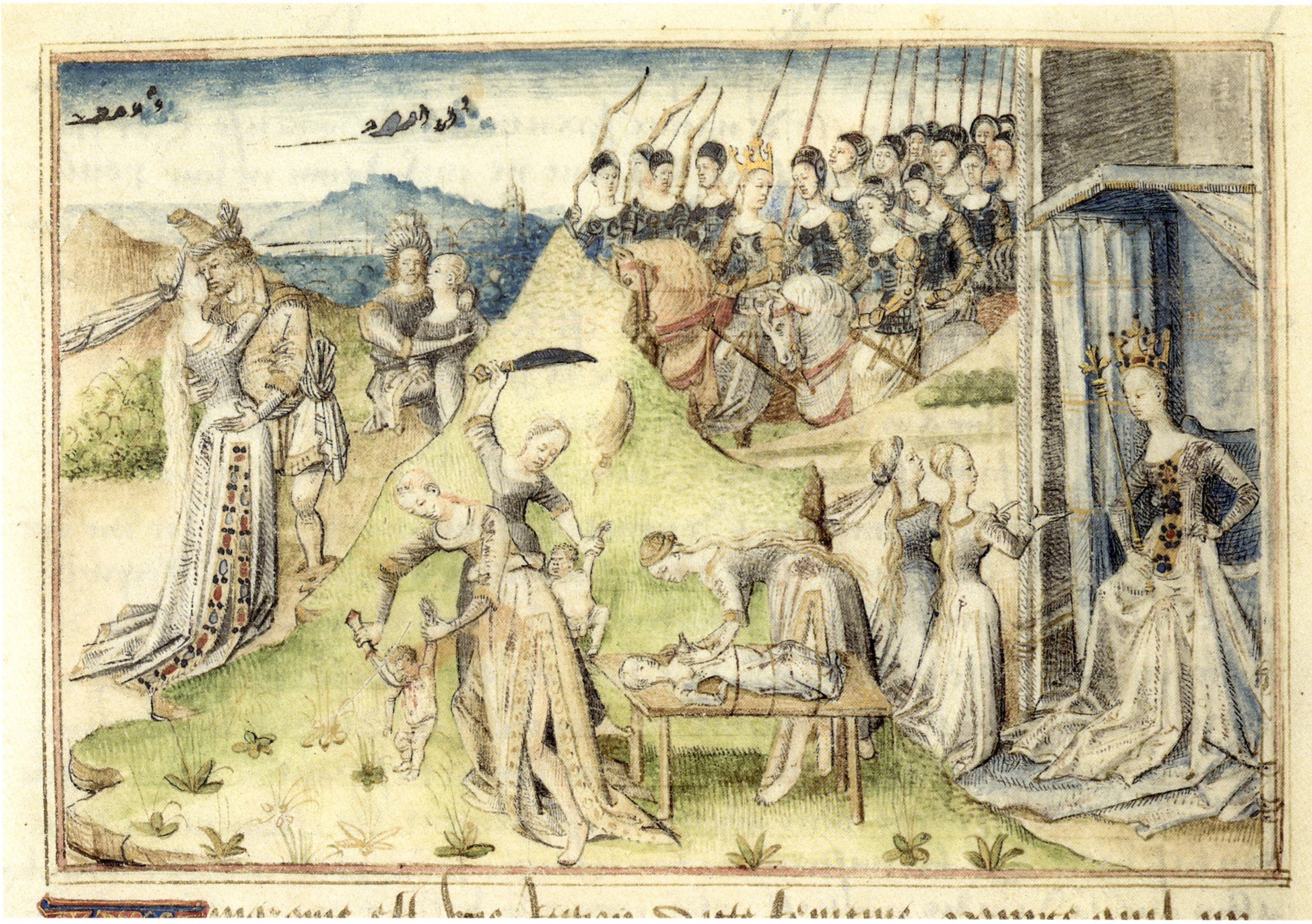

MORGAN, FOL. 5V
(GETTY, MISSING)

PLATE 3

ARABIA

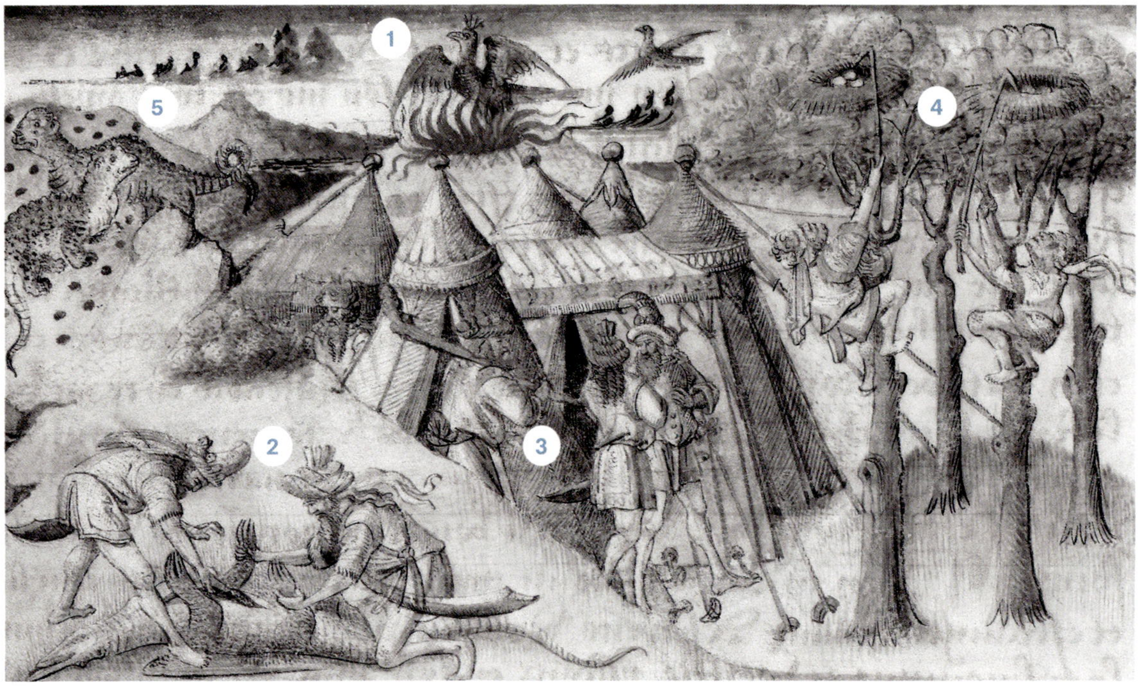

1 *There makes its home the unique and very noble bird that is called Phoenix, which has no equal, nor is it found anywhere else outside of Arabia. . . . [A]fter the Phoenix has lived for a long time and it is time for it to die and come to an end, it makes its nest in a very high spot. . . . And then the Phoenix enters and lies down in the flames and there is burned and consumed and reduced to dust and ashes. And from the ashes that have been produced, because of the bird's natural condition, at the end of three days another Phoenix is bred and created.*

2 *[A]mong these venomous beasts there is a species called the asp. And though they are extremely poisonous, yet they have within their bodies certain stones that are considered very precious and valuable, and the people of this region customarily kill or put to death these asps in order to remove from their bellies these rich precious stones.*

3 *For shelter the people of Arabia use only movable tents and pavilions made and woven from the same sort of hair one uses to make sackcloth, such as hair from the manes of horses and camels or other beasts, and they have no other kind of fabric in this country.*

4 *Solinus says that in Arabia is found a bird called Cinnamologus, and it inhabits only the high mountains and high cliffs and high trees, in which trees it is fond of making its nest. . . . And because the inhabitants of this country cannot reach the nest of this bird to obtain this fine cinnamon, owing to the great height of the trees, they climb up by means of ladders against the trees, and through the use of hooks and scaffolding and other devices, they attack the nests, which are made of the very finest cinnamon flower that exists. And they gather and harvest this cinnamon, and they sell it at very high prices to foreign merchants.*

5 **In Arabia are certain dragons who are of the same condition and properties as the asps of which I have previously spoken in this chapter. For these snakes have within their bellies certain stones that are most worthy and precious. And when the dragons are dead, the people here open them up and seek within their bellies these rich stones, and sell them at a very high price.*

—Figg and Friedman, pp. 185–88 (chap. 4)

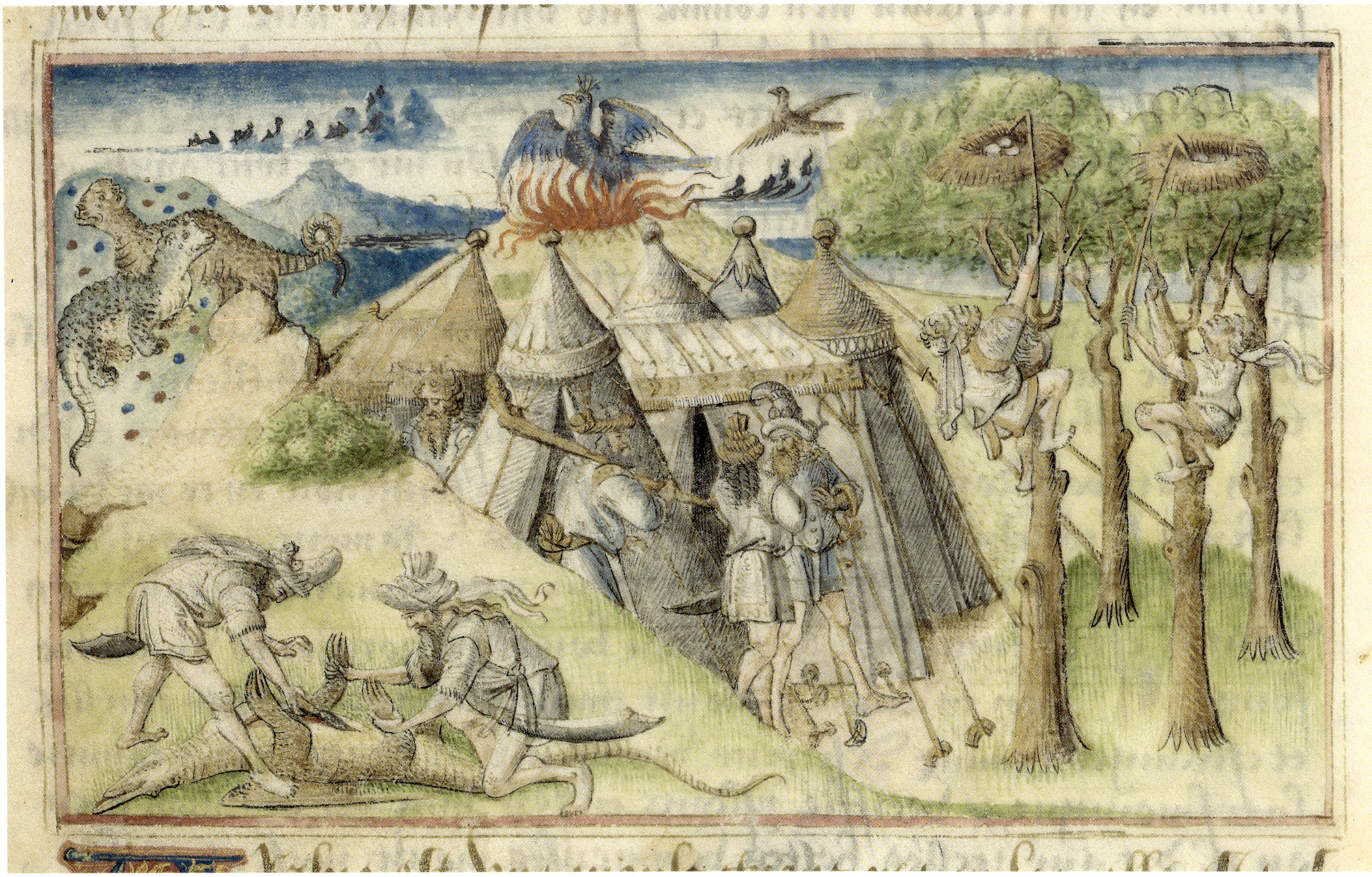

MORGAN, FOL. 10R
(GETTY, MISSING)

PLATE 4

GREAT BRITAIN

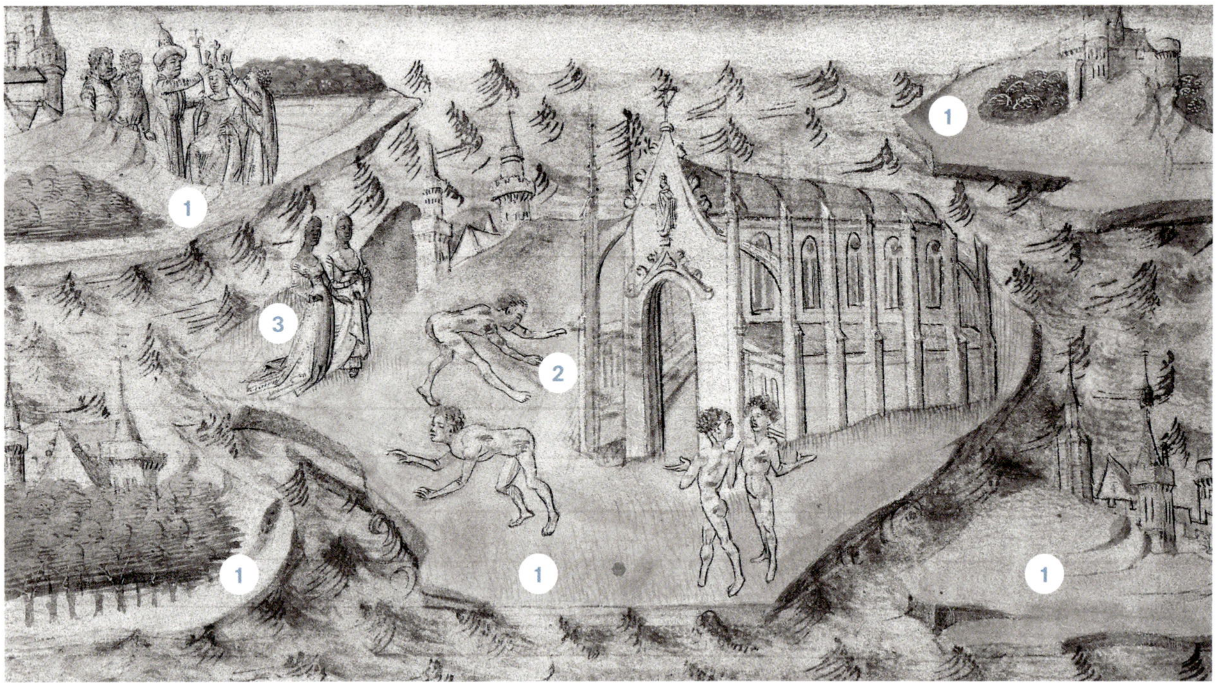

1 *Solinus says that near Great Britain there are five islands, which are called the Hebrides. . . . And their king had nothing of his own, but lived on the commonwealth and thus could appropriate nothing from it for himself or his own profit. . . . And thus the royal power would remain always in the lordship and governance of the common people. And they could take and elect for their king any man from among themselves that they pleased.*

2 *Apropos to this is the story in Holy Scripture in the [second] chapter of the second book of Maccabees, where it is told that [when Nehemiah] the great priest had rebuilt the temple of Solomon, he sent the descendants of the old priests of the law, who were loyal servants of God, to seek out and bring back the temple fire that their forefathers had formerly hidden in a very deep well far away from all men. . . . Solinus says that in Great Britain there used to be certain people that were called beastly barbarians, who under the shadow and color of penitence changed their appearance by adopting bestial manners and qualities. And they governed themselves according to the state and behaviors of certain animals, and they painted their faces and hands and various parts of their bodies with diverse colors in order better to resemble animals. And they did this believing that they made a great sacrifice to God.*

3 *Pliny says that in Great Britain the women customarily anointed themselves with certain herbal juices, and then they became as black as the Moors of Mauritania, and thus they could go wherever they wished without being recognized.*

—Figg and Friedman, pp. 191–93 (chap. 9)

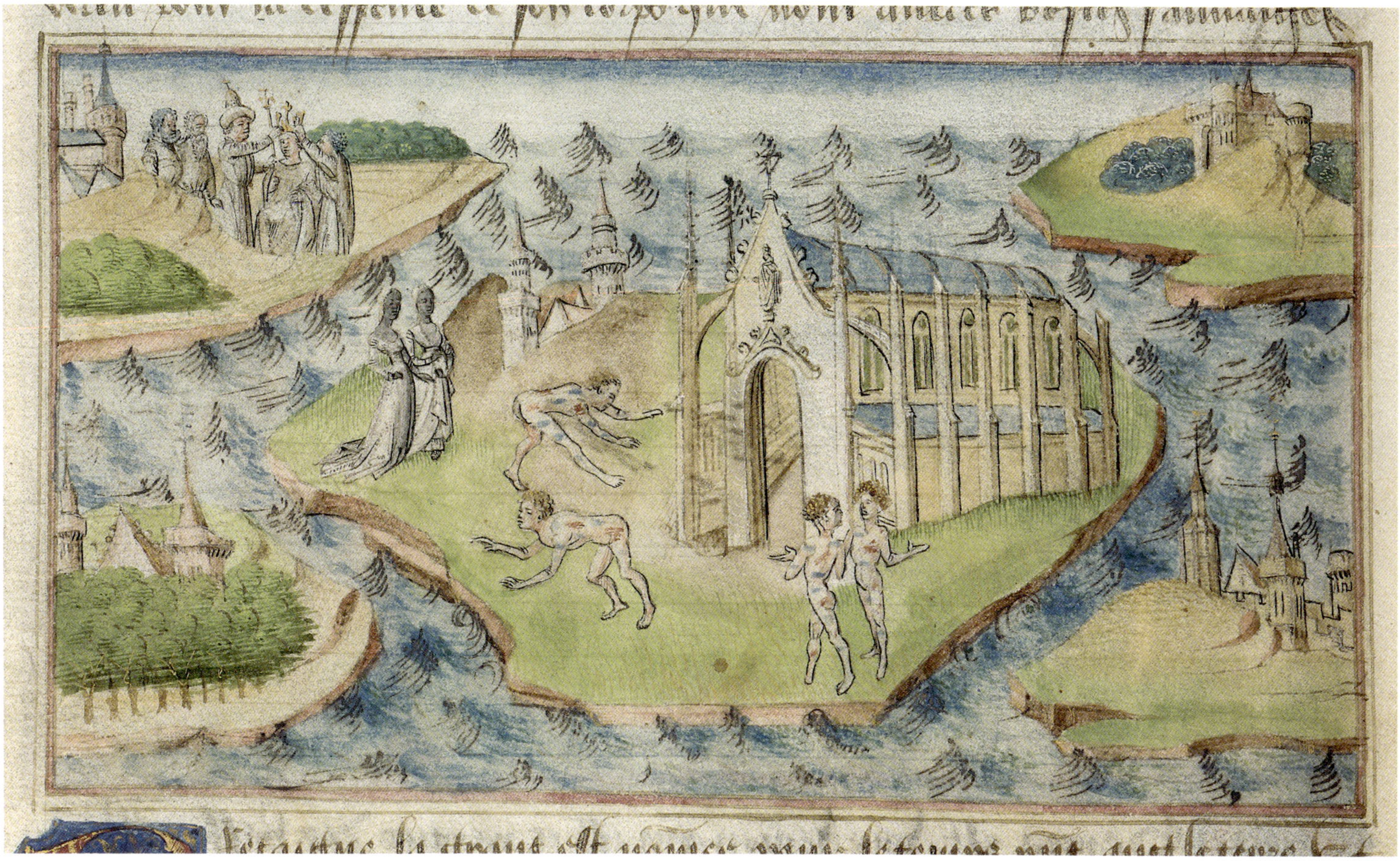

MORGAN, FOL. 13V
(GETTY, MISSING)

PLATE 5

KEDAR [TRIBE IN THE ARABIAN DESERT]

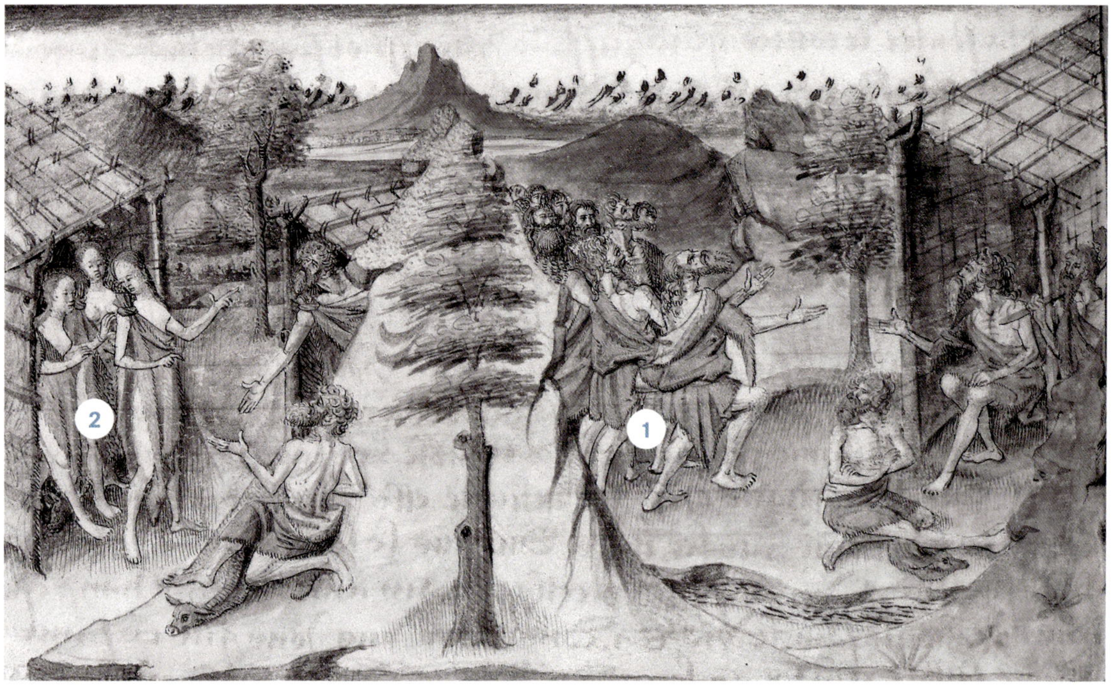

1 **[T]hose of this lineage live in tents and not at all in houses, and they live like savages and beasts. And they go off wandering in the wilderness like lazy people who have no idea what to do in the deserts, and they flee the company of other people as often as they can. For they are so very cruel and wild that there is no bear, leopard, lion, wolf, or dragon that is as cruel and bad and pitiless as these people are. . . . Methodius says that the road these people will travel will be called the Way of Anguish and Misery, for they will bring death and destruction everywhere, to both realms and cities of renown—and to the habitable regions universally. They will overthrow and destroy the churches and the holy places, the tombs of the glorious saints, martyrs, and confessors.*

2 **And they will rape women and virgins. And they will do many other inhuman things that would take too long to recount.*

—Figg and Friedman, pp. 197–98 (chap. 11)

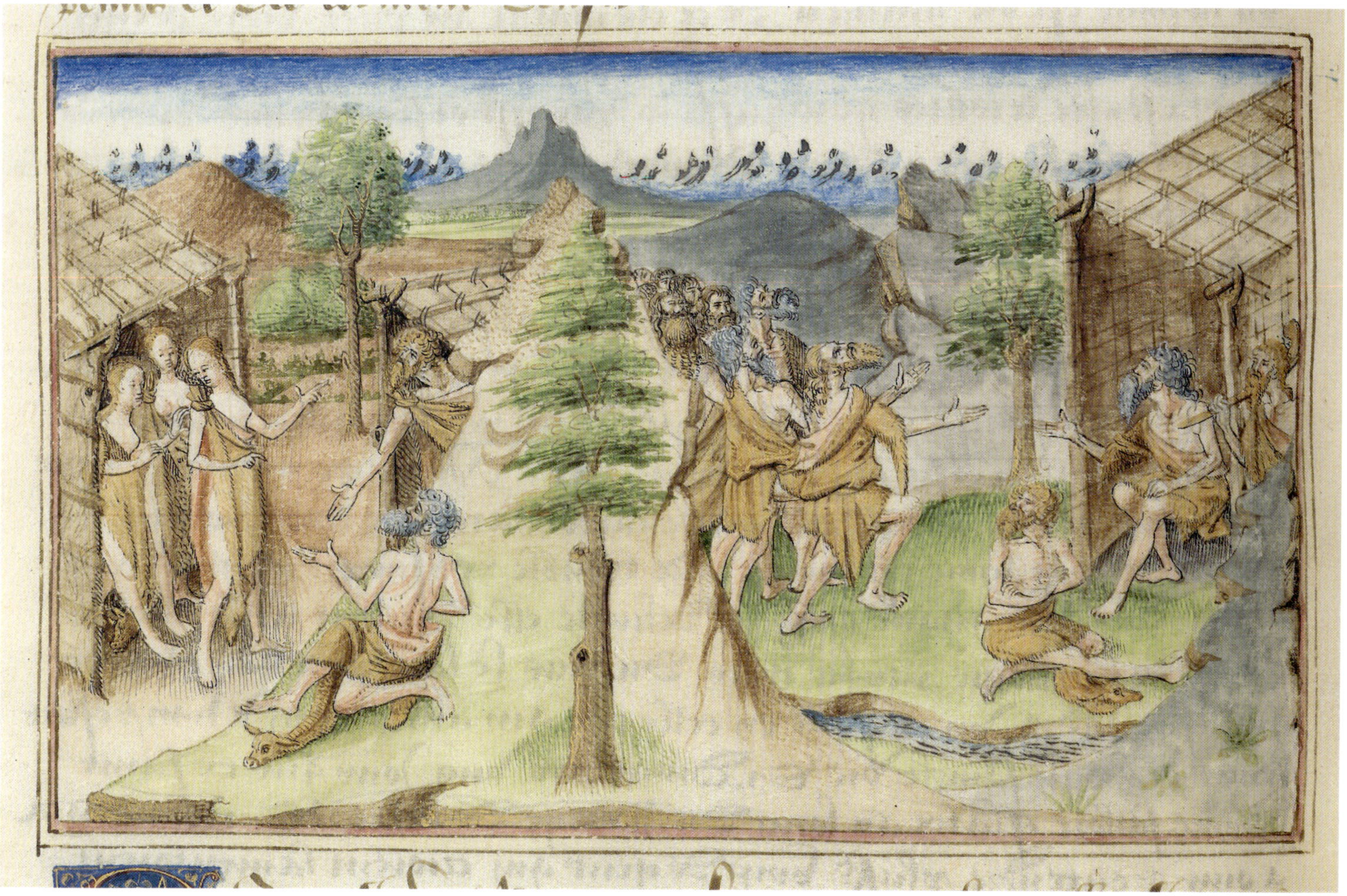

MORGAN, FOL. 17V
(GETTY, MISSING)

PLATE 6

CRETE

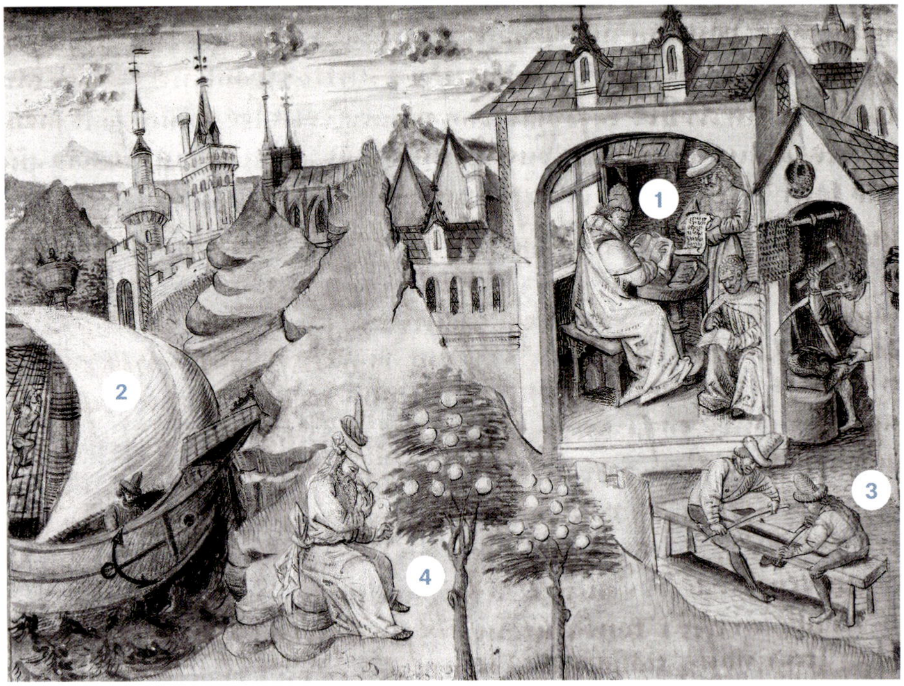

1 *In this region were first invented and developed letters and a method of writing in order to record and set down in words events both past and future, so as to have them in perpetual memory.*

2 *And the Cretans were the first to understand how to go to sea and how to build ships and make sails, ropes, and oars.*

3 *And similarly they were the first who, for the purpose of warfare, came up with the idea of making armaments such as helms, basinets, and other head armor, battleaxes, lances, swords, daggers and knives, shields, bucklers, darts, bows and arrows, crossbows and bolts, and iron body armor.*

4 *Solinus says that on Crete grows a plant of remarkable and marvelous properties that is called allainos. And this herb is of such a nature that if a very hungry person who wished to dine were to eat only one leaf from this plant, he would be satisfied and full and would have no desire to eat for the rest of the day.*

—Figg and Friedman, pp. 200–201 (chap. 13)

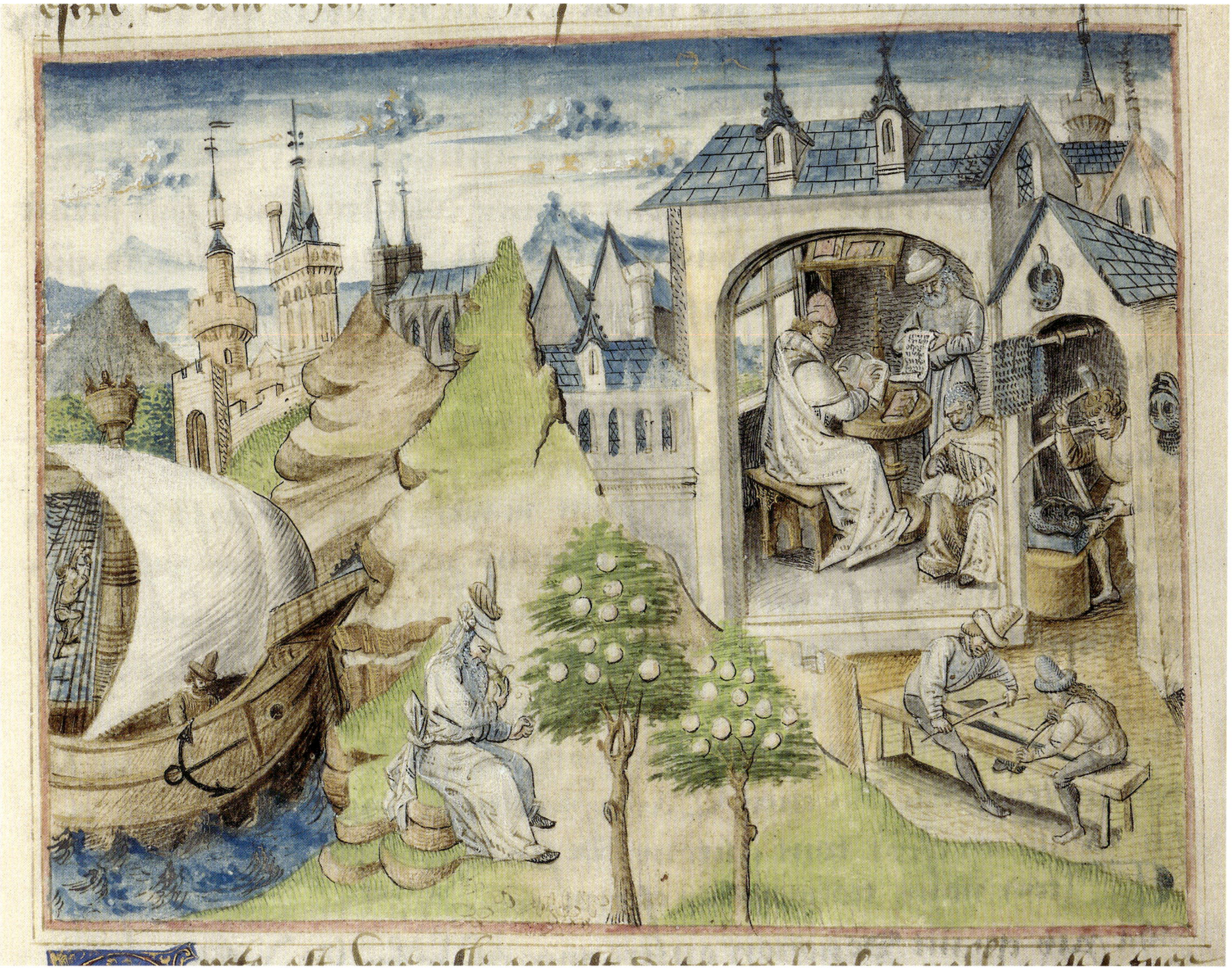

MORGAN, FOL. 19V
(GETTY, MISSING)

PLATE 7

UPPER EGYPT

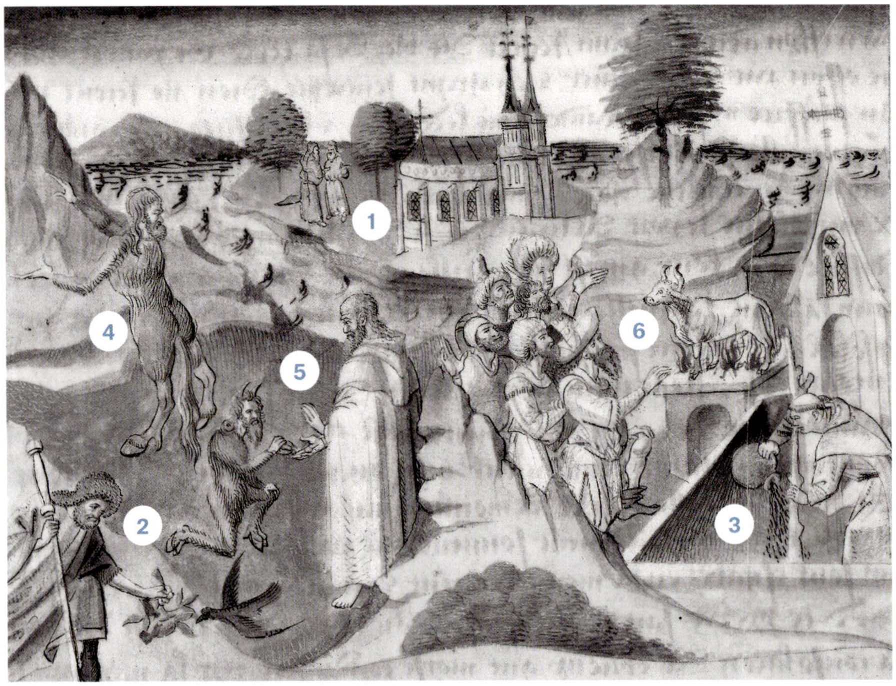

1 **Postumanus speaks of another marvel, for he says that an herb grows there that is sweeter than honey. And it resembles an herb that people call mint. He says that once near this perilous Syrtes he came upon an old man who was living in a small hut, and to honor him, the man gave him this herb for his meal.*

2 *Gervaise said that there was once a knight of Provence who, scorning the joy and prosperity of the world, went as an act of devotion like a hermit on a pilgrimage across the land and went to the high deserts of Egypt. And after he had wandered a long time and endured much poverty and disease, there came and flew to him a crow, who brought him, in his beak, an herb with the root that he had torn from the earth and pulled up, and he placed and presented it at the feet of the knight. This noble knight ate it with great pleasure and found it very sweet and tasty.*

3 *The abbot of this monastery, in order to test the virtue of obedience, commanded a young novice monk that he plant in the cloister of their abbey a dry branch, from which this tree came, and that he water and moisten this dry branch so much that as a result of the watering it would become green and take root in the earth. . . . And when springtime drew near, the young monk noticed that this branch began to bud and that it had taken root in the earth. And soon thereafter it happened that it flowered and brought forth fruit and became a tree.*

4 *Saint Anthony . . . found along the way a very gentle monster or wild animal which had a frightening appearance and seemed to be half man and half horse, man in front and beast behind. And although Saint Anthony did not understand his bestial speech, nonetheless this monster conducted him and set him on the right path by signs and by facial expressions, for which he greatly praised and thanked God. For this monster went before him and always showed him the road with his right hand. And when he had been with him a long time, this monster left him and went away to his dwelling, no one knows where.*

5 *Another similar adventure happened to Saint Anthony in this same region of the Egyptian deserts, for rather soon after this first adventure, he encountered a small wild man, all hairy and naked, who had nostrils almost completely turned inside out, a horned forehead, and feet like a goat. He bowed to Saint Anthony with great reverence, and, to honor him, gave him some dates that he was carrying.*

6 *Pomponius says that the Egyptians in ancient times were idolaters and adored an ox when it was black and spotted with many different colors. And when it was at all different in the tongue and tail from other oxen, they said it was born and engendered in the mother without a father by divine power. And they kept this particular beast for their god. And from the very day of his birth, they adored and celebrated him with devotion.*

—Figg and Friedman, pp. 204–8 (chap. 15)

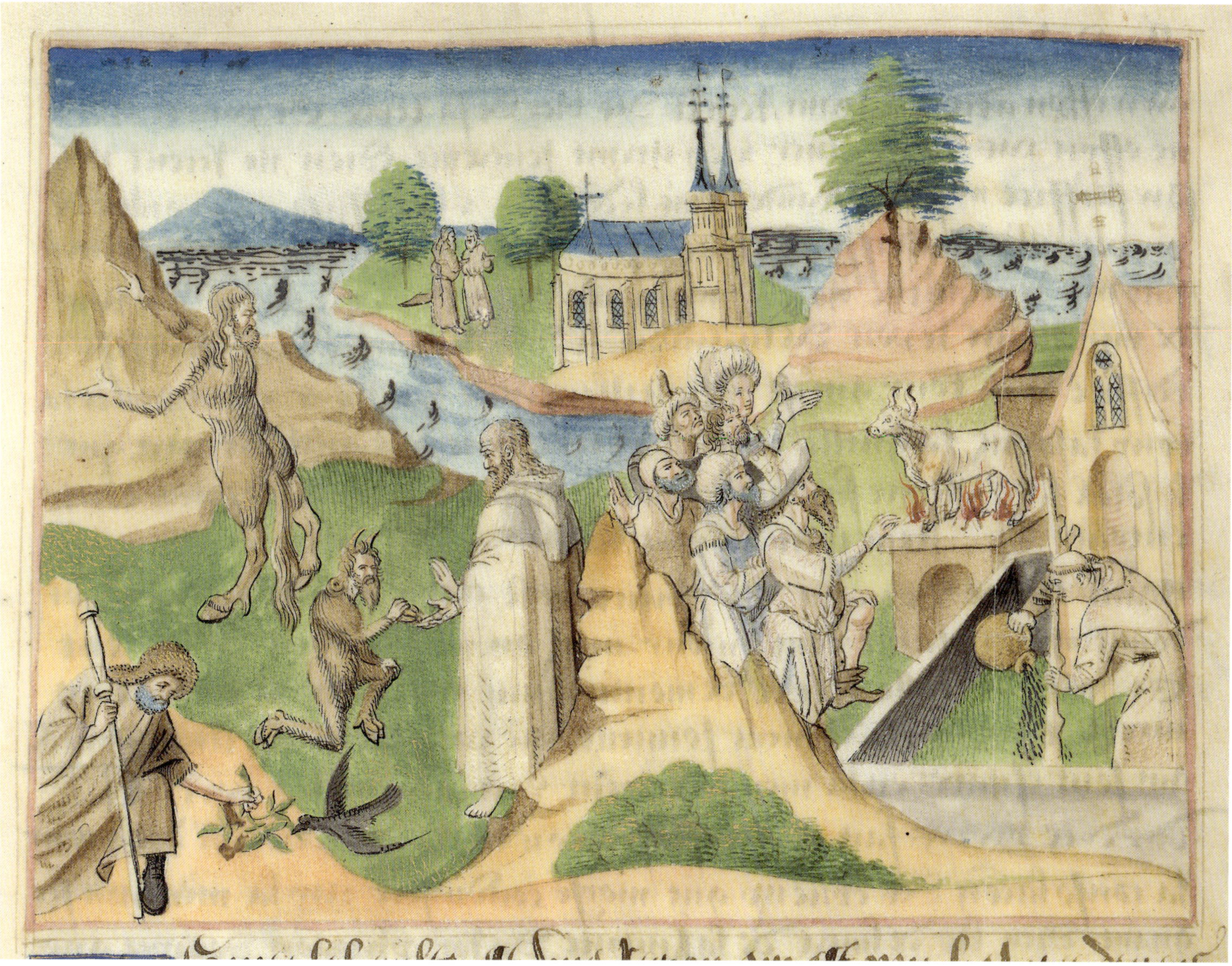

MORGAN, FOL. 22V
(GETTY, MISSING)

PLATE 8

ETHIOPIA

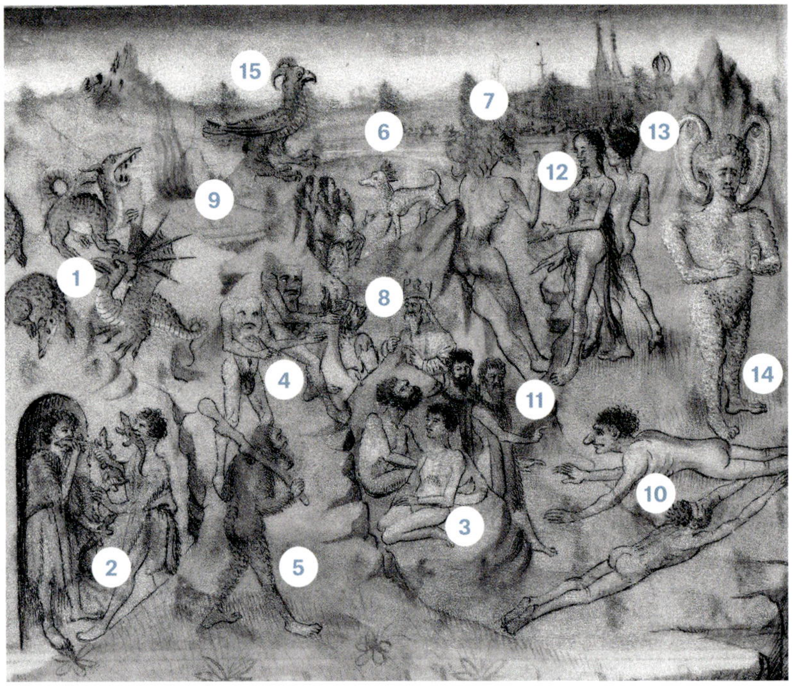

1 *Ethiopia is a region that is situated towards the Southern parts, where there exists a great multitude of venomous beasts, such as serpents, basilisks, great dragons, and asps.*

2 *These men [Troglodytes] live on raw flesh and eat lizards and other small snakes alive.*

3 **In Ethiopia are other marvelous peoples who are named Epaffaphantes. These men are always completely naked and never have any clothes with which to dress themselves.*

4 *In Ethiopia are men who are called Blemmyae. . . . For they have no head on their shoulders, and thus have eyes and a mouth on their chests, and all the rest of their body parts are similar to those of the human body.*

5 *In Ethiopia are other men who are named Sabarines, hairy and without any ears.*

6 *In this land are other people who elect a dog for their king.*

7 *Solinus tells how in Ethiopia there are people named Nerbothes who are of such great height and girth that they are twelve feet tall. And our authority Gervaise says of these people that they are yellow in color and shine like fine gold.*

8 **Gervaise says that in Ethiopia is a type of people who are called Cinophages, and the king of this land has only one eye on his forehead.*

9 *Solinus says that in Ethiopia there is a mountain called Eduhe that burns and blazes at all times of the year, and yet, no matter what fire or flame may be there, the mountain neither wears away nor grows smaller.*

10 *Solinus says that in the high, hot, burned deserts of Ethiopia live other people who are exceedingly marvelous and they are named Etiphages. And they go swimming and floating in the sea like whales and sturgeons and other great fish, and they go about swimming in the sea.*

11 *Gervaise says that in Upper Ethiopia towards the Red Sea is a country that is inhabited by women who are of horrible countenance and frightful customs. For they have great beards which hang down to their breasts. And they are dressed in the skins of animals.*

12 *Gervaise says that in Ethiopia are certain mountains adjacent to the country just mentioned where there are women who are more marvelous than elsewhere. For they have tusks coming out of their mouths like boars, hair black and coarse as the manes of horses and hanging to their heels. And at the end of the spine they have long tails like oxen or cows.*

13 *Pliny says that in Ethiopia there are some savage men who are called Gorgoires. These men are horned like cows and have feet with cloven hoofs like goats.*

14 *He [Pliny] says that in Ethiopia towards the city of Heliopolis are savage and marvelous men who are very large. For they are fully six feet tall and seven feet wide at the shoulders, and they are hairy. . . . And also their heads are disproportionally large and broad. And also their ears are so big and wide that they more closely resemble wings to fly with than ears to hear with.*

15 *He [Solinus] says that another bird lives there called tragoppa, which is bigger than an eagle and which has horns similar to those of a ram with which it defends itself against other birds.*

—Figg and Friedman, pp. 210–20 (chap. 18)

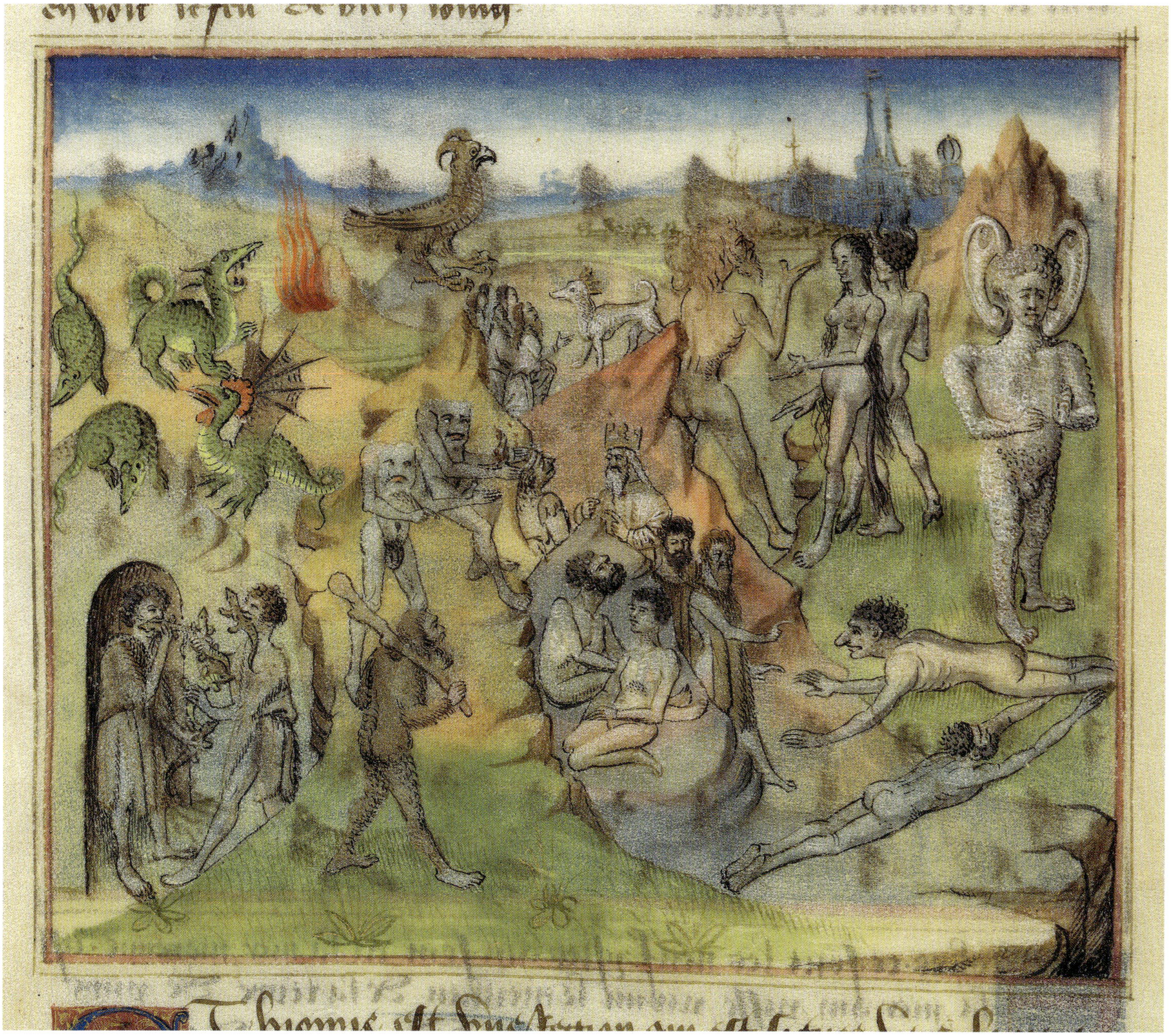

MORGAN, FOL. 26V
(GETTY, MISSING)

PLATE 9

GAUL [FRANCE]

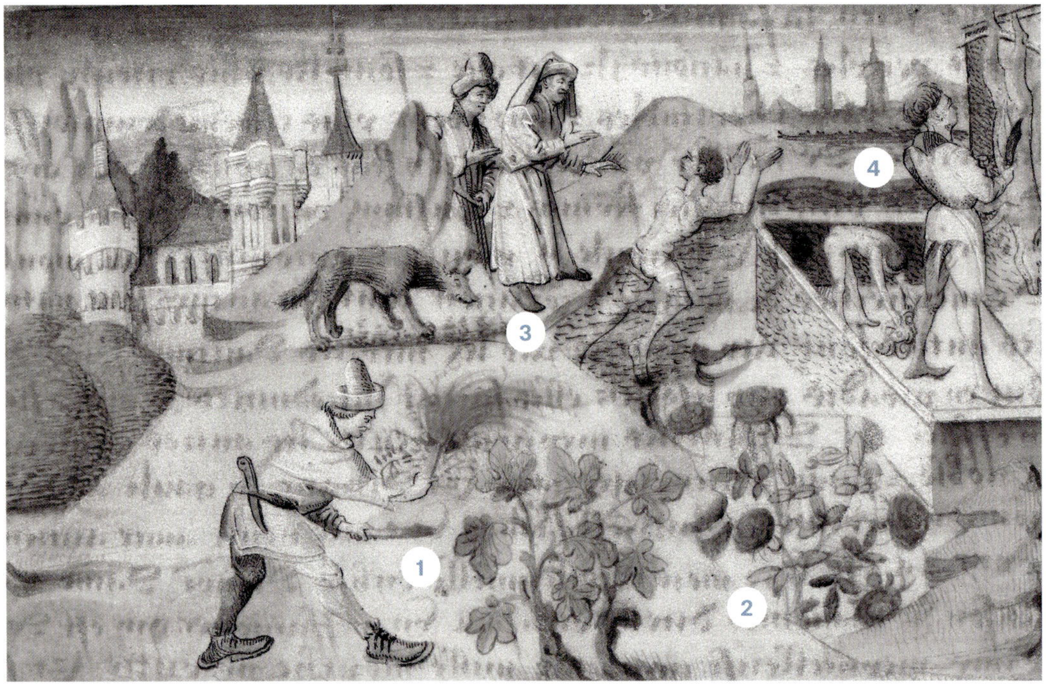

1 *Gervaise says in the province of Narbonne near the castles of Montpellier and Montferrant there is a great marvel. For he says that there is a field full of bracken, briars, thorns, and heath, but when one sets fire to it to burn off these thorns and briars and immediately afterward this field is tilled diligently by the plow, the next year following there will appear and grow vines bearing grapes, without anyone in the world having planted a vineyard or tilled the soil. And in this vineyard grow and are harvested such fine wine grapes that none better grow anywhere in the country.*

2 *[T]here was a similar case of the same sort in the country of Orléans near a castle called Saint Simon in Beauce. And he [Gervaise] says that there is a field which every year is tilled and ploughed two or three times, as thoroughly as if one intended to sow good wheat, to which field come and grow a very great quantity of rosebushes that bear a multitude of beautiful vermilion roses, fine smelling and flowering often.*

3 *Gervaise tells us of another example on this subject and says that near a castle called Calcebara, which is near Viviers, it happened that there was a man of the region who was accustomed at certain times to strip himself nude at the foot of a mountain and leave his clothing there, and then lie totally naked in the sand, and there he would turn and toast himself in this sand. And in doing this he lost his human form and was transmuted and transformed into a wolf.*

4 *In Auvergne there is a castle called Trest where a great marvel occurs every Saturday night. For when the butchers who live in this city have killed any beef, sheep, or other animals to feed the people of the town, they disembowel and clean out all the animals in the middle of a certain public area that is in the town, and in this place they leave all the entrails, blood, and offal of these beasts. But as soon as the butchers have carried off their meat to their shops, there come at night certain invisible spirits that carry off the aforementioned offal and filth, but no one knows where, and they render the place as clean and as dry as it was before, for which the inhabitants of this country have very great joy.*

—Figg and Friedman, pp. 222–29 (chap. 22)

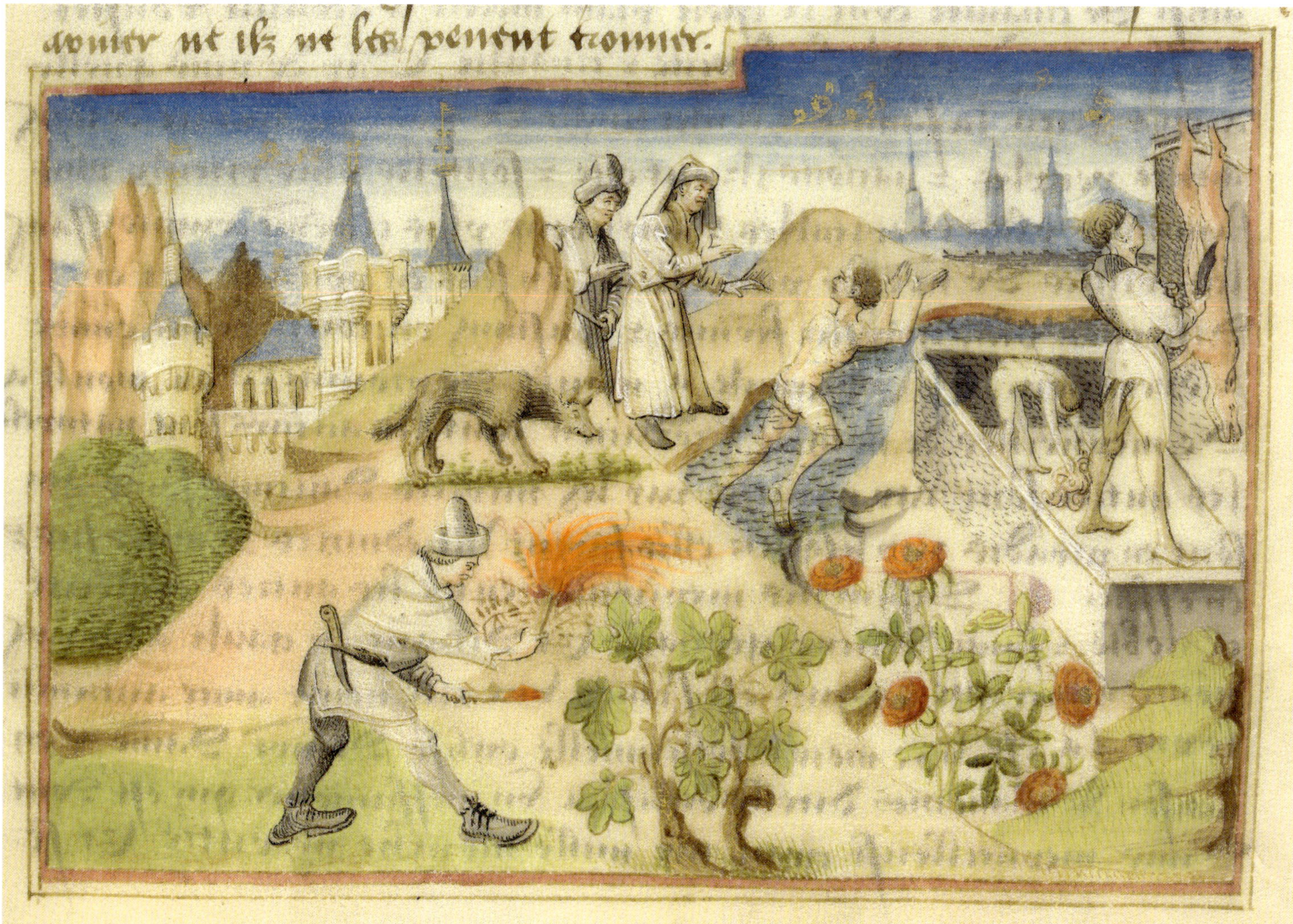

MORGAN, FOL. 33R
(GETTY, MISSING)

PLATE 10

SPAIN

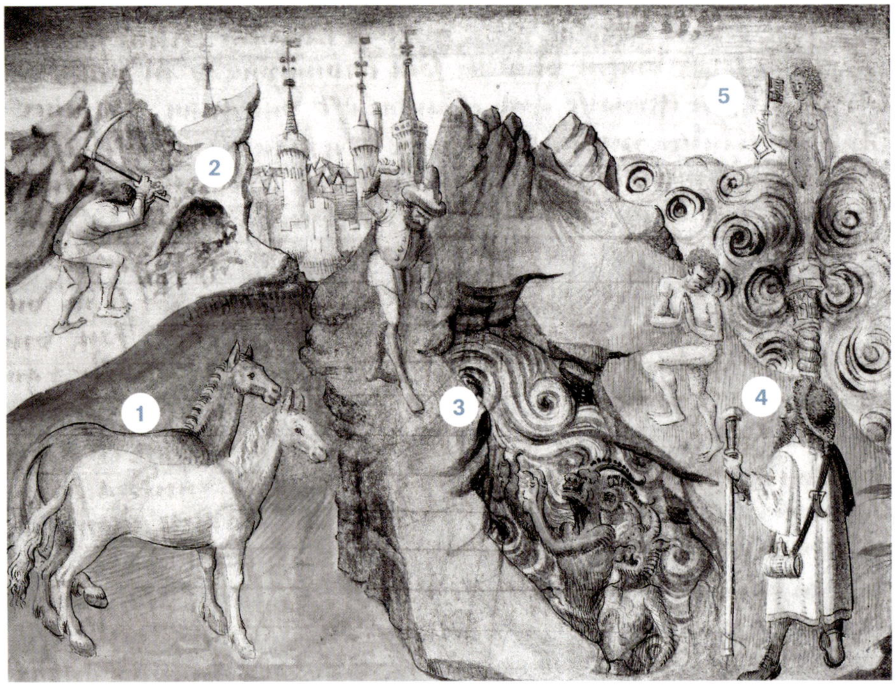

1 *[T]he mares, during the season when the soft and gentle wind Favonius [Zephyrus] is blowing above them, even though they be without the company of their stallions that we call horses and are grazing on the grass of the fields or the mountains all alone, when the month of May comes, they become pregnant by breathing in this wind, without being covered by their stallions.*

2 *[W]hen one has taken some of this salt and made a great ditch in the rocks by means of an iron pickaxe and one has carried the salt away, as soon as there is a sudden downfall of rain on the mountain, the hole that has been made in the rock will be filled up by the water level with the earth, and it will become salt as good and firm as before.*

3 *Gervaise says in Catalonia there is a very high mountain. And at the very top is a lake so deep that no man has ever found the bottom, and its water is hideously black and very frightening to behold. And the inhabitants of the country say that at the bottom of this lake is a palace that is a very marvelous and remarkable edifice. And in this palace live devils from hell. And if it happens that any man throws a stone into this lake, then the devils are enraged and, to avenge their injury, they stir up great rumblings in the form of thunder, lightning, and storms.*

4 *[I]t happened that a pilgrim was passing by this aforesaid mountain where the lake was, and he saw a man who went running and weeping around this mountain, and who expressed many piteous regrets. . . . Then this pilgrim hastened to go tell Peter of the Table the news that he had heard of his daughter. And he counseled him to go to the aforementioned place to implore the devils that they return his daughter. . . . And he conjured and called together the devils and commanded them by God all powerful that they return his daughter to him. And immediately there came the stirring of a great whirlwind and a great storm, in which he was suddenly presented with his daughter.*

5 *[W]hen Charlemagne the great conquered Spain, he destroyed all the pagan and Muslim idols. The exception was one idol that was in the region of Andalus, which he could not destroy or knock down, or act against in any way. This idol was of bronze and seated on a great column of stone and was raised to a great height near the seashore. And it had the right side of its face towards the South and held a key in its right hand. And the ancient Muslims said of this marvelous idol that Mahomet forged and built it. And inside was enclosed a legion of devils which rose to the number of six thousand, six hundred, and sixty-six devils. And he gave to this idol such great authority and power that no Christian could approach it without being quickly trampled and buried in the earth or drowned in the sea.*

—Figg and Friedman, pp. 230–33 (chap. 24)

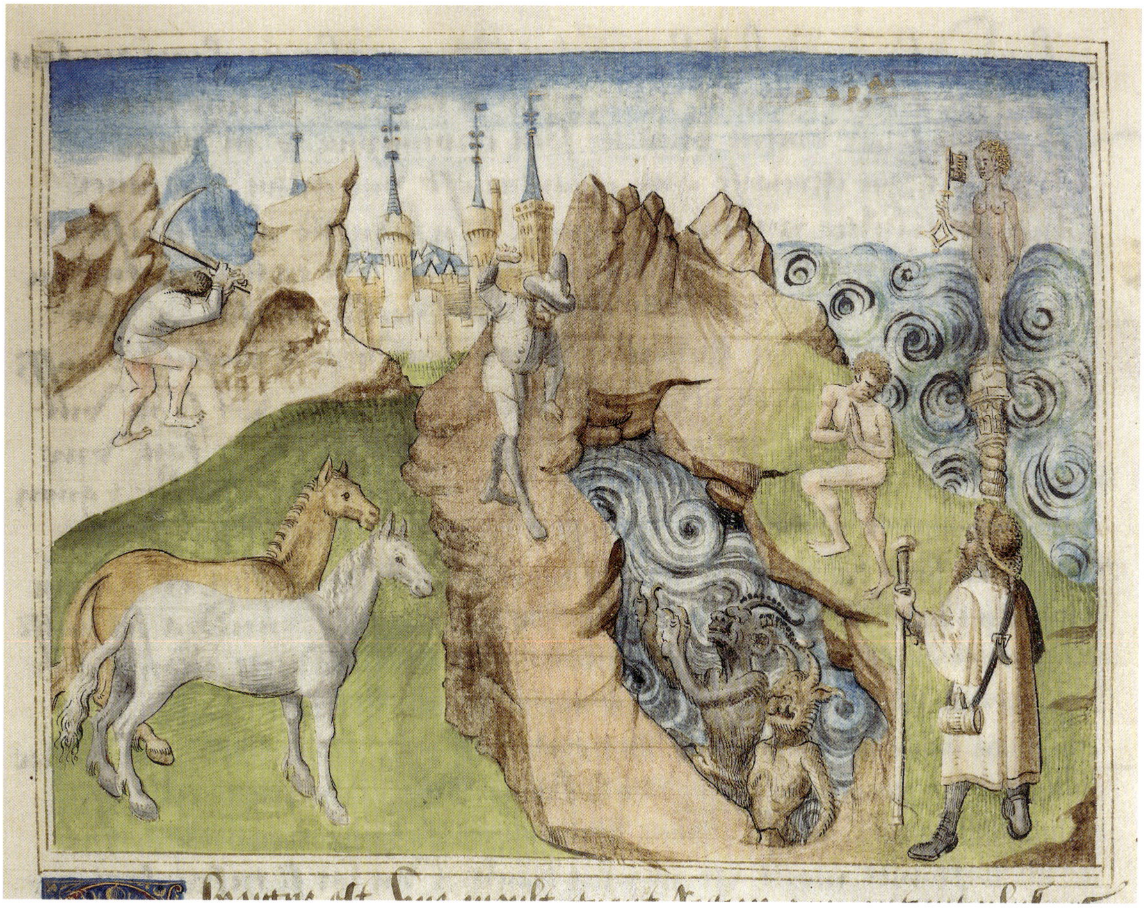

MORGAN, FOL. 38R

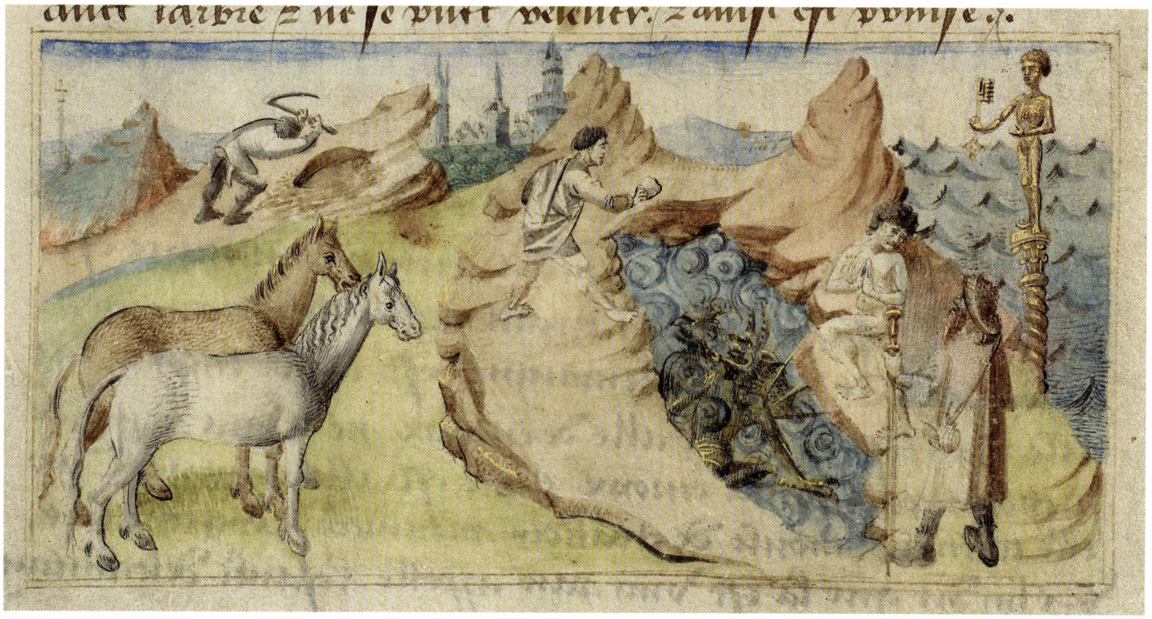

GETTY, FOL. 1V

PLATE 11

IBERNIA [IRELAND]

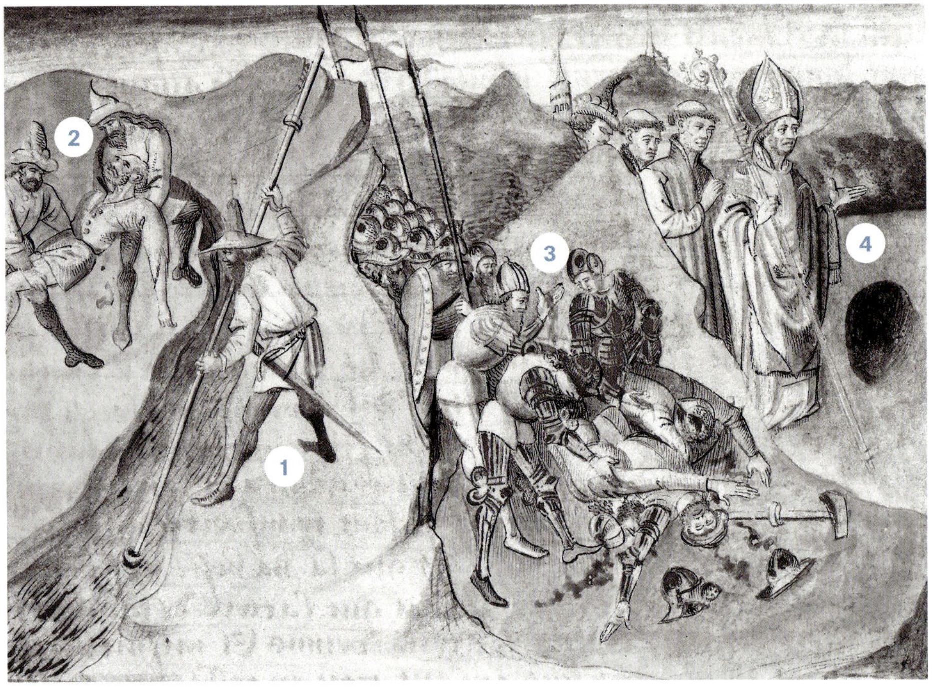

1 *[T]here is a lake that is of a very marvelous nature. For if any one throws or thrusts a lance or other sharp shaft into it, the part that is stuck in the earth is naturally converted and changed into iron. And the part that is in the water is changed into stone. And the other part that remains outside the water stays in its natural state of wood, as it was when it was thrown.*

2 *There is a most marvelous island whose inhabitants' dead bodies, when they are buried there, never rot and remain always whole.*

3 *[W]hen the people of Ibernia have gained any victory over their enemies they drink the blood of the dead and wash their faces and their hands in it.*

4 *Gerald in his book* Marvels of the World *says, in speaking of Ibernia, that near the far end of this island is a province called Monomie, where is to be found a very large opening like the mouth of a very deep well. And he says that it was revealed to the bishop Saint Patrick that this was the entrance to Purgatory and that all Christian men who would enter therein willingly and patiently endure all the dangers there would never have another purgatory.*

—Figg and Friedman, pp. 233–35 (chap. 25)

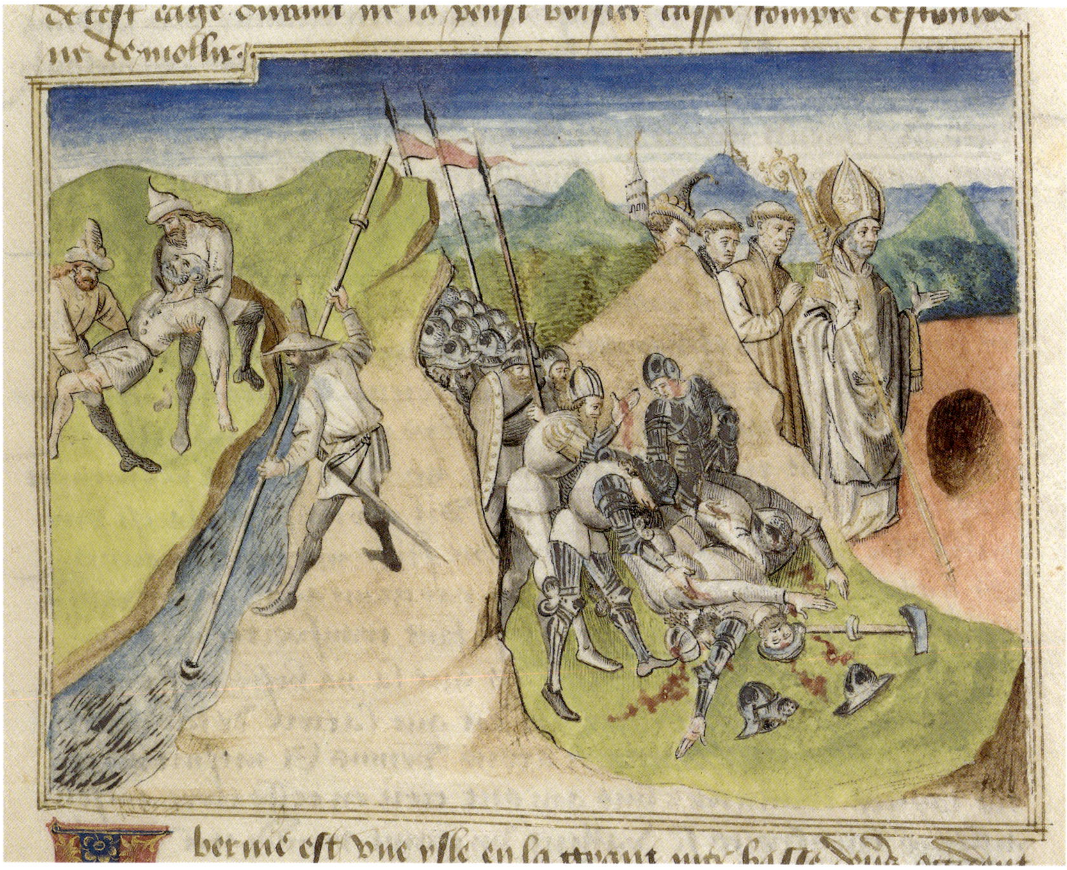

MORGAN, FOL. 40R

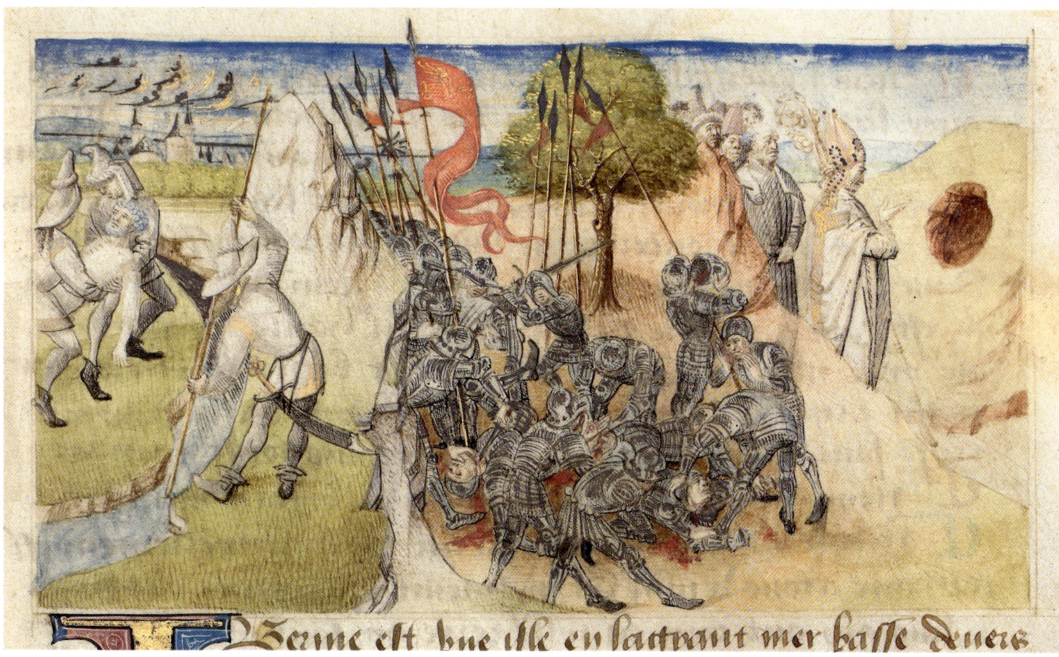

GETTY, FOL. 4R

PLATE 12

INDIA

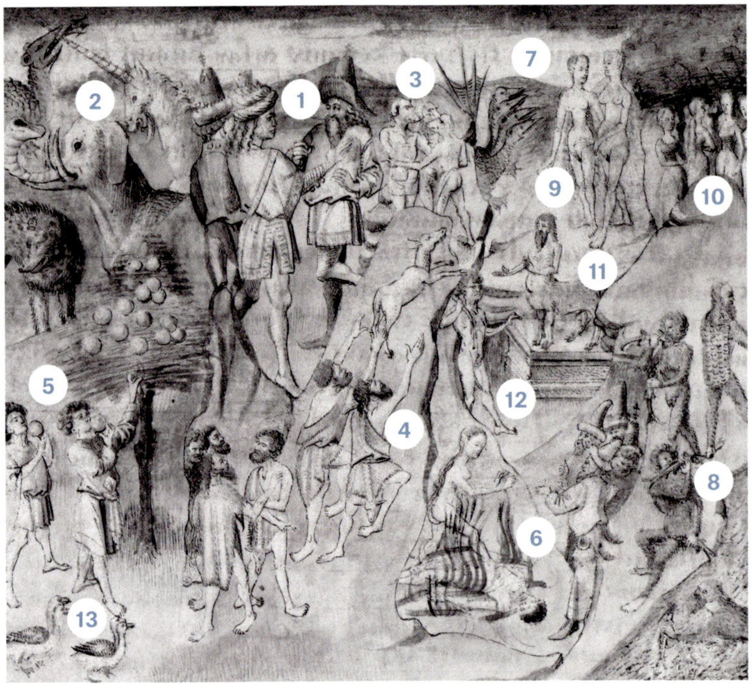

1 *And in this region the men are as large as giants. And they are six or seven cubits in height.*

2 *Solinus says that in India there are unicorns, elephants, and dragons in great numbers.*

3 *Solinus says that in India there are some mountains whose inhabitants have heads and faces similar to the heads and muzzles of dogs.*

4 *Pliny says that there are other men there who have the soles of their feet reversed—that is to say, what is on the top is instead on the bottom. Pliny says that these people have eight toes on their feet and are dressed in the skins of wild beasts that they capture and on which they live.*

5 *Pliny says that in a certain province of India are certain men who have no mouths at all and neither eat nor drink, but live solely on the smells of trees and flowers.*

6 *And when a married man dies and is being burned in a fire, as said before, one of the man's wives [comes] before all the relatives, saying that she has been the most chaste and the most faithful and that she loved her husband best; then she throws herself into the fire of her own free will after her husband, and thus dies.*

7 *Solinus says that in the* Letter of King Alexander, *there are, among the great marvels in India, great serpents and dragons, of which some have three heads and others four, and on each head they have a forked tongue.*

8 *He [Solinus] says that towards the farthest part of India near a great river he saw men as naked and hairy as wild beasts that are always in this river and eat only raw fish.*

9 *He [Solinus] says that in India he found along the banks of the river Odinani huge women, all naked, who were in the river and had hair hanging down to the ground. . . . And when they captured a man . . . they forced him to have carnal company with them. . . . And of this race of women Alexander took just two who were very beautiful and fair.*

10 *[I]n India towards the very farthest region in the East there is a woods that is extremely pleasant and delightful where there live maidens and young women who surpass all other women in beauty.*

11 *There they have an idol of another type that is half man and half ox and is most subtly forged and made of gold and silver.*

12 *They have another marvelous custom in India to adore and sacrifice to their idol. . . . Then the one who wishes to make the sacrifice takes the knife that he hung from his neck and slices a gobbet of flesh from his body. . . . Then he strikes himself with the knife through the heart.*

13 *He [Odoricus] says that in the aforementioned island there are birds that are shaped like geese and have two heads.*

—Figg and Friedman, pp. 235–51 (chap. 26)

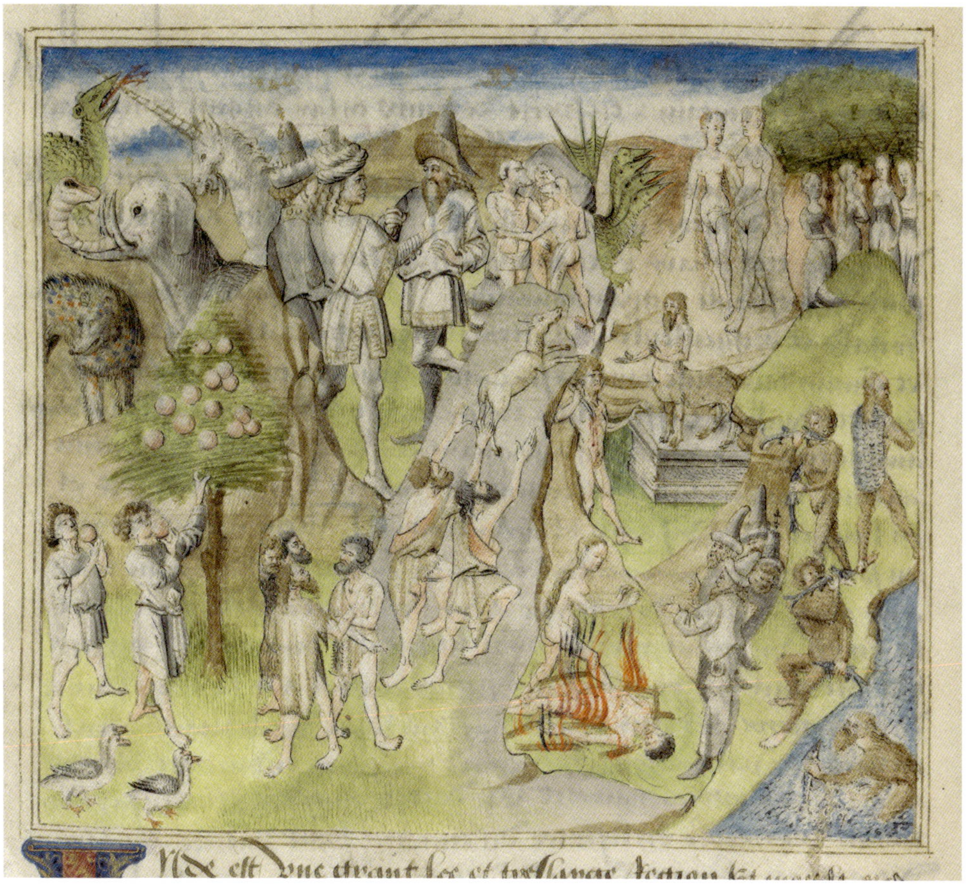

MORGAN, FOL. 41V

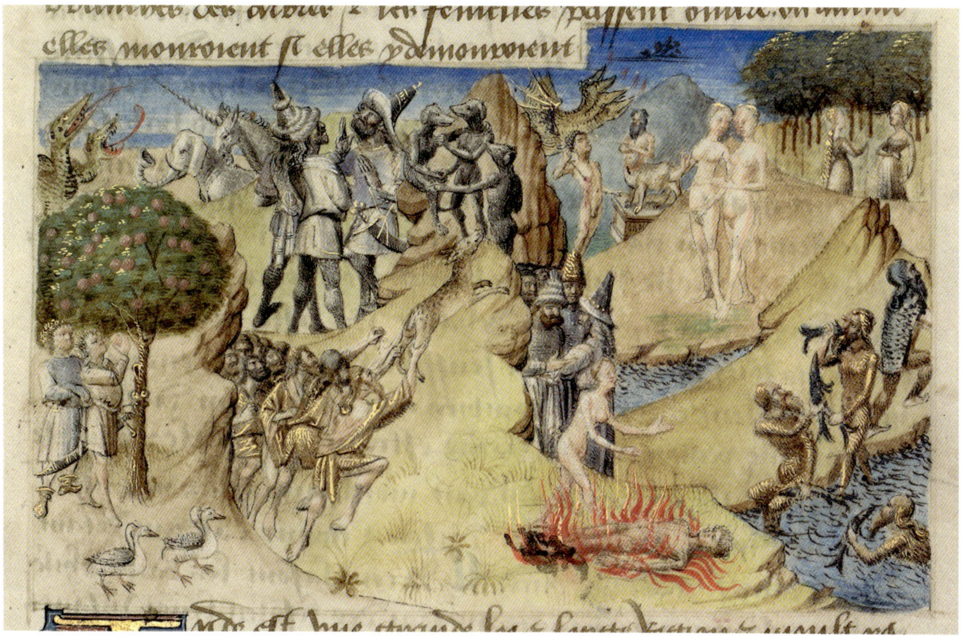

GETTY, FOL. 5R

PLATE 13

ITALY

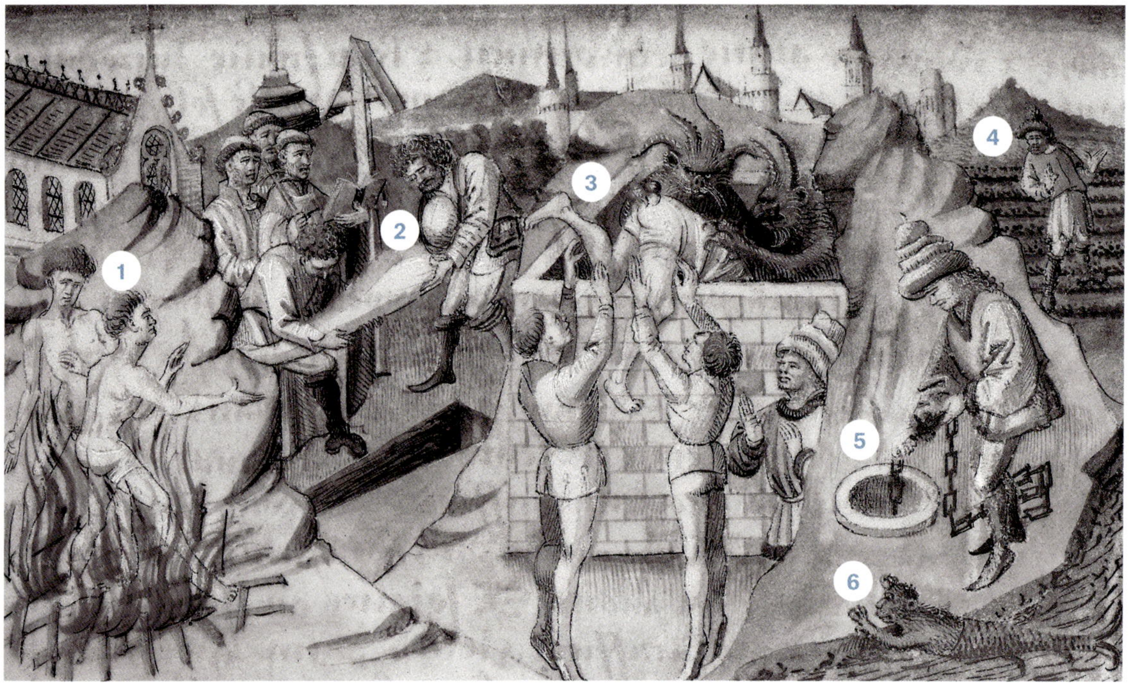

1 *[I]n Italy were once certain people named Hirpes, who were not among the most noble, who had such a power within themselves that they walked and could go and come through a great burning fire without feeling it or having any burns or discomfort at all.*

2 *[I]n Italy in the diocese of Saurinenne there is a cemetery near an abbey where only the monks and religious of the place are buried, and no others, which has a marvelous power and nature. For three days after one will have buried the body of any of the religious of this abbey, if anyone comes to dig or break up the earth in the grave where the body is buried, he will find there no evidence of a corpse, neither flesh nor bones. And one must say that the body has been completely consumed and reduced to nothing or that it has been invisibly transported elsewhere.*

3 *[T]here is a lake that was formerly dedicated and assigned to devils to make their dwelling there. . . . And if any other person were to go there, the devils would immediately and cruelly kill him. And in order to avoid these great perils, high and thick walls were constructed there. . . . [E]ach year the city must, as a mark of tribute and servitude, put a living man over the walls and into the enclosure of this lake, handing him over to the devils who make their habitation there. . . . [T]he people of this city . . . choose and elect an evildoer who is condemned to death for his misdeeds, they keep him until the time that their tribute is due, and then they deliver him to the devils in the manner just described. And if they default in paying the tribute and this tax on the appointed date, the city and all the country around it would be most terribly tormented and persecuted.*

4 *[I]f any laborer, burgess or other person of the country is going to die in a particular year, when his soil is ploughed, in the furrow of the tilled land will clearly appear a great effusion of blood, and this blood signifies the coming death of the person who is the heir of the land where this sign occurred.*

5 *[I]n Italy is a city named Viturbo in which there is a very deep well whose water boils more vigorously within than it would in a cauldron on the fire. . . . And what is more, whoever would throw or cast an iron chain into this well and would immediately after pull it out, would find that from the great heat and warmth of the water of this well the chain will be all reddened and much diminished.*

6 *[I]n the area descending from the mountains called Alps is a lake from which flows a very swiftly running river, and along the banks of the said river lives a beast called beaver, that is half animal and half fish. And, therefore, from the animal portion forward it lives on the earth along the banks of the water. And for the portion in the nature of a fish, it remains swimming in the water.*

7 *Gervaise says that in Italy after the death of Julius Caesar there appeared in the heaven three suns shining in the eastern sky, all in one hour.* [This detail does not appear in the Morgan manuscript but does appear in the Getty manuscript.]

—Figg and Friedman, pp. 253–57 (chap. 29)

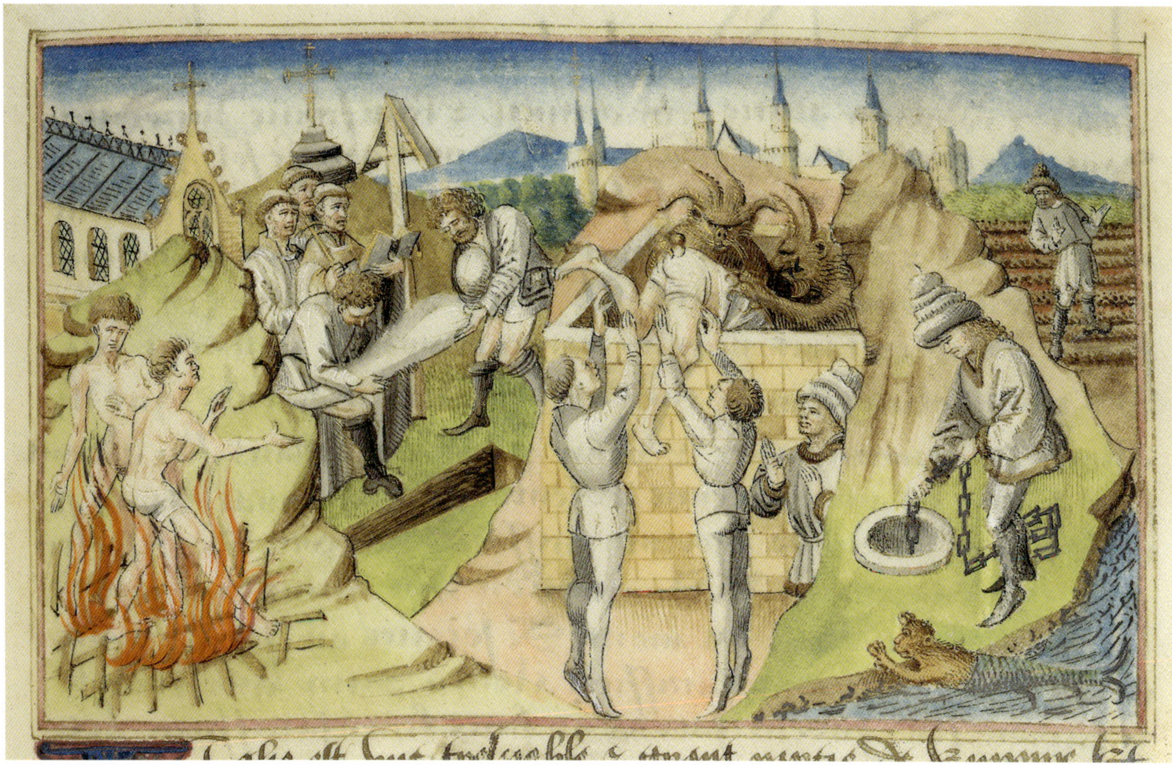

MORGAN, FOL. 51R

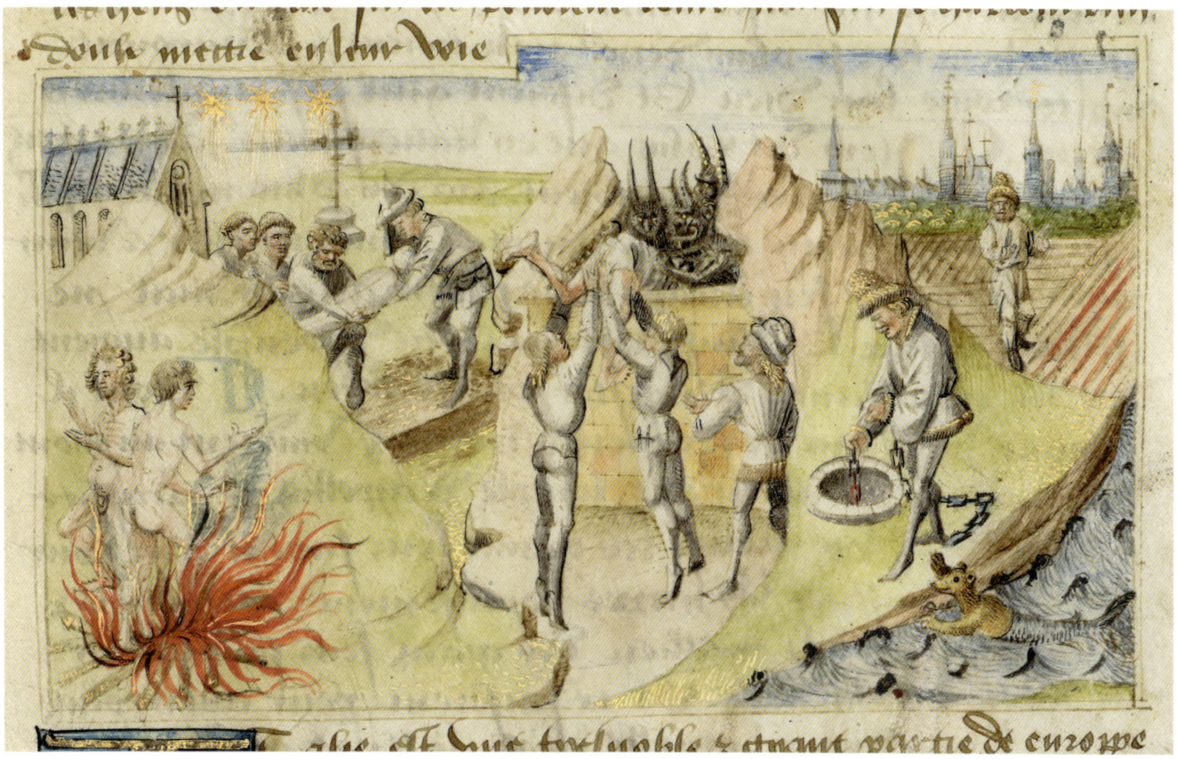

GETTY, FOL. 14R

PLATE 14

PYGMY [IN JUDEA]

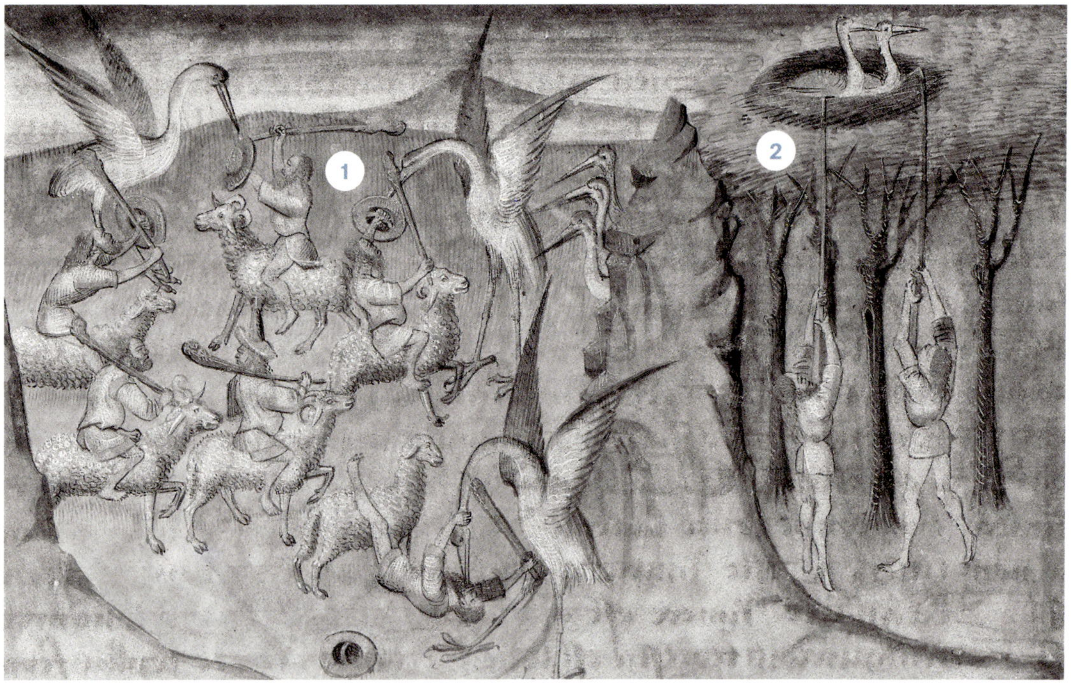

1 *Pigmy is a province in greater Judea of which Pliny speaks and says that the population and inhabitants of this province are of very small height and size. . . . And even though they may be small, they are subtle and of great courage. And in place of horses or of asses they transport themselves on sheep, which they ride just as if they were horses. . . . Pliny says that between this people and the cranes and storks there is a marvelously great war. And, in fact, when it gets to be summertime, these people assemble a great throng mounted on sheep and ewes furnished and strengthened with certain devices and make war against the cranes and storks. And similarly the cranes make war against them.*

2 *And when these people can find their nests, they break and destroy their eggs and kill the young storks in order that they may not grow in number or multiply or that they may not be able to come with great force and power to run or fly against them.*

—Figg and Friedman, p. 267 (chap. 41)

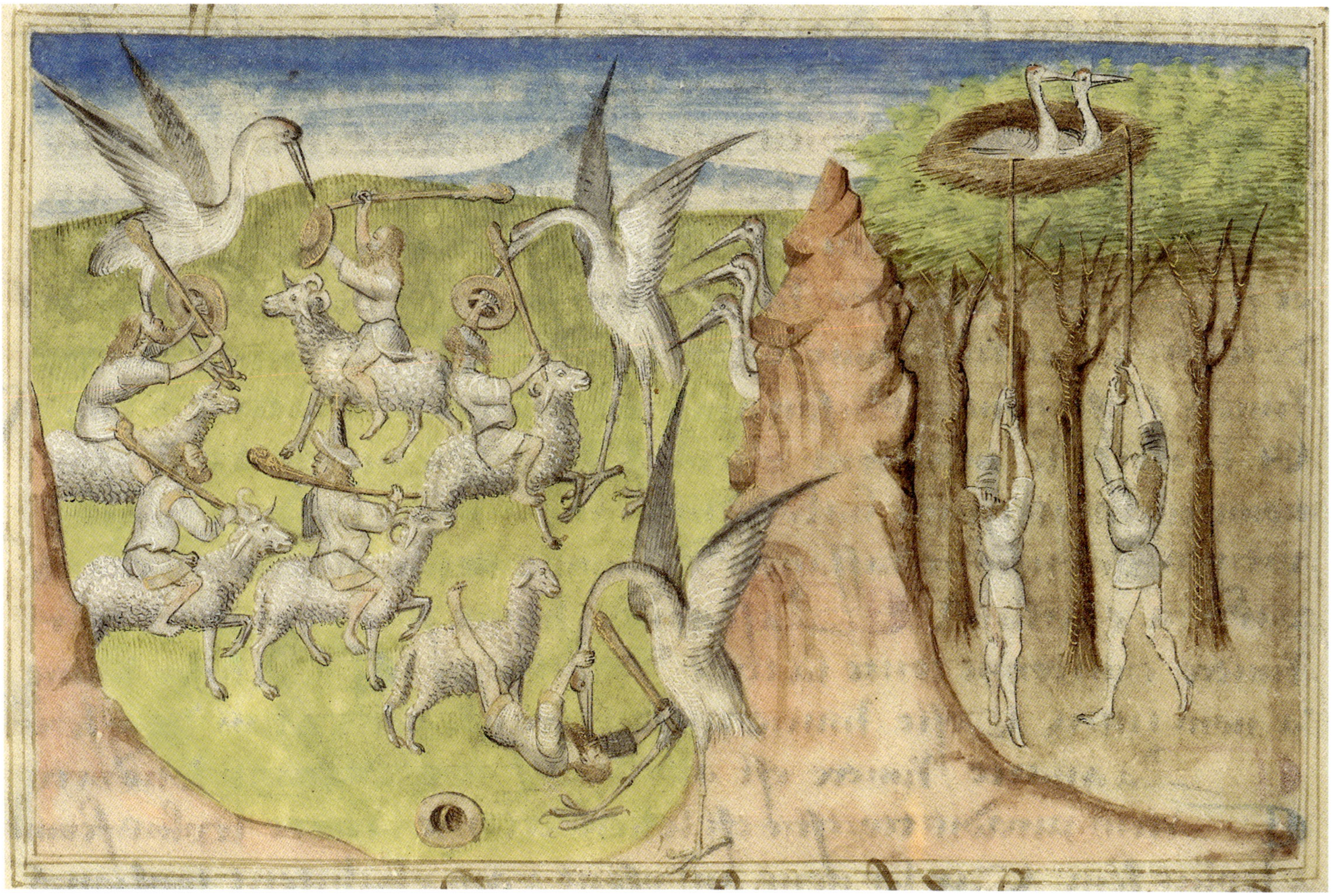

MORGAN, FOL. 61V
(GETTY, MISSING)

PLATE 15

PROVENCE [IN FRANCE]

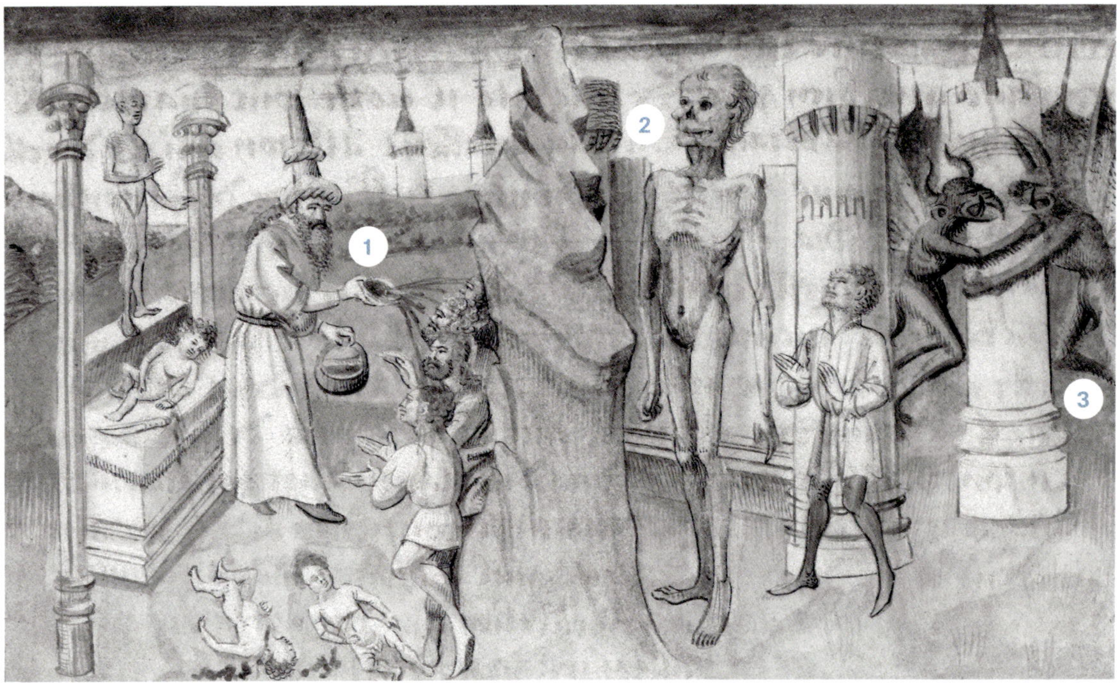

1 *[E]very year, on the first day of May, they bought three young children with the money of the commonwealth, whom they killed and whose bodies they sacrificed to their idols. And all the blood that had flowed from these three young children they scattered and threw on the heads of the people of the city. And they said that the innocent blood was cast on them for the salvation of the people. And they made this sacrifice long ago in a place called The Rock that is in a suburb of this city between two very high columns of stone.*

2 *[T]here was found the body of a giant named Pallas that was complete in the flesh and bones and was in no way abased. And thus for more than a thousand years this great giant had been buried there when he was, by command of the emperor, disinterred, and, through the strength of men, raised and lifted against the walls of Rome, but his height surmounted the height of the walls of the city of Rome. The body of this giant had in his side a wound four feet in length.*

3 *[I]n the city of Vienne there is a tower that the devils brought and put into place there all in one piece. And the ancient sages of the country say that in this tower was once formerly held prisoner a cleric who was expert in magic arts, who thus, as he was enclosed in this tower, convoked and called before him by his arts and knowledge the devils, by whom he had himself carried, within the tower, to the village of Vienne; and this tower is still there.*

—Figg and Friedman, pp. 270–79 (chap. 43)

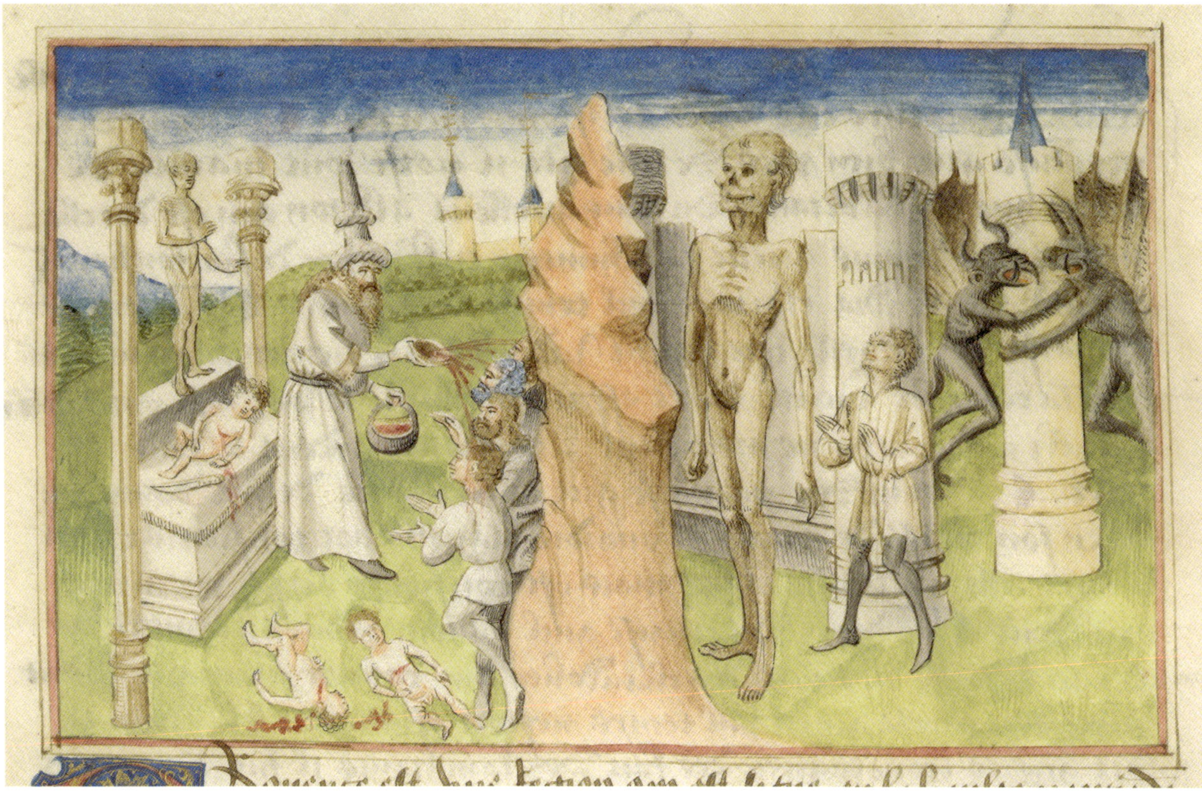

MORGAN, FOL. 64R

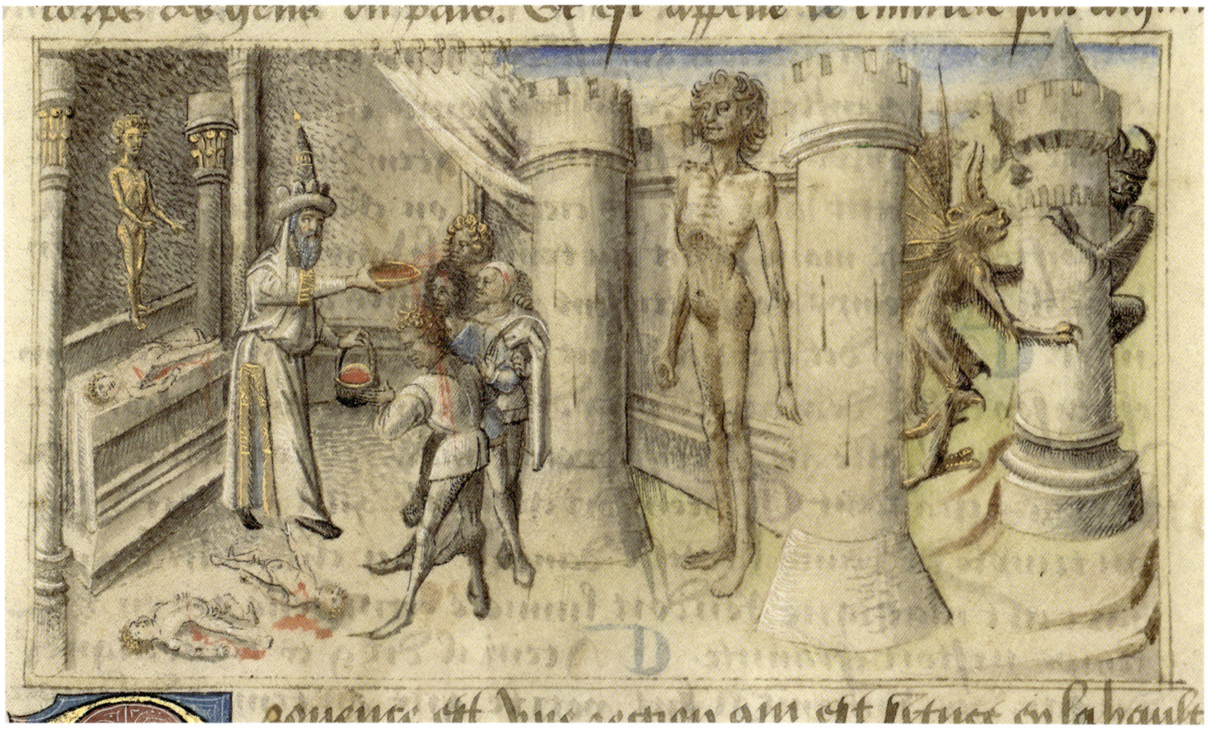

GETTY, FOL. 20R

PLATE 16

SCYTHIA [NORTH OF THE BLACK SEA]

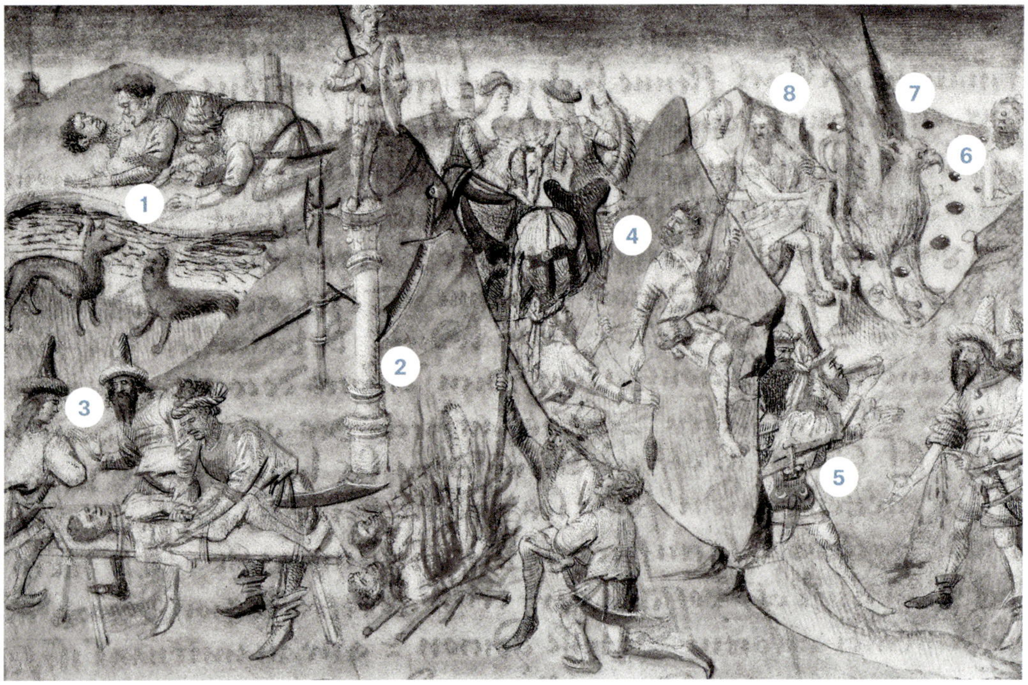

1 *[T]here is a province called Neutria through which flows the river Borriscenes, and on the banks of this river live people who are of such a nature that on certain days of the summertime, when they pass through the waters of this river, they are transfigured and become wolves and live only on raw flesh.*

2 *These men adore for their god the idol Mars, god of battles. And they make to him offerings and oblations of swords, knives, and spears. And they make the fire for their sacrifice from dead men's bones. They offer living men to their god and put them in this fire and burn them up.*

3 *[T]here is a province called Gelonne, otherwise called Anthropophagus, where the inhabitants are of such a condition that when they have overcome their enemies and taken and vanquished them in battle, they skin them alive, and from their skins they make new clothing for themselves and they make caparisons and trappings for their horses, in order to give a particularly horrifying example to their other enemies and frighten them.*

4 *[T]here are certain Sarmathian people who . . . have an amazing custom and way of living, for these men do and carry out all the tasks that women customarily perform elsewhere, such as spinning, combing wool, and making and washing with lye. And the women do all the things that customarily belong to men, such as buying and selling, riding on horseback, and taking arms against their enemies for the defense of their country.*

5 *These people have the custom of drinking one another's blood to seal all of their alliances and all their treaties and promises just as we here reach out to each other our hands as a sign of faith and loyalty and promise, and never, after they have drunk each other's blood, will they break or tear asunder their agreements and promises, even if they must die.*

6 *In Scythia is a region called Gesolithon in which live certain people named Arismappes who have only one eye on the forehead. And they are men of marvelous power and size, and in the high mountains they guard rich precious stones, especially emeralds, so that they will not be taken and carried away.*

7 *In this place are to be found great and horrible griffons who war against all those who wish to go there to attain and carry off the emeralds.*

8 *In Scythia there is an island of people named Ysprodes. . . . [T]hese people have the features and appearance of men and women, according to the dispositions of all the human members—except for their feet, which are like the feet of horses.*

—Figg and Friedman, pp. 281–86 (chap. 47)

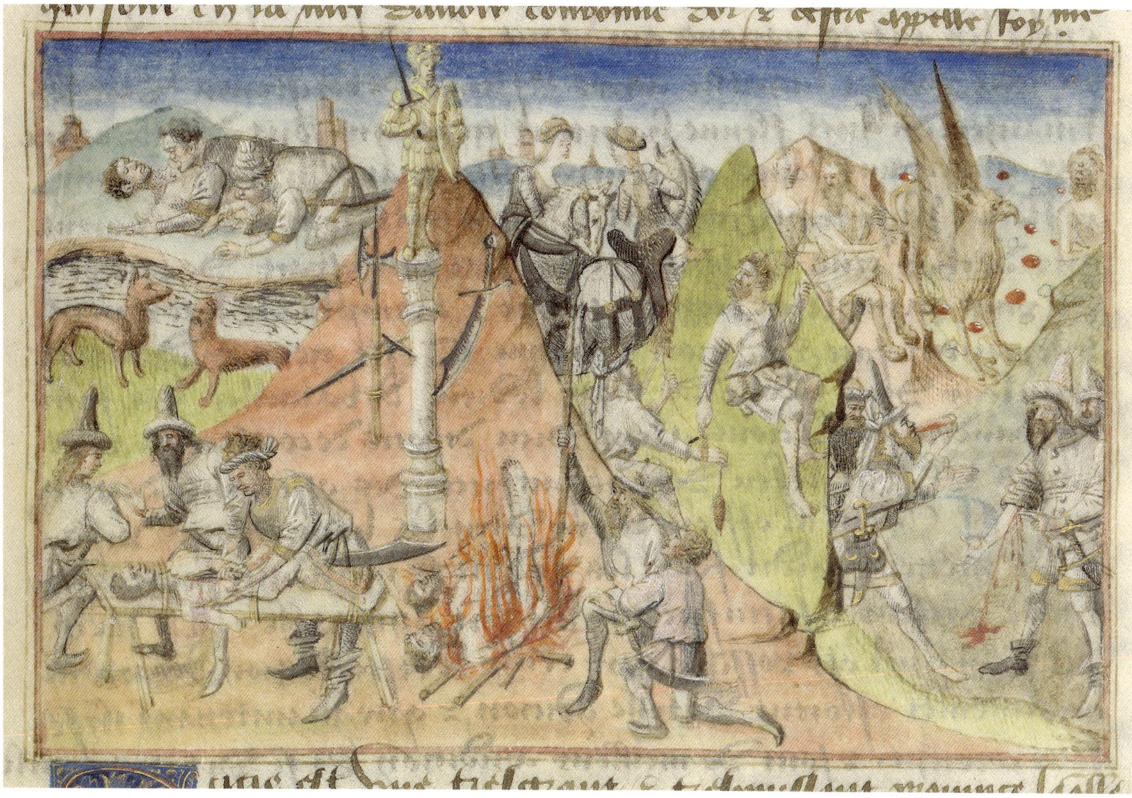

MORGAN, FOL. 70R

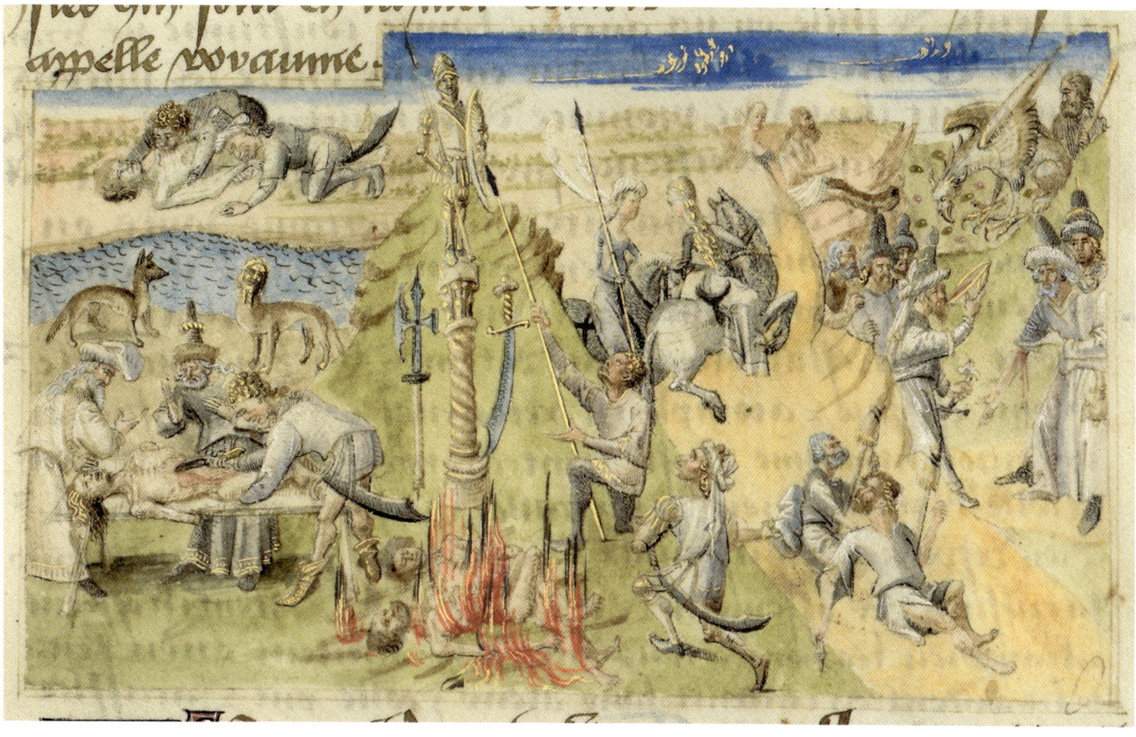

GETTY, FOL. 26R

PLATE 17

SERES [CHINA]

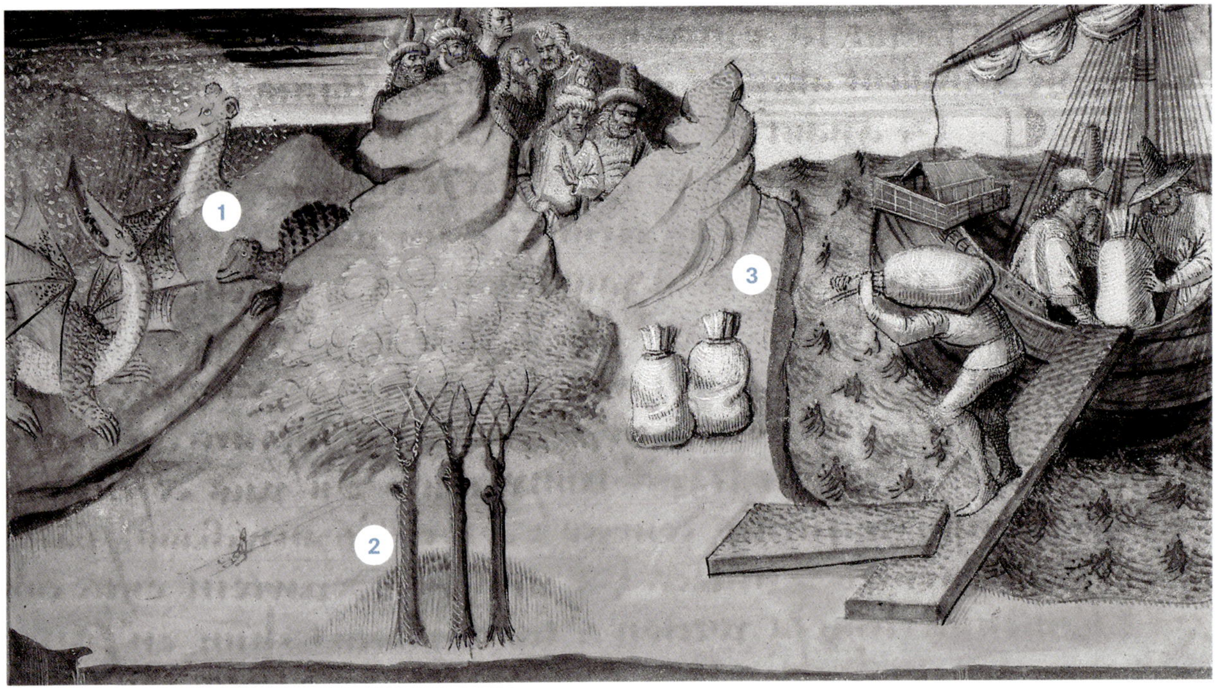

1 *China is a small region situated towards the East which is so extremely far from the habitation of men of other nations or condition that no man can, except with great difficulty and great danger, go there or gain access to it, for several reasons. . . . Also the deserts there are so great and so terrible and so full of ravenous, wild, venomous beasts like tigers, wolves, serpents, and dragons, that no one would be able to go there in a simple way without being killed.*

2 *The region of the Seres is thus named because that is where silk grows in most great abundance in certain trees, and it seems to be a kind of moss, which the men of the country collect and out of which they make cloth and garments for their use.*

3 *[W]hen merchants from other foreign countries come and arrive at any port in the region of Seres in order to do some mercantile business in the country, they do not find anyone to speak with, neither an interpreter nor indeed anyone whatsoever. But when they wish to obtain any of the goods of the country, they deposit on the seashores some grain, some wine, and whatever other merchandise they have brought with them. And then they will leave and will not return there until three days have passed. During this time, the people of the country of Seres come to examine and look over what kind of goods and how many the foreign merchants have brought there and presented to them. . . . And then, according to their opinion and conscience, in the most equitable way they can, they carry to the same place and location on the seashore as much or more of their own goods and merchandise. . . . Then, after the three days, the foreign merchants return from wherever they had gone off to in order to distance themselves, and return to the said port on the seashore and load their vessels with the goods and merchandise that the Seres have brought for them on the seashore.*

—Figg and Friedman, pp. 289–90 (chap. 51)

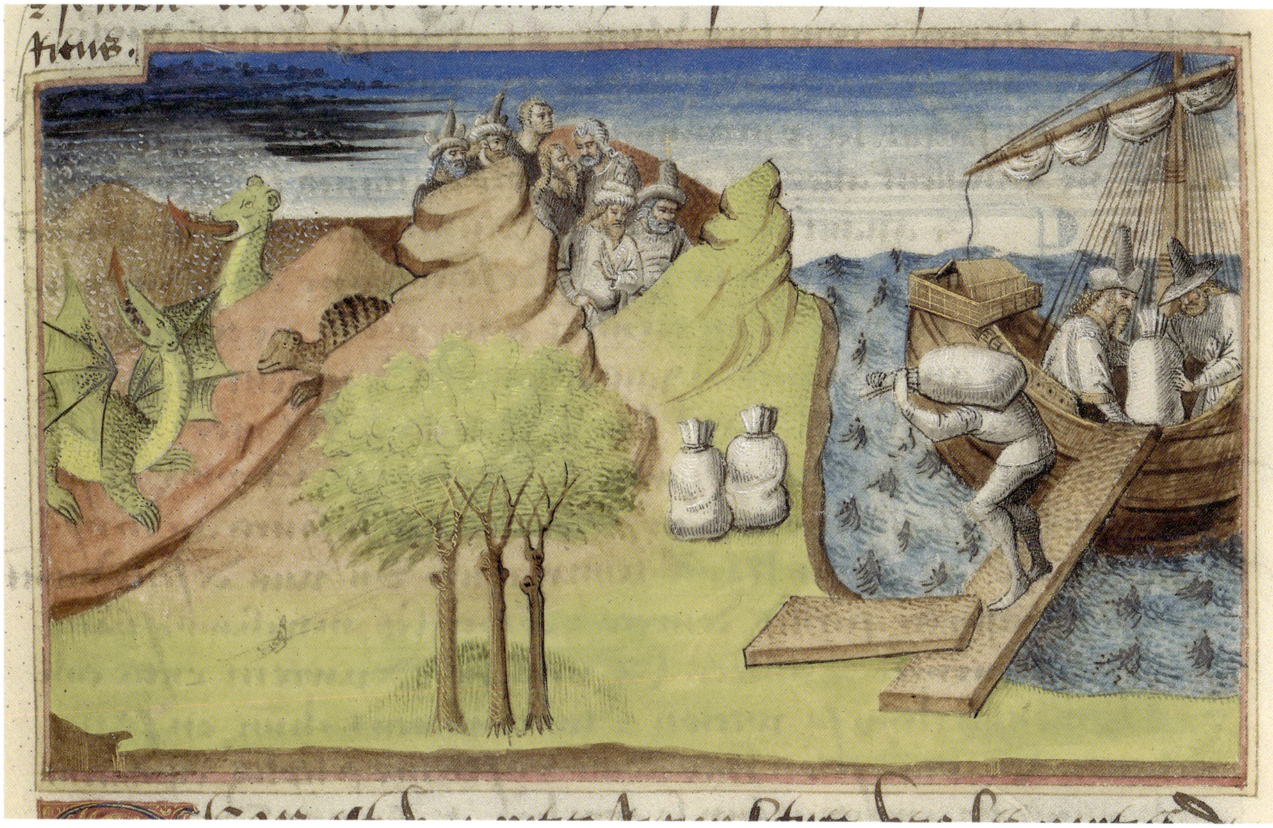

MORGAN, FOL. 75R

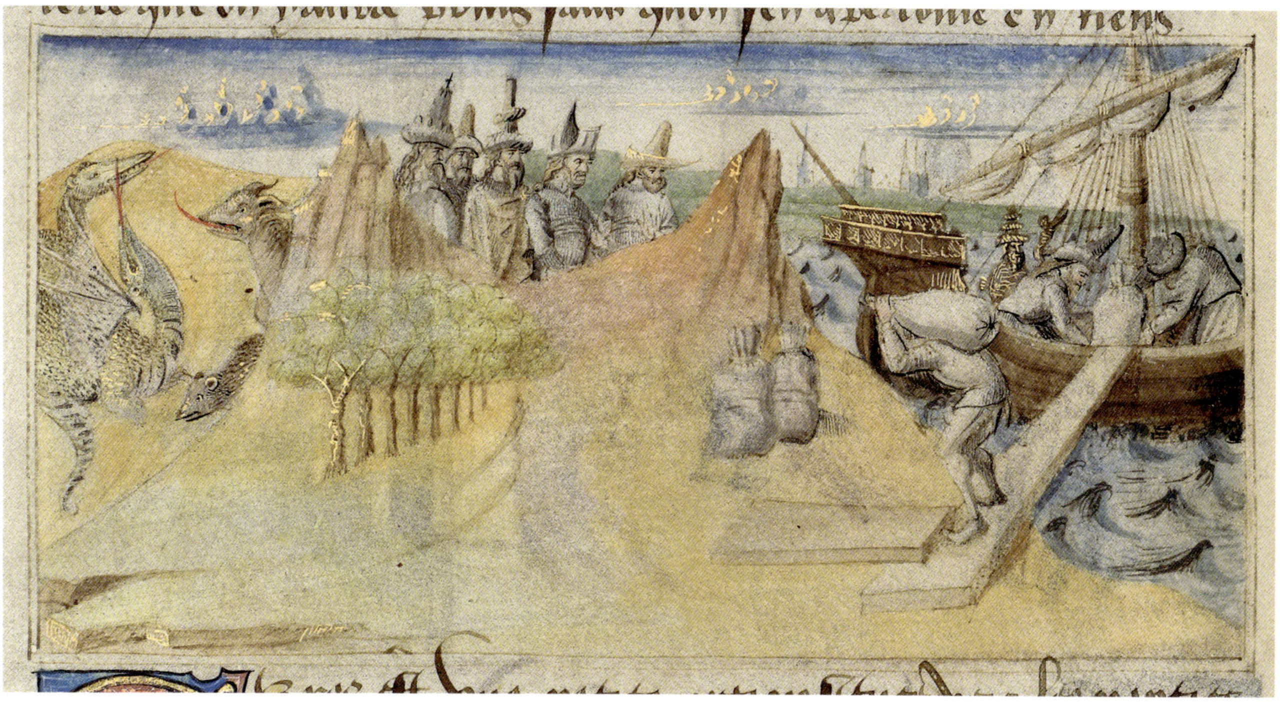

GETTY, FOL. 30V

PLATE 18

THULE [POSSIBLY ORKNEY, HEBRIDES, SHETLAND, OR ICELAND]

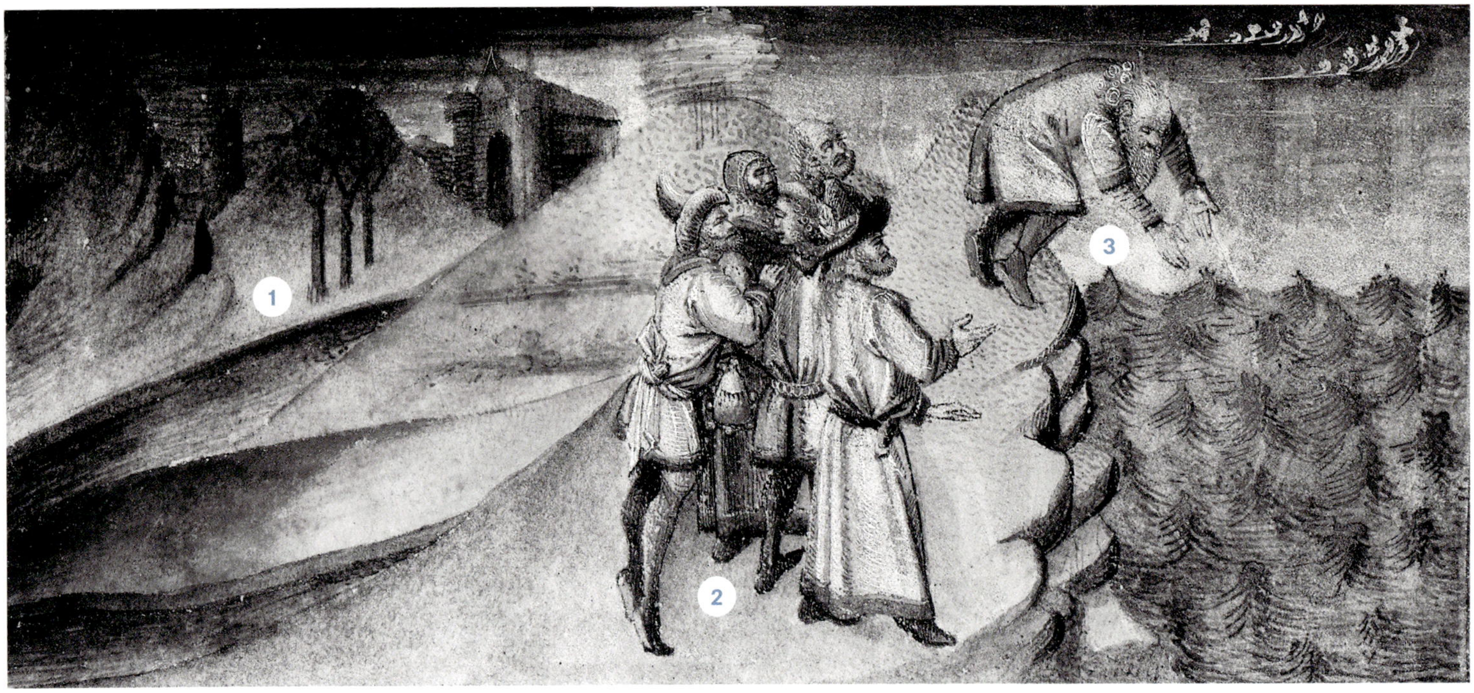

1 *[I]n some part of the North, one sees the sun continually for a period of six months and then, after this half year, for a period of six months one does not see it. . . . For in the summertime, around the middle of the month of June, the sun is always shining at all hours. And when it comes to wintertime, around the middle of the month of December, it is always night and one does not see the sun at all.*

2 *Pliny says that the people who live in this land lead an honorable and good life. For they love peace, unity, and accord, and they hate all war and discord, and they are long-lived and never ill.*

3 *And when the time comes that they are aged and they are very old and decrepit, they throw themselves into the sea and drown. And they say that there is no manner of dying as beautiful and good as drowning oneself in the sea.*

—Figg and Friedman, pp. 290–91 (chap. 53)

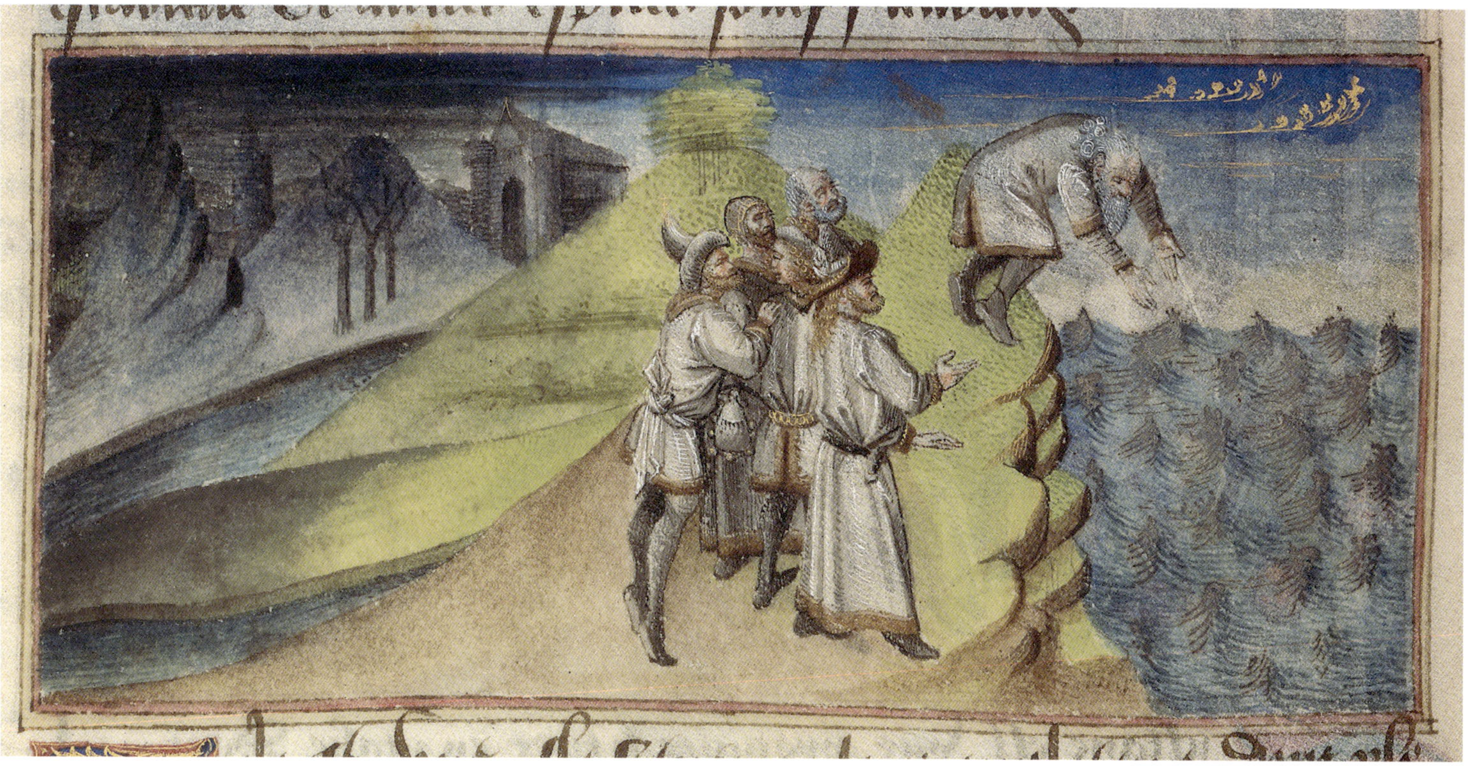

MORGAN, FOL. 76V

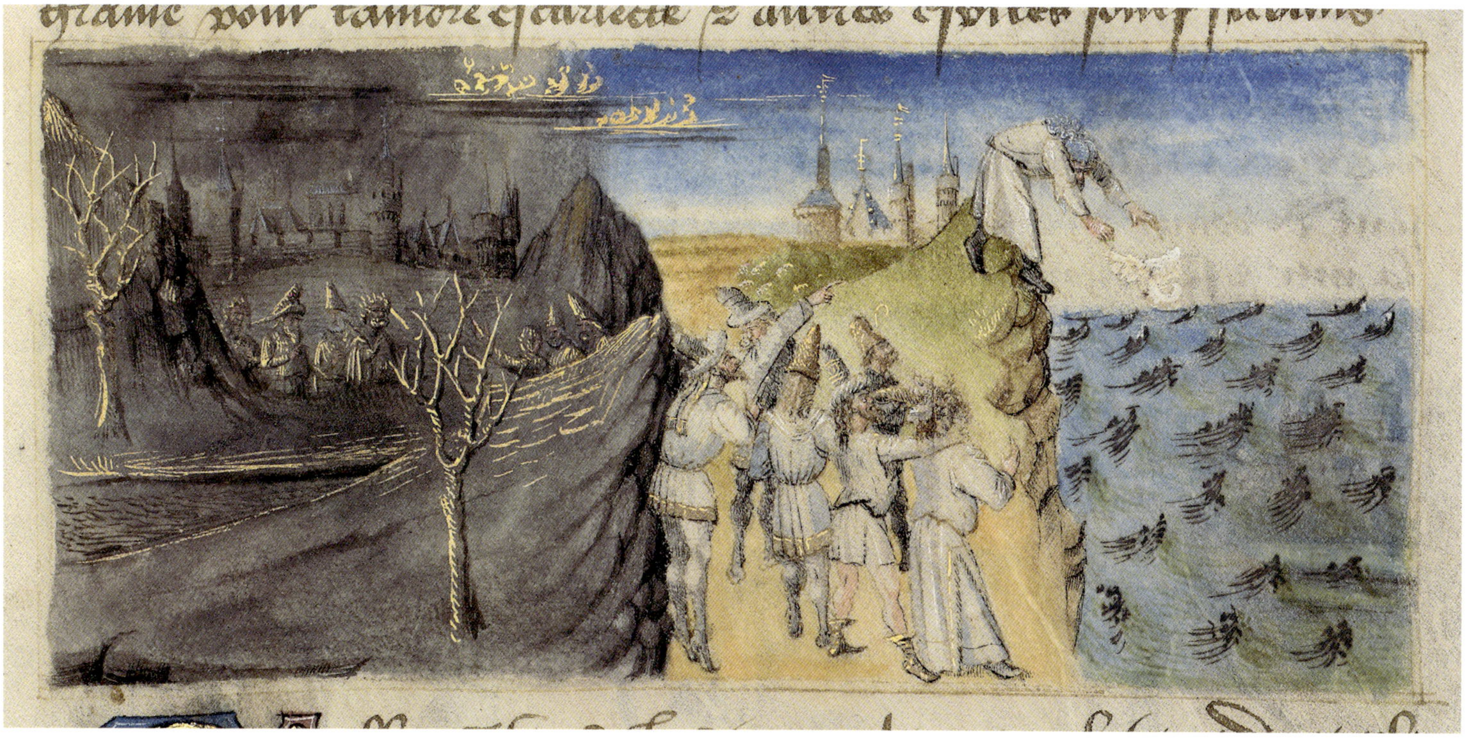

GETTY, FOL. 31R

PLATE 19

TRAPONEE [SRI LANKA]

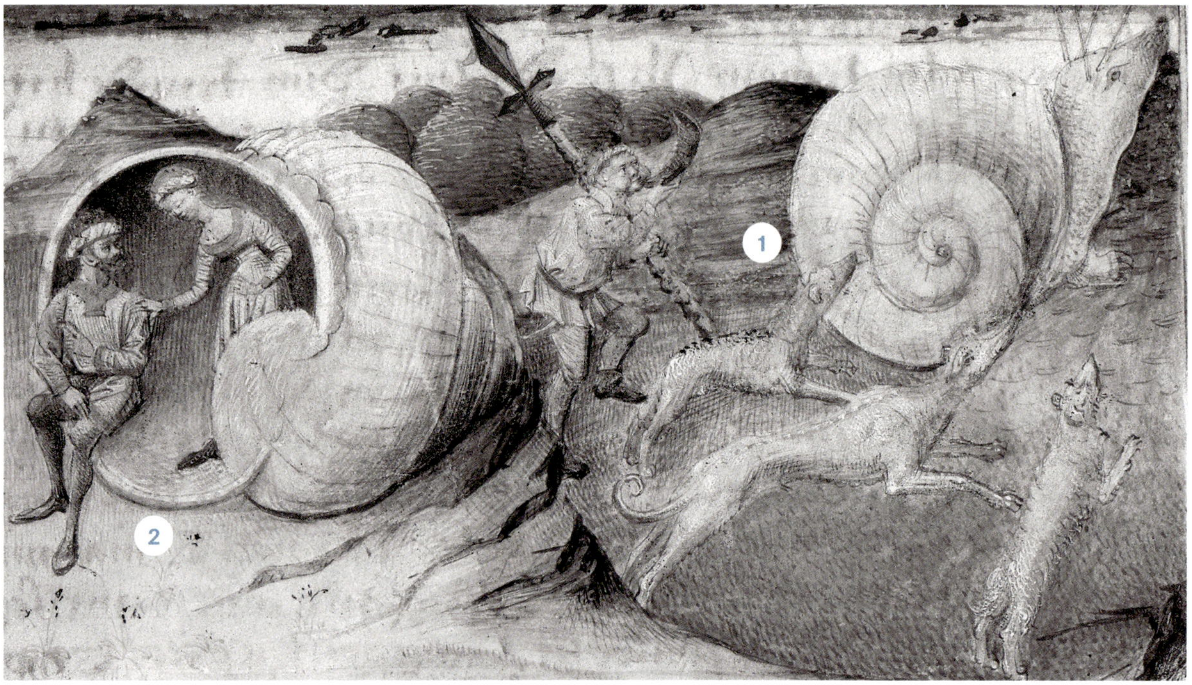

1 *Solinus says that among the progeny of Traponee grow the biggest snails that exist in the world, and they move so quickly that it is a marvel, and the men of the country hunt and chase them as we over here hunt wild animals. And the people of the region live on their flesh.*

2 *And the shells are so big that the men and women of the country live inside them, and they have no other houses or habitations.*

—Figg and Friedman, pp. 292–93 (chap. 55)

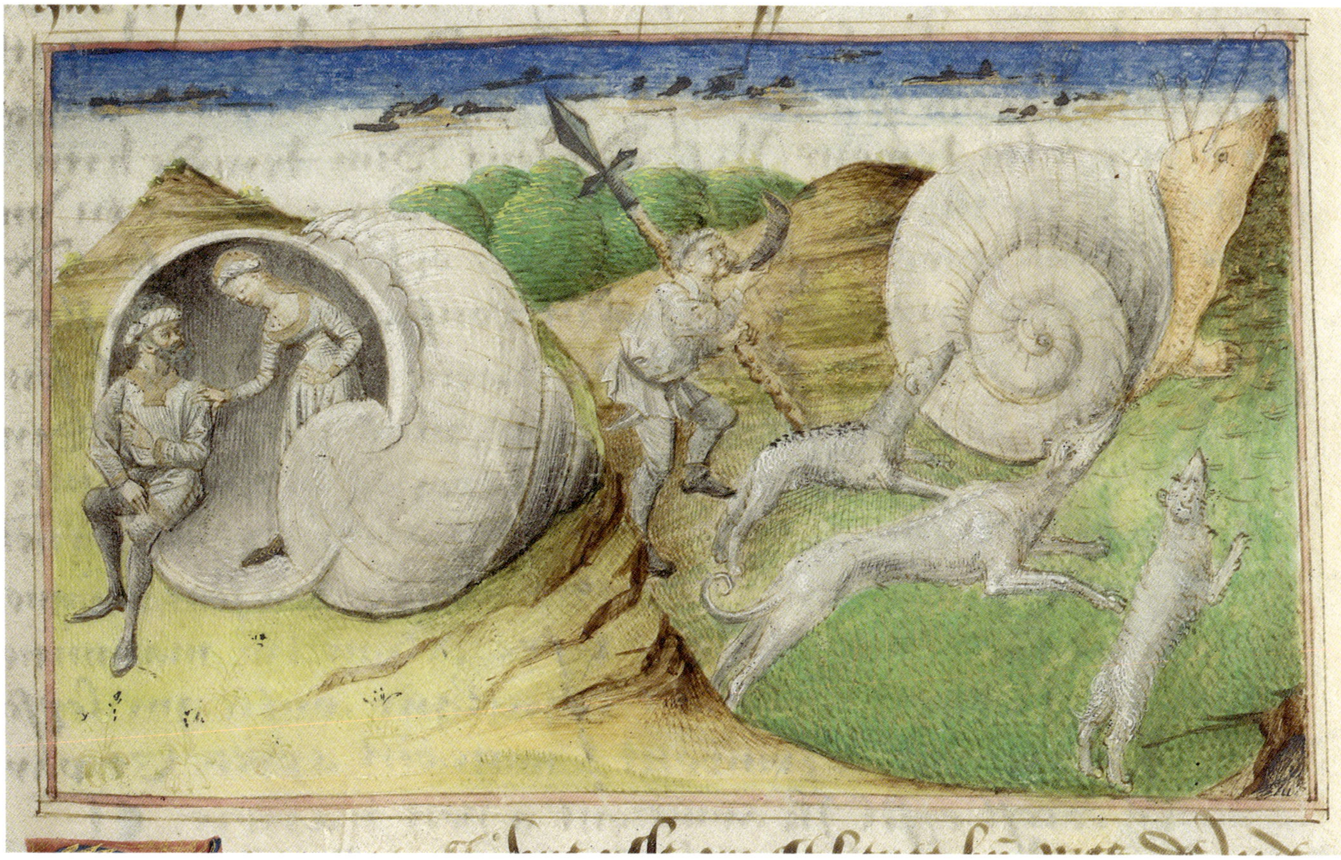

MORGAN, FOL. 78R

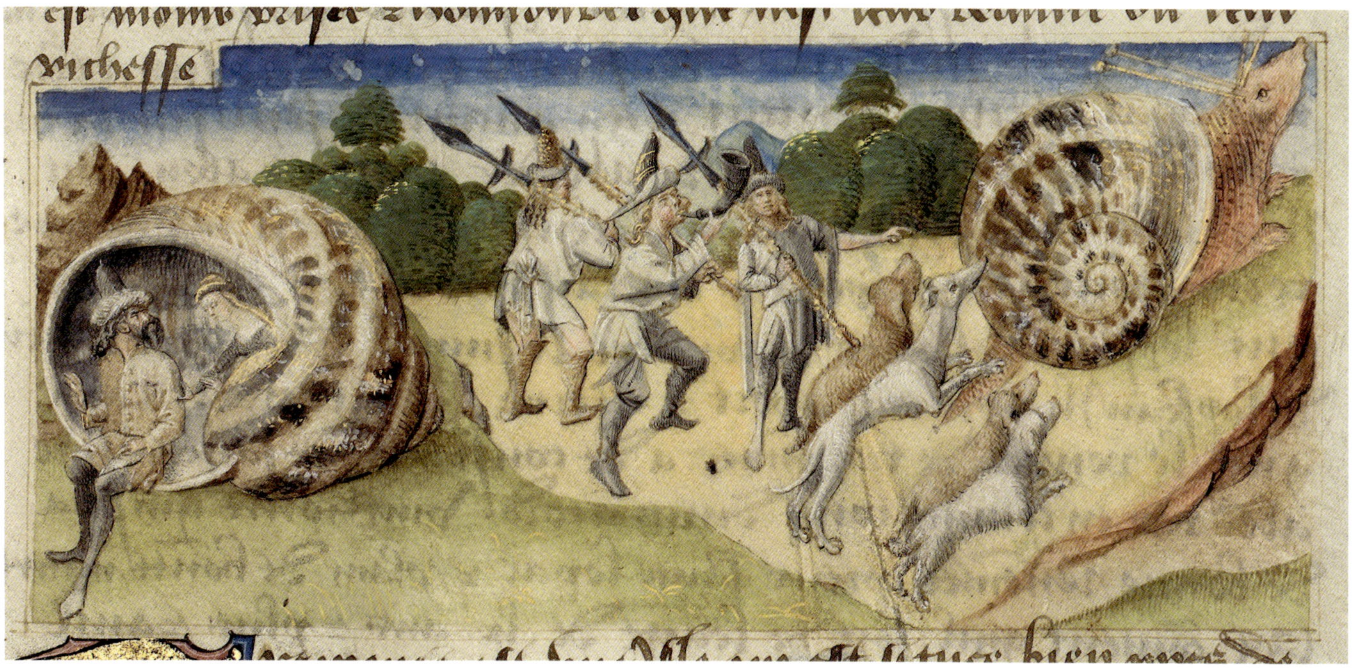

GETTY, FOL. 32R

PLATE 20

ULULAND [IN NORWAY]

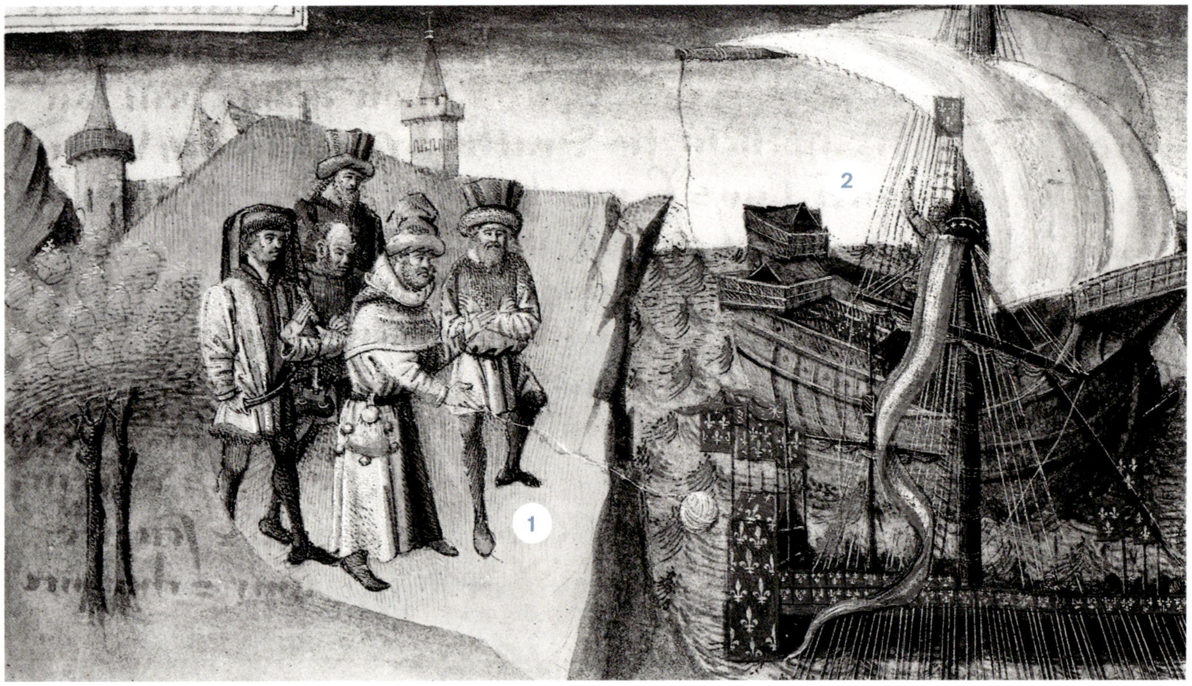

1 *[W]hen the men of Vinland wish to make them have wind, they take a big pile of twine and throw it in the sea, either nearby or far away, according to whether they wish to have a big wind or a small one. Then they call the devils, who immediately come to the ones who move the air and the sea. And they make it blow around the ship of the mariners and merchants, and it seems to the said mariners that it is a good wind that has come to them.*

2 *And when these merchants have gone a little ways into the ocean, then the devils put into motion so great a tempest and so great a raging sea that they are all drowned and their ships are riven, horribly tossed, sunken, and broken to pieces. And thus the poor merchants perish because they believed in the art and science of magic and devilry, and they lose their bodies and souls and all their chattels.*

—Figg and Friedman, pp. 293–94 (chap. 56)

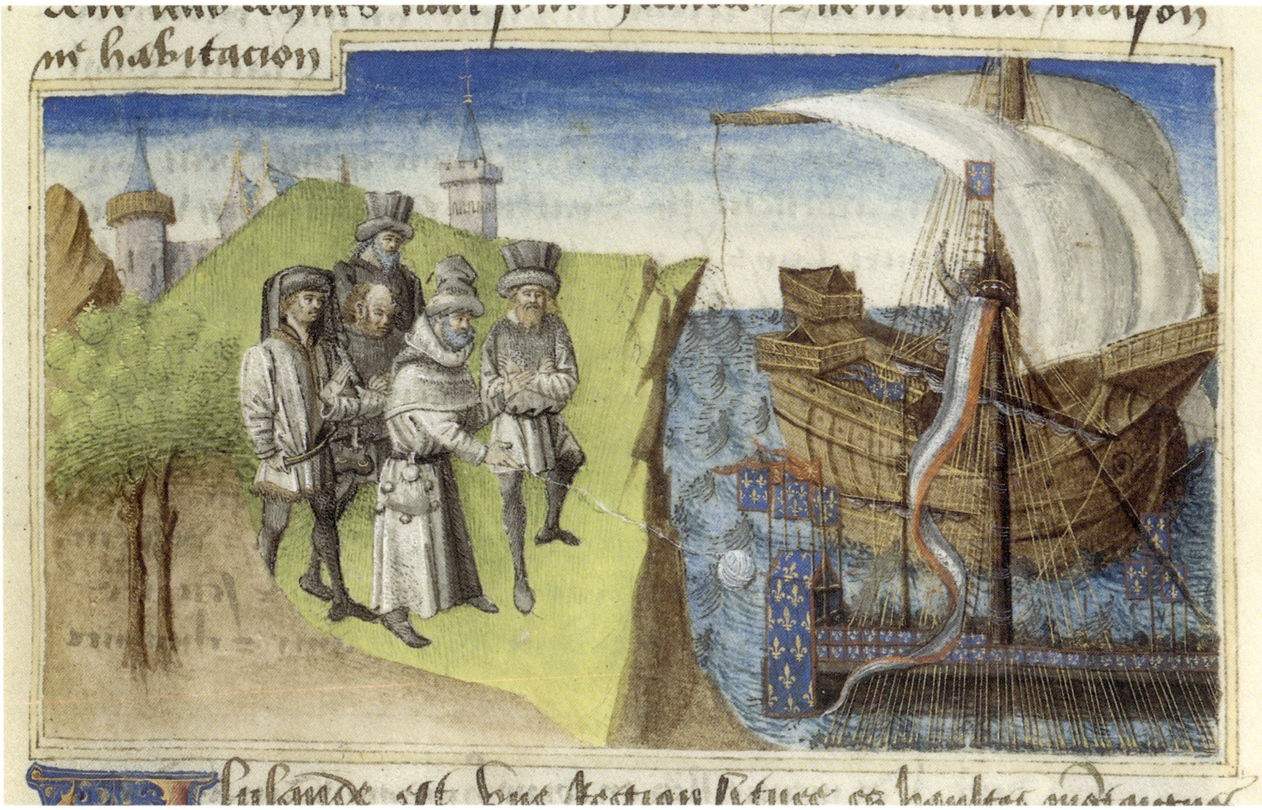

MORGAN, FOL. 79R

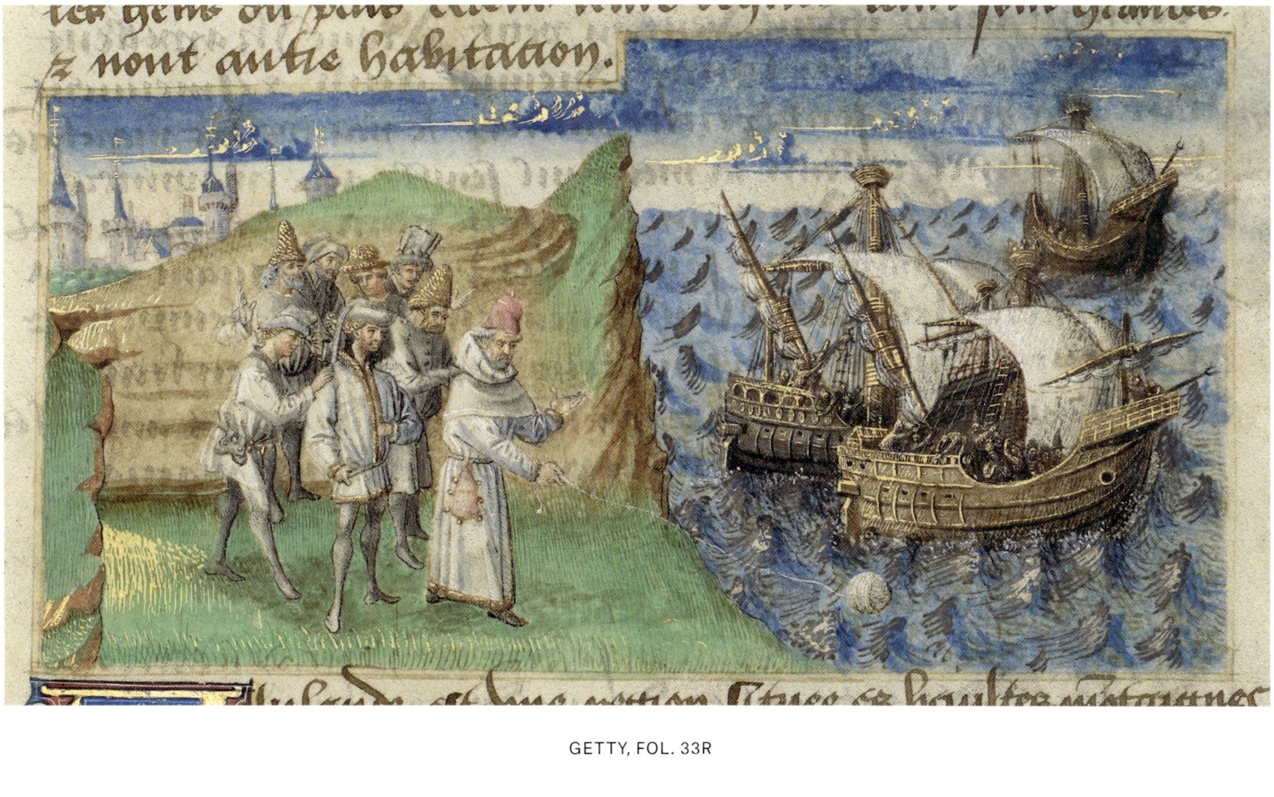

GETTY, FOL. 33R

PLATE 21

WONDERS OF THE HUMAN BODY

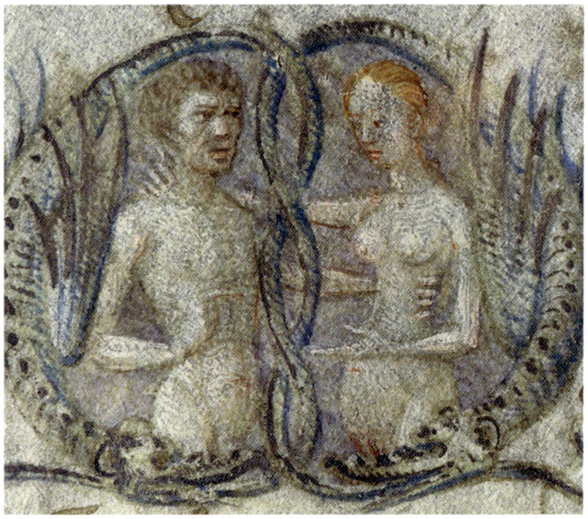

GETTY, FOL. 33V

[A naked man and woman embracing.]

There are many marvels relating to the human body. For as Solinus says, one ought certainly to marvel to hear the wonders of the world recounted. For no one will ever find a man who lived long in this world who did not have and endure more adversity than prosperity.

—Figg and Friedman, p. 294 (chap. 57)

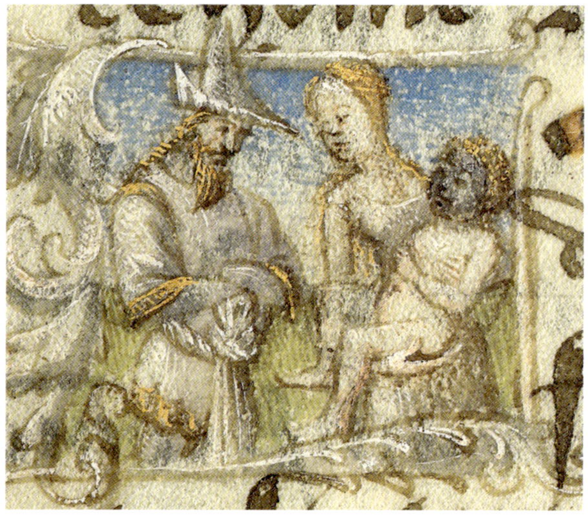

GETTY, FOL. 35R

[T]he imagination and thought of the mother, when she receives the seed, plays an important role in generation. And we can take the example of a woman who conceived and gave birth to a child who was all black like a Moor from the land of the Moors, and this woman was accused of having sexual relations with an Ethiopian—even though she was a worthy woman. But later it was found and verified that at the instant the child was conceived she thought of an Ethiopian that she had seen the previous day, because she had never seen such a man before.

—Figg and Friedman, p. 297 (chap. 57)

PLATE 22

WONDERS OF THE ANIMAL WORLD

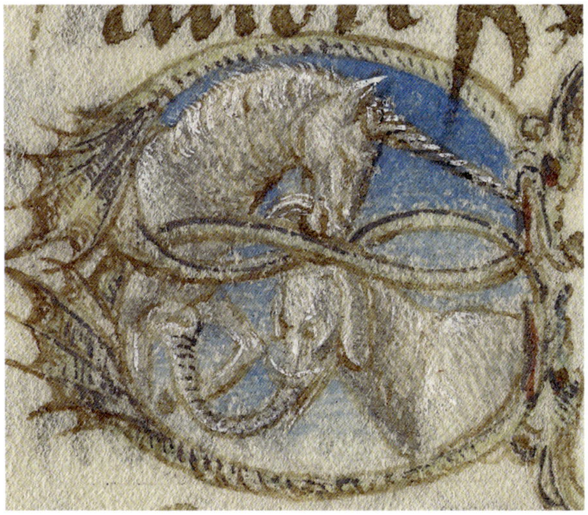

GETTY, FOL. 40V

[A unicorn and an elephant.]

There are many characteristics in dumb beasts. Aristotle speaks of them in his Book of Beasts.

—Figg and Friedman, p. 309 (chap. 58)

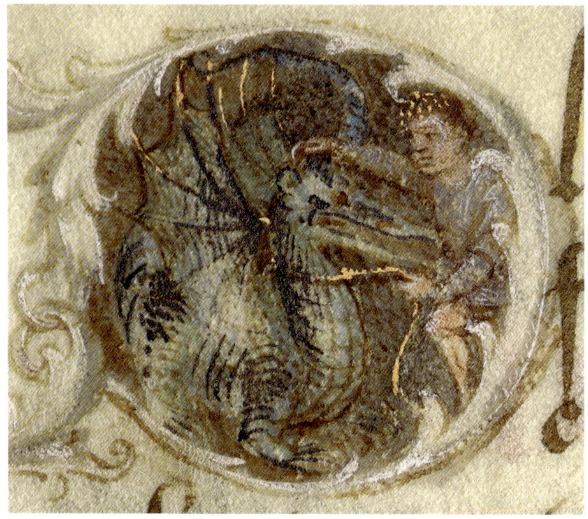

GETTY, FOL. 45R

[T]here was a dragon in the land of Arcadia whom a young man named Dathon nourished from infancy with great pleasure, and he loved it and kept it as a father would his infant. The dragon was so well nourished that he became very large—so much so that the parents of the said Dathon had great horror and dread of the said serpent and blamed their son greatly, requiring him to kill it or to throw it out and chase it away. The boy did not wish to kill it but secretly led it to a distant desert, and there he released it. Then it happened a long time afterward that Dathon was a merchant. And it happened one day that he went into a foreign land on business and, in a woods, was attacked by thieves and murderers who wished to kill and murder him for his goods. This merchant then cried out loudly for fear of death. At his cry the dragon he had nourished came immediately and quickly, having clearly recognized his former master and nurse through his cry and his voice, and he vigorously defended him from the hands of the thieves. And the dragon did this so well that his master passed and escaped safely without having any trouble and without losing any of his goods.

—Figg and Friedman, p. 319 (chap. 58)

PLATE 23

WONDERS OF THE HEAVENS

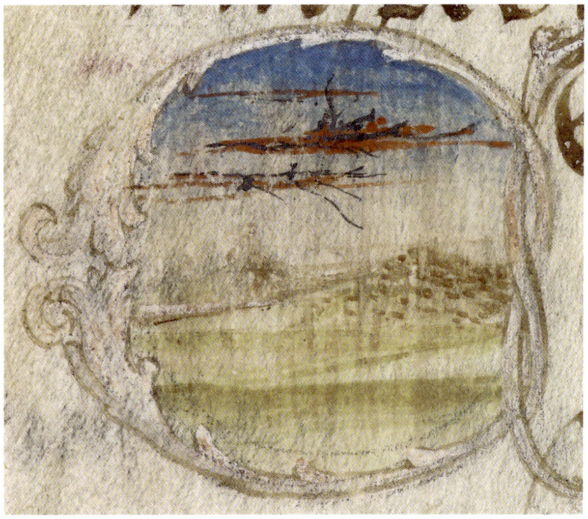

GETTY, FOL. 47V

Celestial impressions are sometimes most marvelous, as Pliny says in his second book, in many forms and diverse fashions. For sometimes one sees a comet so bright and white, shining like burnished silver, that one can hardly see the lines of its tail.

—Figg and Friedman, p. 326 (chap. 59)

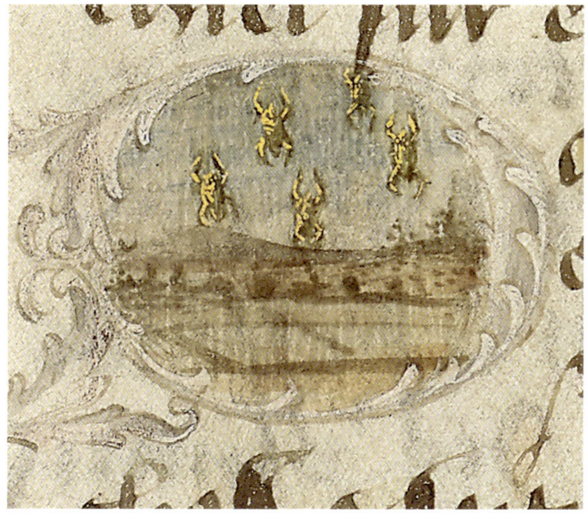

GETTY, FOL. 50R

[S]ometimes a rain has come down in the middle air that is most marvelous and composed of diverse substances, and these have been prodigies and omens of marvels in the past or yet to come, some of which have been natural, others supernatural and demonstrating divine vengeance. . . . [C]ommonly it happens that with the rain that falls from the sky fall small toads and frogs and other vermin which are engendered in the air on high by stormy weather where they have been carried off on high by the winds with earthly vapors.

—Figg and Friedman, pp. 331–32 (chap. 59)

PLATE 24

WONDERS OF BIRDS

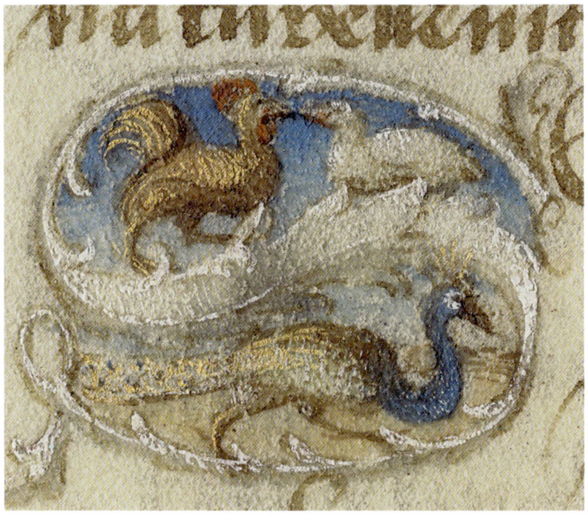

GETTY, FOL. 52V

According to what Pliny says in his tenth book in the twenty-fifth chapter, there are many marvels in the behavior of birds. First, there are some birds that associate with humans at all times of the year like pigeons, peacocks, roosters, hens, geese, ducks, and several other birds. There are some who are around humans only six months in summer, such as swallows, storks, and quail. There are some who are there for a period of three months, such as turtledoves.

—Figg and Friedman, p. 336 (chap. 61)

WONDERS OF THE SEA

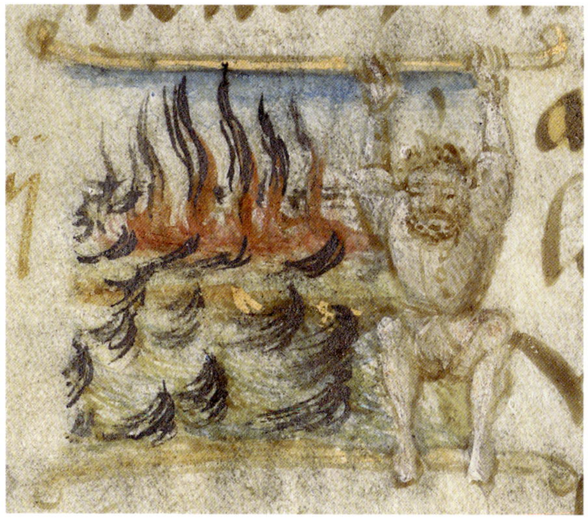

GETTY, FOL. 54R

In olden days it happened, as Pliny says in his second book, that in the high sea of Tusque [an island] arose burning from the depths of the sea. And it appeared above the surface of the water all surrounded with fire, and around the said island were floating fish, of which some were dead and others were extremely weak. And all those who ate of these fish died.

—Figg and Friedman, p. 340 (chap. 62)

WONDERS OF FRESH WATERS

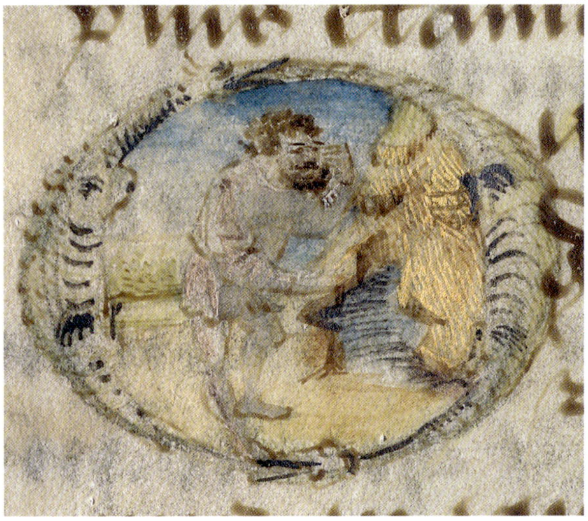

GETTY, FOL. 56R

[A man by a body of water.]

**[A]nd in particular he [Pliny] says that if lead and bronze of equal weight melted together into a mass were put in water, it would sink right to the bottom, and if the mass is flattened and enlarged by beating and forging, it will float on the water.*

**Pliny says that in the region of Cyzicus is a spring that is of such a condition that if man or woman is overcome by disordered and burning love of a sinfully lustful kind, as soon as the person has drunk the water of this spring, the water will make the person forget and cool the person's desire.*

—Figg and Friedman, pp. 344–45 (chap. 63)

WONDERS OF THE EARTH

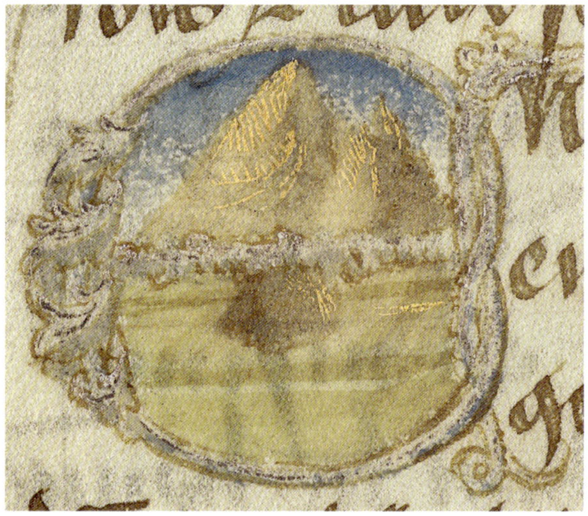

GETTY, FOL. 59R

In the earth are many marvels, as Pliny says in his second book. Among other things, he declares that in the land of Dalmatia is a pit in the earth called Seneta that has a very narrow mouth or entryway as if it were the opening to a small, narrow, deep well. And inside of it is a great marvel. For if anyone lets something drop in there, even if it be light and notwithstanding that the weather be clear and the air calm, as soon as the person has thrown the thing into the mouth of the pit, the prevailing winds will change and become disturbed, and horrible gusts and a great storm will stir themselves up, such that the one who has dropped the thing inside the ditch will be in great peril.

—Figg and Friedman, p. 350 (chap. 65)

Bibliography

The bibliography below includes specific sources cited by the authors in their essays. Together with the "Suggested Further Reading" that follows, this bibliography provides readers an opportunity to gain a wider knowledge of the topics discussed in this volume.

Akbari 2009
Akbari, Suzanne Conklin. *Idols in the East: European Representations of Islam and the Orient, 1100–1450*. Cornell University Press, 2009.

Alexander 1992
Alexander, Jonathan J. G. *Medieval Illuminators and Their Methods of Work*. New Haven and London: Yale University Press, 1992.

Anguissola and Grüner 2020
Anguissola, Anna, and Andreas Grüner, eds. *The Nature of Art: Pliny the Elder on Materials*. Turnhout: Brepols, 2020.

Arjana 2015
Arjana, Sophia Rose. *Muslims in the Western Imagination*. Oxford and New York: Oxford University Press, 2015.

Armstrong 1983
Armstrong, Lilian. "The Illustration of Pliny's *Historia naturalis*: Manuscripts before 1430." *Journal of the Warburg and Courtauld Institutes* 46 (1983): 19–39.

Avril 1996
Avril, François. "Le Livre de Merveilles, manuscrit Français 2810 de la Bibliothèque nationale de France." In *Marco Polo: Le Livre des merveilles: Manuscrit Français 2810 de la Bibliothèque nationale de France, Paris*, edited by François Avril, Marie-Thérèse Gousset, and Marie-Hélène Tesnière, 291–324. Lucerne: Faksimile Verlag, 1996.

Avril and Reynaud 1993
Avril, François, and Nicole Reynaud. *Les manuscrits à peintures en France 1440–1520*. Paris: Flammarion/Bibliothèque nationale de France, 1993.

Bale 2016
Bale, Anthony. "European Travel Writing in the Middle Ages." In *The Routledge Companion to Travel Writing*, edited by Carl Thompson, 152–60. Abingdon, UK: Routledge, 2016.

Banks and Binns 2002
Gervase of Tilbury, Otia imperialia*: Recreation for an Emperor*. Translated and edited by S. E. Banks and J. W. Binns. Oxford: Clarendon Press, 2002.

Benjamin 1935
Benjamin, Walter. *The Work of Art in the Age of Mechanical Reproduction* (first published 1935). London: Penguin, 2008.

Bennett 1954
Bennett, Josephine Waters. *The Rediscovery of Sir John Mandeville*. New York: Modern Language Association of America, 1954.

Betschart 1996
Betschart, Andres. *Zwischen zwei Welten: Illustrationen und Berichte westeuropäischer Jerusalemreisender des 15. und 16. Jahrhunderts*. Würzburg: Königshausen und Neumann, 1996.

Blanks and Frassetto 1999
Blanks, David R., and Michael Frassetto, eds. *Western Views of Islam in Medieval and Early Modern Europe: Perceptions of Other*. New York: St. Martin's Press, 1999.

Booton 2010
Booton, Diane E. *Manuscripts, Market, and the Transition to Print in Late Medieval Brittany*. Farnham, UK: Ashgate, 2010.

Brick 2018
Brick, David. "Sati." In *Martyrdom, Self-Sacrifice, and Self-Immolation: Religious Perspectives on Suicide*, edited by Margo Kitts, 162–81. Oxford: Oxford University Press, 2018.

Brodersen 2014
Brodersen, Kai, ed. *Solinus: New Studies*. Heidelberg: Verlag Antike, 2014.

Bullough and Brundage 1999
Bullough, Vern L., and James Brundage, eds. *Handbook of Medieval Sexuality*. London and New York: Routledge, 1999.

Bynum 1999
Bynum, Caroline Walker. "Miracles and Marvels: The Limits of Alterity." In *Vita religiosa im Mittelalter: Festschrift für Kaspar Elm zum 70. Geburtstag*, edited by Franz J. Felton and Nikolas Jaspert, 799–817. Berlin: Duncker & Humblot, 1999.

Bynum 2001
Bynum, Caroline Walker. *Metamorphosis and Identity*. New York: Zone Books, 2001.

Camille 1989
Camille, Michael. *The Gothic Idol: Ideology and Image-Making in Medieval Art*. Cambridge: Cambridge University Press, 1989.

Camille 1994
Camille, Michael. Review of *Medieval Texts and Images: Studies of Manuscripts from the Middle Ages*, by Margaret M. Manion and Bernard J. Muir. *Speculum* 69, no. 3 (July 1994): 833–35.

Campbell 1987
Campbell, Tony. *The Earliest Printed Maps, 1472–1500*. Berkeley: University of California Press, 1987.

Cavagna 2017
Cavagna, Mattia. *Le* Miroir historial *par Jean de Vignay (Volume 1, Tome 1)*. Paris: Société des anciens textes français, 2017.

Chavannes-Mazel 1988
Chavannes-Mazel, Claudine Albertine. "The *Miroir historial* of Jean le Bon: The Leiden Manuscript and Its Related Copies." PhD diss., Rijksuniversiteit, Leiden, 1988.

Chavannes-Mazel 1990
Chavannes-Mazel, Claudine Albertine. "Problems in Translation, Transcription, and Iconography: The *Miroir historial*, Books 1–8." In *Vincent de Beauvais: Intentions et réceptions d'une oeuvre encyclopédique au Moyen Âge*, edited by Monique Paulmier-Foucart, Serge Lusignan, and Alain Nadeau, 345–74. Paris: Vrin, 1990.

Clark 2006
Clark, Willene. *A Medieval Book of Beasts: The Second-Family Bestiary: Commentary, Art, Text, and Translation*. Woodbridge, UK: Boydell Press, 2006.

Collins 2003
Collins, Minta. *A Medieval Herbal: A Facsimile of British Library Egerton MS 747*. London: British Library, 2003.

Collins and Keene 2022
Collins, Kristen, and Bryan C. Keene. *Balthazar: A Black African King in Medieval and Renaissance Art*. Los Angeles: Getty Publications, 2022.

Cohen 2001
Cohen, Jeffery Jerome. "On Saracen Enjoyment: Some Fantasies of Race in Late Medieval France and England." *Journal of Medieval and Early Modern Studies* 31, no. 1 (2001): 113–46.

Cohen and Wheeler 1997
Cohen, Jeffrey Jerome, and Bonnie Wheeler, eds. *Becoming Male in the Middle Ages*. New York: Routledge, 1997.

Cruse 2015a
Cruse, Mark. "Marco Polo in Manuscript: The Travels of the *Devisement du monde*." *Narrative Culture* 2, no. 2 (2015): 171–89.

Cruse 2015b
Cruse, Mark. "Stories for the King: Narration and Authority in the 'Crusade Compilation' of Philippe VI of France (London, British Library, MS Royal 19 D I)." In *Telling the Story in the Middle Ages: Essays in Honour of Evelyn Birge Vitz*, edited by Kathryn A. Duys, Elizabeth Emery, and Laurie Postlewate, 205–18. Woodbridge, UK: Boydell and Brewer, 2015.

Cruse 2020
Cruse, Mark. "'Pleasure in Foreign Things': Global Entanglement in the *Livre des merveilles du monde* (Paris, Bibliothèque nationale de France, Fr. 2810)." *Mediaevalia* 41 (2020): 217–44.

Cusack 2018
Cusack, Carol M. "Self-Murder, Sin, and Crime: Religion and Suicide in the Middle Ages." *Journal of Religion and Violence* 6, no. 2 (2018): 206–24.

DeVun 2021
DeVun, Leah. *The Shape of Sex: Nonbinary Gender from Genesis to the Renaissance*. New York: Columbia University Press, 2021.

Dutschke 1993
Dutschke, Consuelo Wager. "Francesco Pipino and the Manuscripts of Marco Polo's 'Travels.'" PhD diss., University of California Los Angeles, 1993.

Eisenbeiss and Saurma-Jeltsch 2012
Eisenbeiss, Anja, and Lieselotte E. Saurma-Jeltsch, eds. *Images of Otherness in Medieval and Early Modern Times: Exclusion, Inclusion, Assimilation*. Berlin: Deutscher Kunstverlag, 2012.

Farquhar 1996
Farquhar, James Douglas. "Making Connections in the Irregular Web of Manuscript Production of the Southern Netherlands." *The Journal of the Walters Art Gallery* 54 (1996): 135–46.

Figg and Friedman 2018
Figg, Kristen M., and John Block Friedman. "Transcription and Translation." In *Book of Wonders of the World, Secrets of Natural History: MS fr. 22971: Original Held in the National Library of France, Paris: Studies and Translation*. Burgos: Siloé, 2018.

Fleck 2000
Fleck, A. "Here, There, and in Between: Representing Difference in the Travels of Sir John Mandeville." *Studies in Philology* 97 (2000): 379–400.

Flint 1992
Flint, Valerie I. J. *The Imaginative Landscape of Christopher Columbus*. Princeton: Princeton University Press, 1992.

Fourcade 2021
Fourcade, Sarah. *La noblesse à la conquête du livre: France, v. 1300–v. 1530*. Paris: Honoré Champion, 2021.

Franklin-Brown 2012
Franklin-Brown, Mary. *Reading the World: Encyclopedic Writing in the Scholastic Age*. Chicago: University of Chicago Press, 2012.

Friedman 2019
Friedman, John Block. "The Marvelous Beasts of the *Secrets of Natural History*." *De Medio Aevo* 8 (2019): 1–35.

Friedman 2000
Friedman, John Block. *The Monstrous Races in Medieval Art and Thought*. Syracuse: Syracuse University Press, 2000.

Friedman, Giogoli, and Figg 2018
Friedman, John Block, Kathrin Giogoli, and Kristen M. Figg. "Introduction." In *Book of Wonders of the World, Secrets of Natural History: MS fr. 22971: Original Held in the National Library of France, Paris: Studies and Translation*. Burgos: Siloé, 2018.

Gautier 2017
Gautier, Marc-Édouard. *Les Merveilles du monde, ou Les Secrets de l'histoire naturelle et autres acquisitions récentes du temps du roi René*. Angers: Bibliothèque municipale d'Angers, 2017.

Glendinning 2013
Glendinning, Eleanor. "Reinventing Lucretia: Rape, Suicide, and Redemption from Classical Antiquity to the Medieval Era." *International Journal of the Classical Tradition* 20, nos. 1/2 (2013): 61–82.

Goetz and Wood 2021
Goetz, Hans-Werner, and Ian N. Wood, eds. *"Otherness" in the Middle Ages*. Turnhout: Brepols, 2021.

Gousset 1996
Gousset, Marie-Thérèse. "Un programme iconographique conçu par Jean sans Peur." In *Marco Polo: Le Livre des merveilles: Manuscrit Français 2810 de la Bibliothèque nationale de France, Paris*, edited by François Avril, Marie-Thérèse Gousset, and Marie-Hélène Tesnière, 353–64. Lucerne: Faksimile Verlag, 1996.

Gravestock 1999
Gravestock, Pamela. "Did Imaginary Animals Exist?" In *Mark of the Beast: The Medieval Bestiary in Art, Life, and Literature*, edited by Debra Hassig, 119–35. New York: Garland Publishing, 1999.

Harvey 2012
Harvey, P. D. A. *Medieval Maps of the Holy Land*. London: British Library, 2012.

Hassinger 1927
Hassinger, Hugo. "Deutsche Weltkarten-Inkunabeln." *Zeitschrift der Gesellschaft für Erdkunde zu Berlin* 9/10 (1927): 455–82.

Hedeman 2022
Hedeman, Anne D. *Visual Translation: Illuminated Manuscripts and the First French Humanists*. Notre Dame: University of Notre Dame Press, 2022.

Heng 2018
Heng, Geraldine. *The Invention of Race in the European Middle Ages*. Cambridge: Cambridge University Press, 2018.

Holbrook 2006
Holbrook, Sue Ellen. "The Properties of Things and Textual Power: Illustrating the French Translation of *De Proprietatibus Rerum* and a Latin Precursor." In *Patrons, Authors, and Workshops: Books and Book Production in Paris around 1400*, edited by Godfried Croenen and Peter Ainsworth, 367–403. Louvain: Peeters, 2006.

Horodowich and Nagel 2023
Horodowich, Elizabeth, and Alexander Nagel. *Amerasia*. New York: Zone Books, 2023.

Jones and Sprunger 2002
Jones, Timothy S., and David A. Sprunger, eds. *Marvels, Monsters, and Miracles: Studies in the Medieval and Early Modern Imaginations*. Kalamazoo, MI: Medieval Institute Publications, 2002.

Karnes 2022
Karnes, Michelle. *Medieval Marvels and Fictions in the Latin West and Islamic World*. Chicago: University of Chicago Press, 2022.

König 1982
König, Eberhard. *Französische Buchmalerei um 1450: Der Jouvenel-Maler, Der Maler des Genfer Boccaccio und die Anfänge Jean Fouquets*. Berlin: Gebr. Mann Verlag, 1982.

König 1991
König, Eberhard. *Les Heures de Marguerite d'Orléans*. Paris: Éditions du Cerf, 1991.

König 2002
König, Eberhard. *Das Provost-Stundenbuch: Der Meister der Marguerite d'Orléans in Angers*. Ramsen: H. Tenschert (cat. XLVII [47]), 2002.

König 2009
König, Eberhard. "Le Maître du Boccace de Genève." In *Splendeur de l'enluminure: Le Roi René et les livres*, edited by Marc-Édouard Gautier, 133–43. Angers: Actes Sud, 2009.

König 2018
König, Eberhard. "The Master of St. Jerome: One of the Van Lymborch Brothers." In *Maelwael Van Lymborch Studies 1*, edited by André Stufkens and Clemens Verhoeven, 40–63. Turnhout: Brepols, 2018.

Kosta-Théfaine 2006
Kosta-Théfaine, Jean-François. "Du récit de voyage et de sa mise en image: L'exemple du manuscrit de New York (Pierpont Morgan Library, M.723) du *Devisement du Monde* de Marco Polo." In *Art et littérature: Le voyage entre texte et image*, edited by Jean-Loup Korzilius, 31–59. Amsterdam: Rodopi, 2006.

Lindquist and Mittman 2018
Lindquist, Sherry C. M., and Asa Simon Mittman. *Medieval Monsters: Terrors, Aliens, Wonders*. New York and London: The Morgan Library & Museum, 2018.

Lorentz 2017
Lorentz, Philippe. "Les 'Maîtres' anonymes: Des noms provisoires faits pour durer?" *Perspective: Actualité en histoire de l'art* 1 (2007). https://journals.openedition.org/perspective/3750.

Mandeville 2012
Mandeville, John. *The Book of Marvels and Travels*. Translated by Anthony Bale. Oxford: Oxford University Press, 2012.

Mauntel 2021
Mauntel, Christoph. "The T-O Diagram and Its Religious Connotations: A Circumstantial Case." In *Geography and Religious Knowledge in the Medieval World*, edited by Christoph Mauntel, 57–84. Berlin: De Gruyter, 2021.

McHam 2006
McHam, Sarah Blake. "Erudition on Display: The 'Scientific' Illustrations in Pico della Mirandola's Manuscript of Pliny the Elder's *Natural History*." In *Visualizing Medieval Medicine and Natural History, 1200–1550*, edited by Jean A. Givens, Karen M. Reeds, and Alain Touwaide, 83–144. Aldershot, UK: Ashgate, 2006.

Meier 1997
Meier, Christel. "Illustration und Textcorpus: Zu kommunikations- und ordnungsfunktionalen Aspekten der Bilder in den mittelalterlichen Enzyklopädiehandschriften." *Frühmittelalterliche Studien* 31 (1997): 1–31.

Mittman 2015
Mittman, Asa Simon. "Are the 'Monstrous Races' Races?" *Postmedieval: A Journal of Medieval and Cultural Studies* 6, no. 1 (2015): 36–51.

Morgan and Moodey 2016
Morgan, Nigel, and Elizabeth Moodey. "Grisaille in Manuscript Painting." In *Colour: The Art and Science of Illuminated Manuscripts*, edited by Stella Panayotova, 246–55. London: Harvey Miller, 2016.

Morrison and Grollemond 2019
Morrison, Elizabeth, ed., with Larisa Grollemond. *Book of Beasts: The Bestiary in the Medieval World*. Los Angeles: Getty Publications, 2019.

Morrison and Hedeman 2010
Morrison, Elizabeth, and Anne D. Hedeman, eds. *Imagining the Past in France: History in Manuscript Painting, 1250–1500*. Los Angeles: Getty Publications, 2010.

Murphy 2004
Murphy, Trevor. *Pliny the Elder's* Natural History*: The Empire in the Encyclopedia*. Oxford: Oxford University Press, 2004.

Nirenberg 1996
Nirenberg, David. *Communities of Violence: Persecution of Minorities in the Middle Ages*. Princeton: Princeton University Press, 1996.

Olsen 1985
Olsen, Birger Munk. *L'étude des auteurs classiques latins aux XIe et XIIe siècles*. Vol. 2. Paris: CNRS Éditions, 1985.

Patton 2019
Patton, Pamela A. "Color, Culture, and the Making of Difference in the *Vidal Mayor*." In *Toward a Global Middle Ages: Encountering the World through Illuminated Manuscripts*, edited by Bryan C. Keene, 182–89. Los Angeles: Getty Publications, 2019.

Phillips 2014
Phillips, Kim M. *Before Orientalism: Asian Peoples and Cultures in European Travel Writing, 1245–1510*. Philadelphia: University of Pennsylvania Press, 2014.

Pliny 1938
Pliny the Elder. *Natural History*. Translated by Harris Rackham. Cambridge, MA: Harvard University Press, 1938.

Polo 1958
Polo, Marco. *The Travels of Marco Polo*. Translated by Ronald Latham. London: Penguin, 1958.

Quigley 2009
Quigley, Maureen. "Romantic Geography and the Crusades: British Library Royal ms. 19 D I." *Peregrinations: Journal of Medieval Art and Architecture* 2, no. 3 (2009): 53–76.

Ramey 2014
Ramey, Lynn T. *Black Legacies: Race and the European Middle Ages*. Gainesville: University Press of Florida, 2014.

Reeve 2007
Reeve, Michael. "The Editing of Pliny's *Natural History*." *Revue d'histoire des textes* 2 (2007): 107–79.

Reynolds 2003
Reynolds, Catherine. "Illuminators and the Painters' Guilds." In *Illuminating the Renaissance: The Triumph of Flemish Manuscript Painting in Europe*, edited by Thom Kren and Scot McKendrick, 15–33. Los Angeles: Getty Publications, 2003.

Röhl 2004
Röhl, Susanne. *Der* livre de Mandeville *im 14. und 15. Jahrhundert: Untersuchungen zur handschriftlichen Überlieferung der kontinentalfranzösischen Version*. Munich and Paderborn: Fink, 2004.

Rose 2015
Rose, E. M. *The Murder of William of Norwich: The Origins of the Blood Libel in Medieval Europe*. Oxford: Oxford University Press, 2015.

Rowe 2012
Rowe, Nina. "Other." *Studies in Iconography* 33 (2012): 131–44.

Sáenz-López Pérez 2014
Sáenz-López Pérez, Sandra. *The Beatus Maps: The Revelation of the World in the Middle Ages*. Burgos: Siloé, 2014.

Samaran 1962
Samaran, Charles. "Pierre Bersuire." In *Histoire littéraire de la France*, vol. 39, 259–450. Paris: Imprimerie nationale, 1962.

Samuels 2015
Samuels, Tristan. "Herodotus and the Black Body: A Critical Race Theory Analysis." *Journal of Black Studies* 46, no. 7 (2015): 723–41.

Schramm 1938
Schramm, Albert. *Der Bilderschmuck der Frühdrucke: Die Drucker in Basel*. Vol. 21. Leipzig: Hiersemann, 1938.

Schwartz 1996
Schwartz, Hillel. *The Culture of the Copy: Striking Likenesses, Unreasonable Facsimiles*. Rev. ed. 2014. Princeton: Zone Books, 1996.

Seidel 2017
Seidel, Christine. *Zwischen Tradition und Innovation: Die Anfänge des Buchmalers Jean Colombe und die Kunst in Bourges zur Zeit Karls VII. von Frankreich*. Simbach am Inn: Anton Pfeiler, 2017.

Seymour 1992
Seymour, M. C. *Bartholomaeus Anglicus and His Encyclopedia*. Aldershot, UK: Ashgate, 1992.

Seymour 1993
Seymour, M. C. *Authors of the Middle Ages*. Vol. 1, *Sir John Mandeville*. Aldershot, UK: Ashgate, 1993.

Sotheby's 2017
Sotheby's Paris. *Bacri frères Antiquaires, Paris: Collection Jacques Bacri*, lot 19. March 3, 2017.

Spriggs 1998
Spriggs, James A. "The British Beaver—Fur, Fact, and Fantasy." In *Leather and Fur: Aspects of Early Medieval Trade and Technology*, edited by Esther Cameron, 91–101. London: Archetype Publications for the Archaeological Leather Group, 1998.

Stråth 2004
Stråth, Bo. *Europe and the Other and Europe as the Other*. Brussels: Lang, 2004.

Strickland 2003
Strickland, Debra Higgs. *Saracens, Demons, and Jews: Making Monsters in Medieval Art*. Princeton: Princeton University Press, 2003.

Strickland 2005
Strickland, Debra Higgs. "Artists, Audience, and Ambivalence in Marco Polo's *Divisament dou monde*." *Viator* 36 (2005): 493–517.

Strickland 2008
Strickland, Debra Higgs. "Text, Image, and Contradiction in the *Devisement dou monde*." In *Marco Polo and the Encounter of East and West*, edited by Suzanne Conklin Akbari and Amilcare Iannucci, 23–59. Toronto: University of Toronto Press, 2008.

Terkla and Millea 2019
Terkla, Dan, and Nick Millea, eds. *A Critical Companion to English* Mappae Mundi *of the Twelfth and Thirteenth Centuries*. Woodbridge, UK: Boydell Press, 2019.

Tesnière 1994
Tesnière, Marie-Hélène. "Le *Reductorium morale* de Pierre Bersuire." In *L'enciclopedismo medievale: Atti del convegno*, edited by Michelangelo Picone, 229–49. San Gimignano, October 8–10, 1992. Ravenna: Longo Editore, 1994.

Teter 2020
Teter, Magda. *Blood Libel: On the Trail of an Antisemitic Myth*. Cambridge, MA: Harvard University Press: 2020.

Thomson 2022
Thomson, S. C., ed. *Strangers at the Gate! Multidisciplinary Explorations of Communities, Borders, and Othering in Medieval Western Europe*. Leiden: Brill, 2022.

van Duzer 2019
van Duzer, Chet. *The Psalter Map (c. 1262)*. In *A Critical Companion to English* Mappae Mundi *of the Twelfth and Thirteenth Centuries*, edited by Dan Terkla and Nick Millea, 179–96. Woodbridge, UK: Boydell Press, 2019.

Vernon 2018
Vernon, Matthew X. *The Black Middle Ages: Race and the Construction of the Middle Ages*. Cham, Switzerland: Palgrave, 2018.

Voelkle and Avril 2006
Voelkle, William, and François Avril. *Gaston Phoebus,* Le livre de Chasse*: MS M.1044, The Pierpont Morgan Library, New York*. Lucerne: Faksimile Verlag, 2006.

von Euw and Plotzek 1979–1985
von Euw, Anton, and Joachim M. Plotzek. *Die Handschriften der Sammlung Ludwig*. 4 vols. Cologne: Schnütgen Museum, 1979–1985.

Whalley 1982
Whalley, Joyce Irene. *Pliny the Elder,* Historia naturalis. London: Victoria and Albert Museum, 1982.

Whitaker 2019
Whitaker, Cord J. *Black Metaphors: How Modern Racism Emerged from Medieval Race-Thinking*. Philadelphia: University of Pennsylvania Press, 2019.

Williams and Martin 2017
Williams, John, and Therese Martin. *Visions of the End in Medieval Spain: Catalogue of Illustrated Beatus Commentaries on the Apocalypse and Study of the Geneva Beatus*. Amsterdam: Amsterdam University Press, 2017.

Wolfthal 1993
Wolfthal, Diane. "'A Hue and a Cry': Medieval Rape Imagery and Its Transformation." *Art Bulletin* 75, no. 1 (March 1993): 39–64.

Yeager 2008
Yeager, Suzanne M. "The World Translated: Marco Polo's *Le Devisement dou monde*, *The Book of Sir John Mandeville*, and Their Medieval Audiences." In *Marco Polo and the Encounter of East and West*, edited by Suzanne Conklin Akbari and Amilcare Iannucci, 156–81. Toronto: University of Toronto Press, 2008.

Zumthor 1994
Zumthor, Paul. "The Medieval Travel Narrative." *New Literary History* 25 (1994): 809–24.

Suggested Further Reading

Baumgärtner, Ingrid, Nirit Ben-Aryeh Debby, and Katrin Kogman-Appel, eds. *Maps and Travel in the Middle Ages and the Early Modern Period*. Berlin and Boston: De Gruyter, 2018.

Boletsi, Maria, and Tyler Sage, eds. *Yes: Encounters in the Arts and Contemporary Politics*. Boston: Brill Rodopi, 2018.

Brown, Meg Lota, ed. *Marginal Figures in the Global Middle Ages and the Renaissance*. Turnhout: Brepols, 2021.

Classen, Albrecht, ed. *Meeting the Foreign in the Middle Ages*. New York: Routledge, 2022.

Cohen, Jeffrey Jerome, ed. *The Postcolonial Middle Ages*. New York: St. Martin's Press, 2000.

Cohen, Jeffrey Jerome. *Hybridity, Identity, and Monstrosity in Medieval Britain: On Difficult Middles*. New York: Palgrave Macmillan, 2006.

Davies, Surekha. *Renaissance Ethnography and the Invention of the Human: New Worlds, Maps and Monsters*. Cambridge: Cambridge University Press, 2016.

Eldevik, John. "Saints, Pagans, and the Wonders of the East: The Medieval Imaginary and Its Manuscript Contexts." *Traditio* 71 (2016): 235–72.

Friedman, John Block, and Kristen Mossler Figg. *Trade, Travel, and Exploration in the Middle Ages: An Encyclopedia*. Garland Reference Library of the Humanities. New York: Garland Publishing, 2000.

Giuliani, G. *Monsters, Catastrophes, and the Anthropocene: A Postcolonial Critique*. New York: Routledge, 2021.

Hellyer, H. A. *Muslims of Europe: The "Other" Europeans*. Edinburgh: Edinburgh University Press, 2009.

Karnes, Michelle. "Marvels in the Medieval Imagination." *Speculum* 90, no. 2 (April 2015): 327–65.

Kim, Dorothy. "Introduction to Literature Compass Special Cluster: Critical Race and the Middle Ages." *Literature Compass* 16 (2019): 9–10.

Mauntel, Christoph, Klaus Oschema, Jean-Charles Ducène, and Martin Hofmann. "Mapping Continents, Inhabited Quarters, and the Four Seas: Divisions of the World and the Ordering of Spaces in Latin-Christian, Arabic-Islamic, and Chinese Cartography, 12th–16th Centuries—A Critical Survey and Analysis." *Journal of Transcultural Medieval Studies* 5, no. 2 (2018): 295–367.

Mezzenzana, F., and D. Peluso, eds. *Conversations on Empathy: Interdisciplinary Perspectives on Imagination and Radical Othering*. New York: Routledge, 2023.

Mittman, Asa Simon, and Peter Dendle, eds. *The Ashgate Research Companion to Monsters and the Monstrous*. Aldershot, UK: Ashgate, 2012.

O'Doherty, Marianne. *The Indies and the Medieval West: Thought, Report, Imagination*. Turnhout: Brepols, 2013.

Platt, Peter G. *Wonders, Marvels, and Monsters in Early Modern Culture*. Newark, DE: University of Delaware Press, 1999.

Salazar, Noel B. *Envisioning Eden: Mobilizing Imaginaries in Tourism and Beyond*. Oxford: Berghahn, 2010.

Salazar, Noel B. *Momentous Mobilities: Anthropological Musings on the Meanings of Travel*. Oxford: Berghahn, 2018.

Sonnis-Bell, M., D. E. Bell, and M. K. Ryan, eds. *Strangers, Aliens, Foreigners: The Politics of Othering from Migrants to Corporations*. Boston: Brill, 2018.

ons biens come fruitz z grains ¶ Item ceste terre
nt aucunepart du ciel z de lair du temps est moult bi
erce z atrempee. Et comment lair du temps naturelle
doulx sain z gracieulx. ¶ Item la sont moult bel
eres ruisseaulx z belles fontaines qui sont naturellem
umides z medicinables a ceulx qui dedens se veullent
aigner. ¶ Item la terre de celle prouince est naturell
umide z y croissent certaines precieuses fleurs herbes z ar
omatiques z moult bon flerans z odorans come saffr
ume pour taindre escarlette z autres espices sont flerau

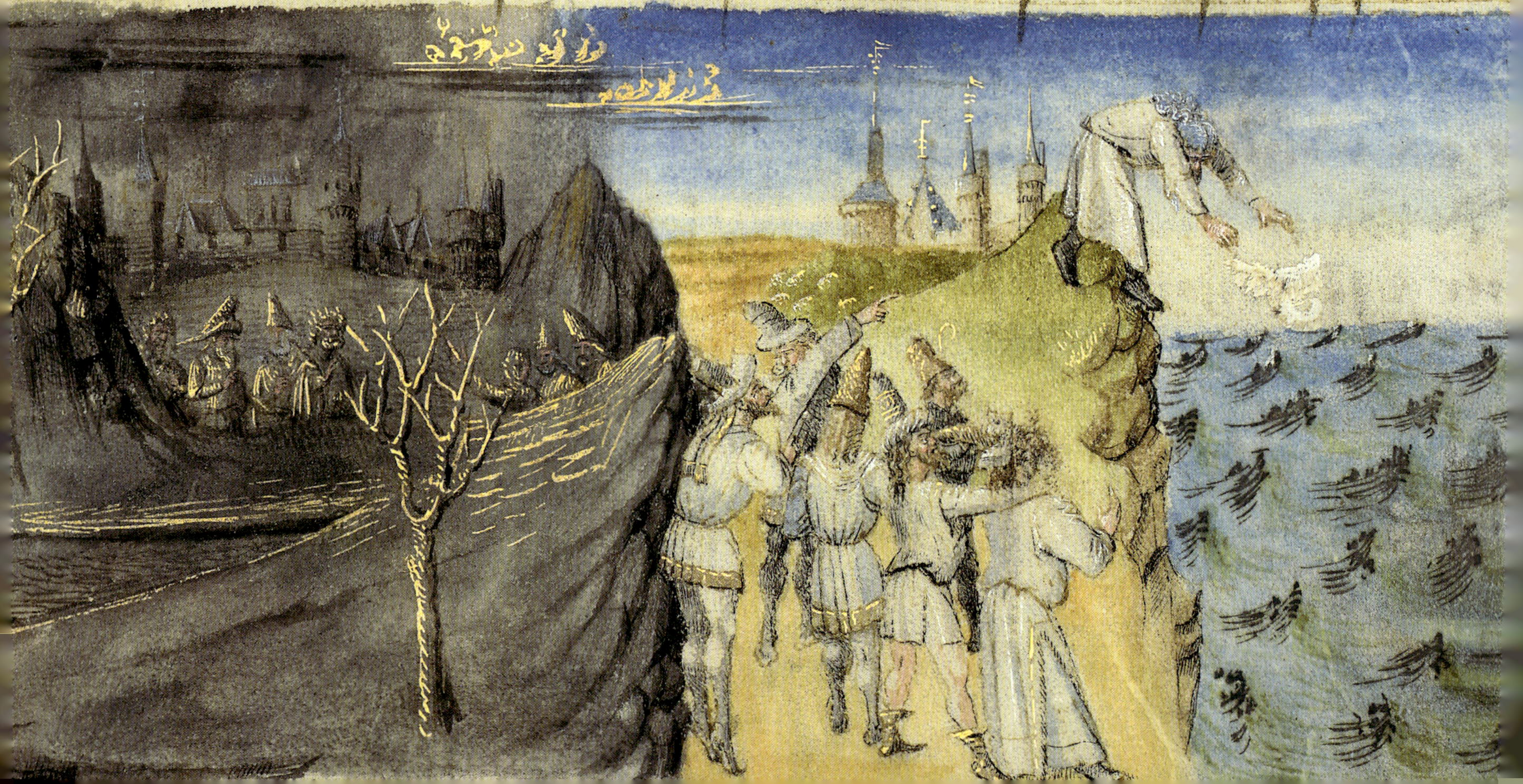

ACKNOWLEDGMENTS

This volume marks a new form of collaboration between the J. Paul Getty Museum and the Morgan Library & Museum. Harnessing the power of these two manuscript collections on either side of the United States, as well as the expertise of their curatorial staffs, we have been able to create a series of essays that explore the twin manuscripts of the *Book of Marvels* in ways that none of the authors could have accomplished on their own. Working together every step of the way, each of us has brought a fresh perspective to the analysis of these manuscripts that not only enriched the individual essays but also informed the thinking and approach to the volume before any words were ever committed to paper. We even called ourselves "Team Marvels" to commemorate our small, cheerful working group. We were excited to welcome Noel Salazar (Katholieke Universiteit Leuven, Belgium), who contributed a thoughtful epilogue that brings a contemporary perspective to the themes explored in our essays.

Of course, the entire project was only possible with the support of our institutions and all the members of the many departments who contributed to this publication and to the exhibitions. At the J. Paul Getty Museum, members of senior leadership gave early and enthusiastic approval for the project, including Timothy Potts, Maria Hummer-Tuttle and Robert Tuttle Director; Richard Rand, associate director of collections; and Carolyn Marsden-Smith, associate director of exhibitions. We relied on the assistance and skill of many colleagues across the Getty: Erin Minnaugh and Marisa Weintraub in Exhibitions; Jessica Harden, Chaya Arabia, and Bre Wucinich in Exhibition Design; Tasia Johnson, Maite Álvarez, Michelle Nordon, Anne Martens, Isoke Cullins, Nia Robertson, and Steve Gemmel in Interpretive Content; Nancy Turner, conservator of Manuscripts; Kanoko Sasao, Haley Clayton, and Jennifer Garpner in the Registrar's office; Johana Herrera, Kayla Kee, and Aleia McDaniel, who assisted with photography; Mary Miller, David Brafman, and Marit Coyman-Myklebust at the Getty Research Institute; and Mike Mitchell and his incomparable team in Preparations.

Likewise at the Morgan, this project received support and encouragement from senior leadership, including Colin B. Bailey, director; John Marciari, curatorial chair and Charles W. Engelhard Curator and head of the Department of Drawings and Prints; and Elizabeth Abbarno, director of Exhibition and Collection Management. Roger S. Wieck, Melvin R. Seiden Curator and head of the Department of Medieval and Renaissance Manuscripts, provided guidance and feedback from the earliest stages of the project onward, as did other department members, including Deirdre Jackson and Juliana Amorim Goskes. Marilyn Palmeri, director of the Imaging and Rights Department, played a crucial role in organizing new photography for the publication, which was expertly undertaken by Janny Chiu and Carmen González Fraile. Additional thanks go to Maria Fredericks, Frank Trujillo, Reba Snyder, Rebecca Pollock, and Michael Caines, Thaw Conservation Center; Lauren Stakias and Kirsten Teasdale, Development and Membership; Erika Hernandez Lomas, Walsh Hansen, and Sholto Ainslie, Exhibitions and Collections Management; Nicholas Danisi, Financial Services; Philip Palmer, Literary and Historical Manuscripts; John McQuillen, Printed Books and Bindings; Karen Banks, Publications; and Peter Gammie and Sima Prutkovsky, Reference Collection.

This beautiful publication was the result of much appreciated time and effort by our team at Getty Publications. We wish to extend our gratitude to publisher Kara Kirk and editor in chief Diana Murphy, who were both keen sponsors of the project. Former editor in chief Karen Levine provided crucial advice about shaping the volume. Managing editor Nola Butler ably shepherded the project through the approvals process, while Leslie Rollins and Nancy Rivera obtained the crucial rights for the translated text and images. Rachel Barth was our heroic editor and kept us on track and in good spirits, and manuscript editor Alexandra Bonfante-Warren skillfully assisted with the language and tone of the volume. Jon Grizzle provided the elegant design. We would also like to thank design and production manager Clare Davis, production coordinator Molly McGeehan, proofreader Anne Canright, and indexer Do Mi Stauber.

Colleagues across America and Europe kindly provided vital ideas, knowledge, and aid in the execution of this project. We especially thank Ariane Adeline, Suzanne Akabari, Charlotte Denoël, John Friedman, Marc Edouard Gautier, Anne D. Hedeman, Sandra Hindman, Eva Hoffman, Amy Landau, Tal Nadan, Alain Terrienne, Madeleine Viljoen, and Eric White. In addition, GIL DE SILOÉ, S.L., generously allowed us to republish portions of Kristen Figg and John Friedman's superb translation of the original medieval French text into English.

Finally, we would like to express our deepest thanks to our three anonymous peer reviewers, whose insightful comments were instrumental in helping us to define the original medieval audience for the manuscripts while always keeping our modern one in mind.

Larisa Grollemond
Assistant Curator of Manuscripts
J. Paul Getty Museum

Kelin Michael
Former Graduate Intern, Manuscripts
J. Paul Getty Museum

Elizabeth Morrison
Senior Curator of Manuscripts
J. Paul Getty Museum

Joshua O'Driscoll
Associate Curator of Medieval and Renaissance Manuscripts
Morgan Library & Museum

Index

Italic page numbers indicate illustrations.

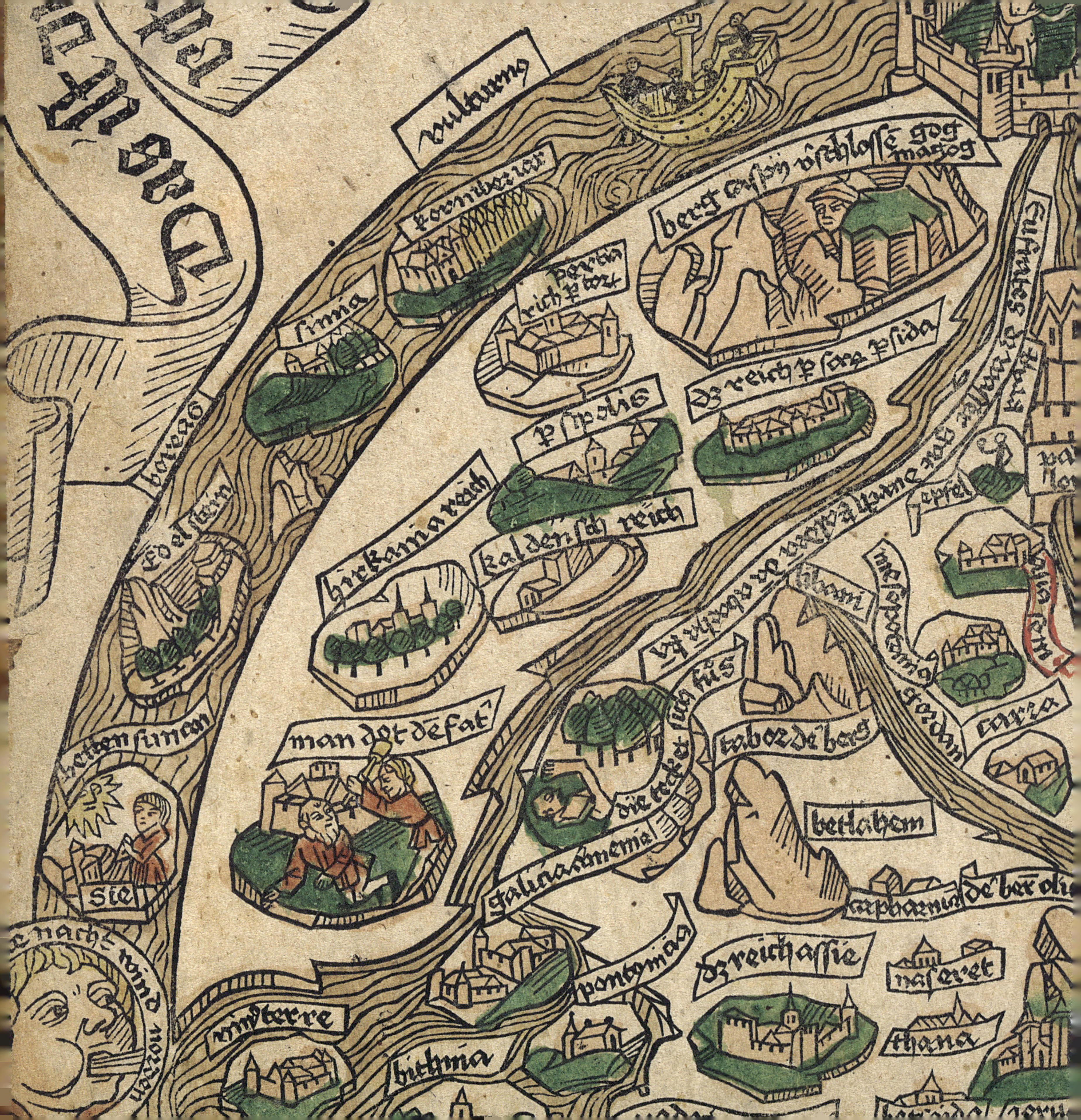
vulturnus
gog magog
berg caspij
persia reich
boreas
Edelstein
hirkania reich
persepolis
man dot dē fat
tabor dē berg
bethlehem
libanū
jordan
caria
galicia armenia
Sie
nacht wind
bithinia
Dz reich assie
naseret
thana
capharnaū
Eufrates